# THE
# DOULOS
# STORY

# Dedication

Dedicated to Prisca (Jung-Ro) Ahn from South Korea (1955–1987), Karen Goldsworthy from New Zealand (1972–1991) and Sofia Sigfridsson from Sweden (1972–1991), who gave their lives in faithful service aboard *Doulos*.

'Well done, good and faithful servant. . . .
Come and share your master's happiness'

Matthew 25:21,23.

# THE DOULOS STORY

## ELAINE RHOTON

OM
publishing

Copyright © Elaine Rhoton 1997

First published in the UK 1997 by OM Publishing
Reprinted 1998, 1999

03  02  01  00  99        7  6  5  4  3

OM Publishing is an imprint of Paternoster Publishing,
PO Box 300, Carlisle, Cumbria, CA3 0QS, UK
http://www.paternoster-publishing.com

The right of Elaine Rhoton to be identified as the Author of this Work has been
asserted by her in accordance with the Copyright, Designs and Patents Act 1988

*All rights reserved. No part of this publication may be reproduced,
stored in a retrieval system, or transmitted in any form or by any
means, electronic, mechanical, photocopying, recording or otherwise,
without the prior permission of the publisher or a licence permitting
restricted copying. In the UK such licences are issued by the
Copyright Licensing Agency,
90 Tottenham Court Road, London W1P 9HE.*

**British Library Cataloguing in Publication Data**
A catalogue record for this book is available from the British Library

ISBN 1-85078-269-5

Unless otherwise stated, Scripture quotations are taken from the
HOLY BIBLE, NEW INTERNATIONAL VERSION
Copyright © 1973, 1978, 1984 by the International Bible Society.
Used by permission of Hodder and Stoughton Limited. All rights reserved.
'NIV' is a registered trademark of the International Bible Society
UK trademark number 1448790

Typeset by WestKey Ltd, Falmouth, Cornwall
Printed in Great Britain by Mackays of Chatham

# Contents

# 1

## The Ship

Sprawled on top of a mountain of goods in the back of a large truck of indeterminate age, eight or ten young men made half-hearted attempts to while away the long hours. A couple of them, stretched out on sleeping bags near the open back door, were struggling to focus on the contents of books propped up in front of them — a task complicated by the lamentable condition of the roads. Less ambitious or less disciplined members of the party lounged lazily and engaged in desultory conversation working up to spirited enthusiasm punctuated with bursts of laughter which lapsed gradually into periods of silence. Two men, snoring, were oblivious to everything: they had been on driving and navigating duty throughout much of the previous night.

The group had set out from England a couple of weeks earlier in high spirits which they were determined to maintain, but seemingly endless days spent on the long road to India had taken their toll. The roughest leg of the journey had started as they reached eastern Turkey at the onset of winter and made their way along snow-covered roads swept by strong and bitterly cold winds. Further east they had emerged from the snow to find a barren wilderness of mountains, hills, rocks and little else. The road, such as it

2

was, could hardly be distinguished from the rest of the landscape in places. Tiny villages offered welcome breaks from the monotony of travel; as bodies unfolded and descended from the truck, limbs were stretched and the travellers swarmed into a local teahouse or cleared out a good proportion of the contents of a tiny bakery, primitive and dirty but emanating the irresistible aroma of freshly-baked bread. The newly-purchased loaves would be carried back to the truck and liberally spread with peanut butter and jam or covered with cheese, and another meal would be under way.

The travellers were part of a small convoy carrying workers with Operation Mobilisation (OM), an international mission that recruited young people for short-term evangelistic outreach, mainly in Europe and Asia. Many university and Bible College students used their holiday time to go out on small teams to distribute Christian literature and talk personally with anyone who would listen. Some young people even set aside a year or two to work with OM.

Among the travellers in one of the trucks was a thin, wiry American with an air of suppressed nervous energy. He was George Verwer, director of OM, who in 1957 at the age of nineteen, had initiated the evangelistic outreach by talking two fellow students from Maryville College in the United States into going with him to Mexico during their summer holidays. Their mission outreach was repeated in subsequent holidays, the number of participants increasing each time. By the time of this trip to India in the early sixties, the work had grown into a more established mission organization with several hundred workers year-round and many, many more during holidays.

In the truck, George shifted his body, trying to find a more comfortable position while his thoughts moved ahead to India where the action would begin. *What a waste of time this trip is*, he complained to himself impatiently. Three, four weeks, maybe even more, with nothing to do but lie around while people in India were suffering and dying without knowing the good news that God loved them.

*If only we could fly to India and cut out this long trip*, he thought wistfully. But of course, that was out of the question. There was no money for such things. And even if there had been, the money would be better spent on Bibles and Christian literature. No, flying could not even be considered. The weeks of time wasted in travel were inevitable.

*What we need is a ship*, he thought and smiled to himself. Suddenly he snapped to full mental alertness. *A ship! Think what we could do with a ship!* The trip to India might take longer — it probably would — but the time wouldn't be wasted! They could hold training sessions for new workers. They could stop in a port and let the workers go ashore to practise what they had learned. Then they could sail on, get more training and stop again. A floating Bible school! And think of all the supplies they could transport to India! The Christian literature! Tons of it!

George's excitement grew. Literature was his great passion.

That was the beginning of an idea that fired the imagination of OM leaders some time later in England and finally resulted in the purchase of a 2319-ton ship which was christened *Logos*. (The story of this ship is told in *The Logos Story*.) After its first long voyage in 1971 with around one hundred and fifty workers on board, however, the ship was not used to transport people or goods to India, although it did become a base for training Christian workers and for going ashore to put that training to use. Beyond the training aspect, it was used in ways that George had never imagined, as daily hundreds and even thousands of visitors streamed aboard to purchase books from the unique floating book-shop or to attend various meetings open to the public. Well-attended receptions were held for government offi-cials, foreign diplomats, military officers and other influen-tial people outside the sphere of influence of most missionaries and local Christian workers. Personal friend-ships were forged between Logos people and individuals living ashore. Whereas a hundred Christian workers enter-ing a city might become lost in the crowd, the ship provided a high profile that attracted the interest of the local populace and was welcomed by them. God had given OM a powerful vehicle for ministry.

That was one side of the story — the great blessings. The other side was the problems, pains, stresses, uncertainties and failures that came along with the blessings. The burden fell most heavily on George Verwer. That's why he reacted as he did when a British marine engineer meeting him at an OM conference in 1972 exclaimed enthusiastically, 'Hey, George, we're praying for another ship. Did you know that?' and went on to tell of a small prayer band of half a dozen people who met to pray especially that God would provide a second ship to expand the ministry of *Logos*.

Taken aback, George was silent for a moment before responding huskily, 'You don't know what you're talking about. You've never even seen Logos. You have no idea of all the tears and heartbreak that have gone into it.'

George was definitely not ready to go through it all again.

But others in OM, seeing what God was doing with Logos, began to think about what could be accomplished if OM had two ships instead of just one. Enthusiasm for the prospect continued growing until even George himself was caught up in it. But he was not yet ready to relinquish his resistance.

'One of the problems I see,' he pointed out, 'is the leadership needed. Who is going to carry the responsibility for a second ship if we get it?'

No one had an answer to that.

In the meantime, an OM team led by Dale Rhoton was ministering to Christians behind the Iron Curtain. Dale, an American, had accompanied George on his first evangelistic trip to Mexico and had worked with him in the subsequent development of OM. Like George, Dale was slim and fairly tall, but in temperament he was totally opposite. Whereas George was a fireball burning with energy and sparking out ideas fast and furiously, Dale was a phlegmatic who carefully considered each prospective move. He was slow to offer an opinion, but when he did, it had substance. Close friends, he and George offered a valuable counterbalance to each other.

After working for several years in the Middle East, Dale had moved with his family to Austria in 1968 gathering around him a small team to smuggle tens of thousands of

Bibles and other Christian books to Christians living in communist eastern Europe. Although he found the work challenging and immensely satisfying, by 1973 he was beginning to sense that he had worked himself out of a job. The team he had assembled was functioning so well that his leadership was no longer needed. It was time to move on.

But where? That was the question which occupied his thoughts as he tried to conjure up in his mind the various possibilities and evaluate them.

'I can imagine us fitting into just about any area of OM ministry,' his wife assured him. 'Except the ship ministry. That's definitely out.'

Eight months of waitressing work aboard a small cruise ship to earn money for university had made her fully aware of the intense pressures of living and working with a lot of people in a confined space. It was not an experience she wished to repeat nor to subject her family to.

By the time of the annual conference for OM workers held in September in England, Dale was no closer to a decision about his next move. Near the end of the conference George asked him to fly out to *Logos* in India for a couple of weeks. The ship would soon be sailing into the Persian/Arabian Gulf and those on board needed orientation for the Muslim world.

One evening shortly after Dale had left for India while his family remained at the conference, a *Logos* worker gave a report to the conferees and showed slides. *This is not ship life as I know it*, Dale's wife realized as she watched and listened spellbound. *Why this is exciting, breath-taking! God is obviously at work!*

Meanwhile, Dale arrived in Bombay tired from the long flight and the inevitable jet lag. On his first morning in India he woke with an almost mystical sense that something important was going to happen that day.

*Strange*, he thought, *I've never felt anything quite like this before.*

Later that day he went for a boat ride with one of the *Logos* leaders who began to relate enthusiastically some of the things God had been doing through the ship. Suddenly it was as if a bright light flashed on in Dale's mind.

*This is it!* he thought. *The ship is the place where God wants us!*

When he returned home a couple of weeks later, he brought up the subject rather diffidently, remembering his wife's strongly expressed aversion to the idea of ship life. To his amazement, she nodded and agreed calmly, 'Yes, I think God may want us there.'

God had put his man in place.

When OM leaders met to discuss business in September of the following year, 1974, Dale's decision was a major factor in their agreeing that the time to purchase a second ship had arrived. George Miley, an American who had been director of *Logos* for three years, would assume the oversight of both ships. Dale would work with George and eventually become director of the new ship.

The search for a ship was on. A Christian broker in Great Britain heard about it and offered his services. Every remotely possible ship was brought to the attention of Mike Poynor, OM's expert on marine affairs. Ship drawings were pored over and promising ships visited, but all were too big, too expensive or simply unsuitable for the type of ministry.

In 1977 word came about *Franca C*. Built in the United States in 1914, she had started her career as a cargo ship named *Medina* and had later been rebuilt into a passenger ship, rechristened *Roma*. Eventually she was upgraded to a cruise ship after purchase by Costa Lines in Italy.

Mike Poynor, along with another veteran *Logos* worker and a German married couple, drove to Italy to inspect the ship.

As they turned a corner in Venice and headed towards the port area, they spotted a pristine white passenger liner, a giant vessel boasting three funnels.

'Oh!' exclaimed the woman excitedly, 'What a beautiful ship! Isn't God wonderful to give us such a lovely ship?'

Mike Poynor, a bit more down to earth, looked beyond the great luxury liner to a smaller scrubby-looking vessel listing strongly to port. Pointing it out, he remarked dryly, 'That one's more typical of an OM ship.'

It was *Franca C*.

The group didn't have time to dwell on the subject. Their appointment with the owners was at 11 am and they were running late because they had been held up by traffic. It was already 10:30 and they still needed to park their car on the mainland and take a boat over to the old city. The pressure of time grew as they located a car park and found themselves at the end of a long line of cars waiting to enter. After a very brief discussion, Mike hopped out of the car and dashed off to get a boat so that he, at least, would be on time. The others followed later.

Their initial impressions gleaned from a tour of the ship were positive.

As deliberation continued in the coming weeks, Mike was offered an opportunity to sail on one of *Franca C's* regular cruises to the Greek Islands.

'Why don't you take your wife with you?' suggested some of the OM workers. 'You could give her a little holiday and do your work at the same time.'

'Humph,' grunted Mike, a large, dedicated Texan and a man of few words, 'Rex Worth would be more useful.'

So it was Rex, a British engineer, who went. This was business after all, not pleasure. Instead of drinking in the beauty of the Greek islands, the two men spent their time exploring the engine room and other sites of technical importance on the ship. A vast amount of work would be needed they could see, but their overall impression was favourable.

On their recommendation OM leaders decided to purchase the ship.

On the morning of 28 October, 1977, *Franca C* sailed for the last time into her home port of Genoa. On board for a final inspection as a basis for negotiating a price were Mike and Rex, along with Stan Thomson, a British marine electrician of considerable experience, Jonathan Stewart, who had been captain on *Logos*, and Ebbo Buurma, a big burly Dutchman who would be chief steward.

As the ship neared the pier, the OM delegation spotted their boss, George Miley, on the quayside waving wildly. With him was a German businessman, chairman of the board of directors for the company which would become legal owners of the ship.

A couple of hours later in the office of Costa Lines the negotiations began. Costa Lines was asking just under $900,000. The OM delegation countered with a bid of $700,000. Back and forth they went, bidding and counter bidding, discussing what items could be removed by the sellers to bring down the price. Soon after lunch they reached an agreement on $770,000 and discussion moved on to other important details.

A contract was drawn up and signed on 13 November and the a deposit of $77,000 was paid. Another six weeks would be needed to take care of formalities stipulated in the contract. But finally on 29 December an OM delegation met with Costa representatives to pay the remainder of the purchase price and claim possession of the ship. There was another expense at this time, one that had been foreseen but not calculated up to this point. In taking possession of the ship, OM needed to pay for whatever fuel and 'lube' oil remained on board. And that led to an embarrassing situation.

The OM account contained enough to cover the cost of the ship and almost all the fuel. *Almost* all. The OM men went through their pockets pulling out all the cash they had on them and laying it on the table. They were still $300 short.

'Forget the $300,' responded the Costa representatives magnanimously.

'Oh, no,' answered Ebbo as he pulled out his personal Eurocheque book and began to write a cheque. With a flourish he signed his name and handed it over. 'Now we have paid to the last penny,' he announced proudly.

As the OM men left the office, the Costa lawyer invited them for a cup of coffee at one of Genoa's many coffee houses. While they were drinking their coffee, the lawyer asked curiously, 'Tell me, Mr. Miley, did you have the money for the ship when you signed the contract back in November?'

George looked at him. 'No,' he admitted after a brief hesitation as he thought back over the many financial gifts that had poured in during the past month, 'no, we didn't have the money when we signed the contract.'

'I *knew* it! I *knew* it!' exclaimed the lawyer.

**2**

# A New Name and a New Start

With the transference of ownership, *Franca C* surrendered her name. For months long-term OMers, as OM workers were often called, had been submitting ideas for a new name, such as *Morning Star, Light, Messenger, Friendship, Charis, Doulos*. Each suggestion was weighed and discussed until a majority of opinions gravitated toward the name *Doulos*.

The word *Doulos* best expressed what the ship ministry was all about, they decided. A Greek word appearing many times in the New Testament, it meant slave or servant. The apostle Paul called himself a *doulos* of the Lord Jesus Christ. Writing to the Corinthian church, he said, 'For we do not preach ourselves, but Jesus Christ as Lord, and ourselves as your servants [*doulous*: variant grammatical form of *doulos*] for Jesus' sake.'

That was what OMers wanted: to be utterly committed to serving Jesus Christ as their Lord and Master and, in doing this, to become servants of the people to whom they would preach Christ. They wanted a name that would remind them that they were not going forth to distribute largesse grandiosely or to proclaim pompously all the answers to life's problems. They were going out to learn and to serve.

They had a unique model. The Lord Jesus Christ himself set aside all the glory, wealth, comfort and privileges of his position in heaven and, in the words of the apostle Paul, 'made himself nothing, taking the very nature of a servant [*doulou*], being made in human likeness.'

And so the 'new' OM ship became *Doulos*, and her people committed themselves to serving. Not superficially as paid servants who could leave any time something displeased them, but deeply committed as slaves to their Lord and Master, Jesus Christ.

As they went out with this attitude, they were to discover something astonishing, incredible, awesome. They may have viewed themselves as slaves, but Jesus received them as friends. It was just as he had said to his disciples in the Gospel of John, 'I no longer call you servants [*doulous*], because a servant [*doulos*] does not know his master's business. I have called you friends. . . .'

As they went out to serve, they discovered that their Master shared in their elation. He put a comforting arm around them when they were in pain. When they floundered, he came to their aid. He accepted them for what they were while seeing in them what they could become. He involved them in the things that lay close to his heart. He met them as friends.

Servants and friends. That would be the story of *Doulos* repeated again and again in an ever-changing array of situations.

And so *Doulos* came into being. And *douloi* [plural form] came aboard to overhaul her engine and do a lot of other work necessary before the ship could be given the safety certificates required for sailing. A dozen men had already been living and working on the ship before the purchase was completed. Afterwards more came. Director George Miley wrote in a report of those first two months:

> Then people started coming. From the USA, from Canada, from Great Britain, from Switzerland, from Germany, from other places they came. We knew some were coming. Others just came. Some had never been on ships before. Some had been at sea for years. Some we had been counting on all along. Many others we did not even know about when we signed the contract of purchase. Soon we had thirty-five people on board. Then it jumped to fifty. Before we knew it we were eighty. And before we finally sailed from Genoa, we were around 150 people — more on the maiden voyage than we had ever had on *Logos*!

One of those who came was a friend of Chief Engineer Rex Worth. He was from Switzerland and spoke little English but certainly had a will to work. Rex went to the engine room early one morning at 6:00 and there was Rudi, faithfully working.

'Rudi,' exclaimed Rex in surprise, 'have you been here all night?'

'Yes,' he said and went on to explain, 'I can't preach. I can't teach. But I can serve the Lord with my lathe.'

Another person who came — and ended up staying for years as chief engineer — was a Dane named Johannes Thomsen. According to another *doulos*, 'He came aboard, showed his face and disappeared into the engine room, where he has been ever since.' Once he was asked to say something about himself in group devotions.

'If I worked as badly as I talk,' he replied, 'you wouldn't need me on this ship.'

And with that he disappeared into the engine room again.

Mike Poynor, who had been heavily involved in finding the ship and inspecting her, moved aboard with his wife and four daughters, two of whom were six-week-old twins. His wife, Carol Ann, gives an idea of what family life involved at that time:

> When we moved on there was no water. A hose from ashore was run up to the galley where I used to go every morning to get a bucket of water. I'd heat it in a kettle and give the twins a bath in a little plastic basin.
>
> It was freezing cold on the ship since there was no heat. When you slept on a bunk that was along the ship's side, you froze. And as you were breathing, the moisture in the room would condense along the steel side of the ship.
>
> We had to send all the laundry ashore and pay by the piece, but having all these tiny bits of clothes for the babies got a bit expensive, so I washed them by hand and tried to dry them on the ship.
>
> After the babies were washed and fed and put to bed, Vera Buurma [another mother on board] and I would start cleaning the ship. Our first job was to unplug all the toilets. The watchmen who'd been staying on the ship [in a little hut temporarily erected on the poop deck] would come in and use a toilet until it blocked up from not being flushed and then move on to use another one till it too blocked up. Vera's and my first job was carrying around buckets of water to pour down the toilets because there was no running water to flush them. That was because the ship was 'dead' and not generating any power.

Vera, her Dutch co-worker, recalls the laundry system:

> All our laundry went on shore. We saw quite often a woollen shirt come back small. I remember one evening a man appeared for supper wearing a shrunken woollen shirt which would now fit a child. It was hilarious.

16

Chief Engineer Rex Worth brought his wife, Ros, and their one-year-old daughter to the ship a few weeks later when the ship was in dry dock. Ros was given a key to the ladies' toilets on the other side of the dock, about two hundred yards away. Each day she would bundle up her baby in a blanket, walk down the gangway and around the dry dock through the bitter cold to unlock the ladies' toilets, where there was hot running water. She would bathe the baby, wrap her up and return to the ship.

'It didn't seem strange then,' she explained later. 'It seemed the most natural thing to do. We coped with all sorts of things. It was exciting to be working with a new project.'

That was life on the ship until *Doulos* came out of dry dock at the end of January and the ship's generators were finally ready to be started up. Power was restored to the ship and life became slightly easier.

One place on the ship was relatively warm and cosy all along. That was the engineers' mess, which served as dining-room for all on board. A cable from ashore brought in electricity and heat emanated from an electric stove on which the cook prepared the meals. The mess became the 'living-room' of the ship. Each morning prayers were held there, including prayers for the day's activities.

The venue for devotions changed, however, when George Miley moved aboard in January.

'Let's do things now the way we plan to do them later,' he urged, 'instead of forming lax habits which will have to be unlearned.'

Accordingly, devotions and prayer meetings were moved to the auditorium, known as the main lounge. Thirty or thirty-five workers filed in, huddled around in a room large enough to seat five hundred and shivered miserably in the cold. Soon, however, the rows began to fill up as more and more workers arrived.

Like many of the workers on board, Rex Worth liked to spend time alone with God before starting his day's activities. One morning he read from the book of Ezra in the Old Testament about the Jews returning home from exile and rebuilding their temple. As Rex read, he was impressed with a principle he saw there. In doing God's work, whatever was necessary would be provided as it was needed.

Rex got so excited and caught up in his own personal devotions that he lost track of time. Suddenly he realized he would be late for group devotions. He closed his Bible and dashed down to join the others who had already started their meeting. At the first opportunity, he eagerly jumped up to share what he had read that morning.

Everyone started to laugh.

Rex looked around perplexed. 'Well, I don't think it's funny,' he finally said defensively. 'This is what God said to me.'

'Yeah, we know,' someone enlightened him, 'but we've already heard your message. The electrician has just given it.'

'Oh,' said Rex weakly and sat down.

Prayer was an integral part of all that was going on. In the early *Logos* days tension had developed between the engineers and deck-hands. Determined not to allow that to happen on *Doulos*, leaders decided that every evening when work was finished (at 10 pm!), the two departments would get together to discuss the day's work and pray about it.

Prayer was not just a spiritual discipline exercised by the group; it was also a very personal thing. Stan Thomson, as chief electrician, had been busy getting the electrical system in order. Late one afternoon a fault developed in the emergency lighting system. It couldn't have happened at a much worse time. The safety surveyor was due the next morning to inspect the electrical system and give the safety certificate required.

Stan and his team of five electricians searched determinedly for the source of the fault that was tripping the circuit-breaker and blacking out an entire section of the emergency lighting. They investigated everything they could think of, but in vain. They couldn't find the fault.

Supper time came and everyone else went to the dining-room, but Stan was too occupied with his problem. *I've tried everything!* he told himself in frustration. *I just can't think what to do. The fault could be in hundreds of different locations.*

Suddenly he realized that he hadn't prayed about the matter. He had relegated it to the realm of practical matters to be solved by his own wisdom. And that was wrong, he concluded.

Finding an empty cabin, he went in and prayed, 'Lord Jesus, your word tells me that you are the creator of all things — seen and unseen. That includes the structures of mass, the very atoms of air we're breathing and even this fault I'm looking for. Lord, you know all things. You know the trouble this is causing me. Could you please help me find out where the problem is?'

He narrates what happened after that:

> I didn't feel anything, but it was amazing how in a way I was guided. I left the cabin, walked up the port side of the ship and crossed over to the starboard side to walk aft again. I went down to a lower deck and on to the end of the passageway. There I ducked into a cabin to get a bunkbed ladder, which I carried out into the alleyway and climbed up to the last fluorescent light fitting, also containing the DC emergency lighting. As I dismantled this, I found at the back a big black mark. A short circuit had burned the cable off. Within fifteen minutes the fault was rectified. When the surveyor came in the morning, everything was working perfectly.

A short time after dry-dock, *Doulos* people held a reception for the dry-dock workers and showed them what had been done with *Logos* and what was intended for *Doulos*. Everyone in the port area knew how much the *Doulos* dry-dock bill had been. They knew that the crew and staff had been praying for the money. At the reception the head of the dockworkers' union spontaneously took off his hat and passed it around; dockworkers put in money to help pay the bill. They were almost as excited as the *Doulos* workers when shortly afterward some stock that had been given to the ship ministry was sold, bringing in the remaining $80,000 needed.

All told, the cost of overhauling the ship to pass surveys cost around $100,000. The Costa company, when they had been contemplating keeping the ship, had budgeted $300,000 for the job. When the Costa engineer in charge of the technical aspect of the company's ships heard about the amount *Doulos* had paid, he jokingly said he'd get into trouble because he had predicted it would cost so much.

Then he turned serious and asked, 'Do you pray for everything?'

'Oh, yes,' Carol Ann Poynor assured him. 'The children are praying now for snow.'

'Snow? But it never snows in Genoa,' protested the man. The next day he couldn't come to the ship as planned because of the snow.

The Costa engineering superintendent proved very helpful with various suppliers and manufacturers in getting the spares needed for *Doulos*. When a large quantity of spares for the main engine were obtained from the Fiat company that had made the engine, the Fiat manager began to get a bit nervous. He called up the Costa engineering superintendent and said, 'These people are ordering a lot of spares. Do you think they will be able to pay for them?'

The superintendent's answer was, 'If they pray, they pay.'

*Doulos* people did both. On 28 February, 1978, they sailed to Bremen with all bills paid.

In Genoa work had been concentrated on bringing the ship up to the standard necessary to pass safety surveys and obtain safety certificates. In Bremen the focus was on renovating and equipping the ship for ministry. Two of the major items on the agenda were building a roof over the book exhibition which would be located on the top deck aft and putting in a lift where the swimming pool was currently located, so that books could be transported easily to and from the storage holds several decks below.

Mike Poynor was responsible for this work. He drew up the plans and did a great deal of the actual work himself. Rex Worth relates a couple of incidents that showed God's hand in it all:

> Mike had designed the elevator. The cage was all done and the shaft was ready. He was puzzling out how we could build the machinery to get the thing to run up and down. We were all in his cabin talking about it when there was a knock on the door. The man standing there said, 'Excuse me for disturbing you, but I've been an elevator manufacturer for the last twenty-four years. I wondered if you needed any help with your elevator machinery.'
>
> It was the same again when Mike designed and virtually built by himself the roof over the book exhibition. When the roof was finished, a big truck came alongside the ship with all sorts of equipment. In the truck was a Christian roof expert who'd come to help make the roof watertight.

Adults were not the only ones working. Some of the half dozen older children were workers too, outside school hours. Or perhaps entrepreneurs would be a better word. They went up on the top deck where the swimming pool was being removed and collected bits of tile. They added bits of metal slag that had fallen from various welding jobs. In the Poynor cabin, which had previously belonged to the purser, they turned up a trove of Costa ash trays, postcards and so forth. With all these treasures, the children set up a little stand inside the foyer of the ship and sold their wares to German visitors. With an eye for publicity, they stationed the Poynor twins in their 'Jolly Jumper' swing hanging from hooks in the deckhead above. People would stop to look at the bouncing babies and fall prey to the sales pitch of the young vendors. The profit was then invested in a German toy-range called Playmobil.

Hospitality played a large role during that time in Bremen. Busloads of Christians would come from all over the country to see the ship and to hear about its proposed ministry. *Doulos* people not involved in practical work were kept busy entertaining them in cabins, showing them around and preparing meetings for them.

At Easter time three hundred visitors came down from Sweden for the weekend. At the same time a number of German ladies came with eggs to be coloured for Easter. *Doulos* children were mobilized, along with several mothers. Six hundred eggs were boiled in the galley and carried down to the mess, where the children coloured them and then rubbed them with bacon in the traditional German way. On Easter Sunday everyone, including the three hundred Swedish guests, received an Easter egg.

Not everyone who came to the ship in Bremen was a visitor. Many came as volunteers to help out with practical work in any way they could. One of these was an older

German woman. *Doulos* people were not sure just how they could use her.

'What kind of work have you done?' she was asked.

'Oh, I've worked in a laundry.'

'In a laundry? Now that's interesting. In our laundry here on the ship we have a big ironing machine that no one knows how to use. . . .'

The woman knew exactly how it should be used.

'She came in and commanded us around like a drill sergeant,' Carol Ann Poynor remembers. 'She taught us how to do the tablecloths and napkins. Made sure we turned them up the right way. It was very good.'

With the steady flow of visitors, it was extremely helpful to be able to keep on hand a freshly ironed supply of the table linens that had come with the ship when it was bought. And it was a new experience for the ship people who had served previously on Logos. As Carol Ann commented, 'We'd never had even paper napkins on our ship because we had felt that was wasteful of money. It was rather exciting to have cloth ones now.'

The alterations on *Doulos*, the purchase of equipment and supplies all cost money. German friends took much of this on as their own special project. At a conference one weekend Chief Steward Ebbo Buurma was at the coffee bar serving some guests when a lady handed him an envelope.

'Here,' she told him, 'this is for *Doulos*.'

Ebbo thanked her heartily, stuffed the envelope into his breastpocket and kept working. And forgot about the gift.

Much later in the day as he was talking with a good friend who was a produce seller in Bremen, he suddenly remembered the envelope. He drew it out of his pocket and opened it. There lay 10,000 DM (Deutchmarks worth approximately $5,500 US).

'Oh, look,' exclaimed Ebbo excitedly to his friend, 'God is answering prayer!'

God continued to answer prayer as the German friend said, 'Oh, that's wonderful! Here's another 5,000 DM to add to it.'

*Doulos* people never learned the identity of the lady who gave the 10,000 DM so they were never able to get back to her and thank her. But they were confident that God knew.

When the time in Bremen came to an end after three months, a special commissioning service was held in co-operation with a local church that was very closely linked with the ship. *Doulos* then sailed off for ministry, first to a port in France, then on to Spain and Portugal.

Dale Rhoton with his family joined *Doulos* in Bilbao, Spain. In Málaga he got his first taste of directorship when George went away for a couple of weeks or so. Before George left, he asked Dale to go for a walk with him on shore to discuss ship business. As they set out, Dale recalled an occurrence on his first visit to *Logos* when he had also talked with George about the ship ministry. As he was leaving George's office at that time, he had asked casually, 'Got any particular needs you'd like me to pray about?'

'Well, as a matter of fact, there are three things we need before we sail in three days,' George replied matter-of-factly. 'Our captain is leaving and we don't know who we can get to replace him. Then our doctor has already gone and we can't sail without a doctor. Finally, we can't leave port until we've paid our bills here and frankly, we don't have anywhere near enough money.'

Dale gulped and said weakly, 'Sure, I'll pray for that.' He paused a moment and, in spite of himself, blurted out, 'And you're going to sail in three days?'

'Right,' said George.

Three days later *Logos* sailed, with captain and doctor on board and all bills paid.

That had been several years earlier. And now George was going away and Dale would have to deal with any problems that arose on *Doulos*.

'So in a few days we sail to London,' Dale remarked to get the conversation moving. 'What sort of things need to be taken care of before then?'

'Well, Dale,' drawled George in his soft Virginian accent, 'you need three things: a captain, a doctor and money to pay the bills. . . .'

'It seems the ship ministry hasn't changed much in the last decade,' commented Dale.

'No, but God hasn't either,' replied George.

*Doulos* too set sail on schedule for London.

That was in Spain. Carol Ann Poynor has some memories of Great Britain, which followed Spain and Portugal in the itinerary:

26

I remember the first ladies' conference. The lounge was absolutely packed with ladies. I was introduced to speak. As I stood up in front and looked out at all the people, I began to cry. That's all I could do. Just cry out of thankfulness that we had this ship, that we had space and didn't have to turn people away like we had done so often on *Logos* [a much smaller ship].

In Scotland I can remember sharing about discipline in a conference. I talked about disciplining children and about self-discipline. I told the ladies I was toilet-training my twins right then and I realized it wasn't so much their problem as it was my problem to be disciplined.

The next day a florist arrived with a big bouquet of roses for me. It was from a lady who was trying to toilet train one child. She thought if I was trying to train two while living on a ship, I needed some encouragement, so I got this beautiful bouquet of roses.

In another port our ship's washing-machines broke and our laundry was forced to close down. Two older ladies knew that I had small babies. They used to come every day to the ship to pick up the dirty clothes from the twins. The next day they would bring them back washed and dried.

*Doulos* workers had come to serve and found themselves being served, supported, encouraged, loved.

# EUROPE and LATIN AMERICAN TOURS 1977–1986

**1978**
Italy
West Germany
France
Spain
Portugal
United Kingdom
United States
Mexico

**1979**
Mexico
Colombia
Venezuela
Barbados
Trinidad
Argentina
Uruguay
Brazil
Portugal (Madeira)
Spain
West Germany
United Kingdom
Holland

**1980**
United Kingdom
Portugal (Azores)
Barbados
St. Vincent
St. Lucia
Venezuela
Netherland Antilles
Colombia
Panama
Ecuador
Peru
Chile

**1981**
Argentina
Uruguay
Brazil
Barbados
Puerto Rico
Jamaica

**1982**
Mexico
Bahamas
United States
Puerto Rico
Venezuela
Netherland Antilles
Colombia
Panama
Ecuador
Peru
Chile

**1983**
Chile
Argentina
Uruguay
Brazil
Spain
United Kingdom

**1984**
United Kingdom
West Germany
Norway
Denmark
Sweden

**1985**
West Germany
Holland
United Kingdom
Belgium
Portugal
Spain
Italy

**1986**
Italy
Malta
United Kingdom
(Gibraltar)

# 3

## Under Way at Last

As the 1970's drew to an end, Latin America sat poised for a period of political turmoil and upheaval. Argentina, Brazil, Chile, Peru, Cuba, Nicaragua and El Salvador were under the tight control of dictatorships. During the next decade and a half, all except Cuba would move toward democracy, but the road would not be easy.

The eighties rode in on a crest of economic exuberance with money open-handedly and irresponsibly dispersed. National debts piled up and the inevitable day of reckoning crashed down upon country after country, leaving them reeling from shock.

That decade saw Argentina going to war for the first time in a hundred and twenty years, as she challenged Great Britain for the Malvinas (Falkland Islands) and was forced to back down.

These were the startling, defining movements that caught the attention of the world. But another change of even greater significance passed largely unnoticed until its magnitude finally forced acknowledgment. This was the explosive growth of the evangelical church from a tiny despised minority in the fifties and sixties to a pervasive presence throughout much of Latin America. In fact, the growth was so rapid that churches faced a crisis of leadership. There were not enough mature trained Christian leaders to keep up with the demand of the new congregations springing up.

As *Doulos* was obtained and prepared for ministry, most of her people were unaware of the situation in Latin America and not much interested. Their eyes were on Asia. That's where *Doulos* would be heading.

A small OM team that had been travelling through part of Latin America upset their plans.

'Before we head out to Asia for the next few years, why don't we first make one short trip to South America just to get an idea of the situation there?' suggested Bob Clement, leader of the small team.

This suggestion stirred up a storm of controversy. Finances were a major concern; the Atlantic crossing alone would cost a staggering sum. And who knew whether Latin Americans would help to bear the economic burden through purchase of books — *extensive* purchase of books — and gifts? Who knew whether Latin Americans would even find the ship of interest?

Greater than anxiety about financial disaster or an indifferent reception, however, was the fear that the ship might be too well received, igniting an interest in OM. The OM work had already spread too rapidly and thinly for its own good, leaders felt. It needed to be consolidated and put on a sound footing rather than being extended even more.

After much discussion a decision was reached by consensus. *Doulos* would go to the Caribbean and South America for one brief survey trip. That was all. Absolutely no new OM work would be started in any country in that part of the world.

On 24 October, 1978 *Doulos* left England for Latin America.

30     One little detour, however, was too tempting to resist. *Doulos* could not pass so close to her birthplace without calling in at Newport News, Virginia, or at least as close as she could come to it.

A highlight for the ship in the United States was the visit of an older woman, little known to the world at large but very special to the ship: Mrs. Parramore. On an August day in 1914, as a teenager, she had stood on the quayside of a shipyard in Newport News, Virginia, smashed a champagne bottle against the hull of a new ship and christened her Medina. The intervening years had brought changes in name and appearance to both the sponsor and the ship which was now named *Doulos*, but the two grand old ladies were able to meet again and renew their acquaintance.

Mexico was the next country on the itinerary, with the small commercial port of Tampico and then Veracruz a few miles to the south. Latin America at last! Bubbling with a heady mixture of curiosity and enthusiasm, tempered with perhaps a degree of apprehension, all off-duty crew and staff — and even a few on-duty ones – slipped out one by one onto the decks to line the rails and watch the sliver of land on the horizon grow larger and larger until individual buildings and landmarks became distinguishable. Then began the guessing game which in time would become a familiar one: where would the ship berth? The first clue was a collection of towering cranes and a concentration of ships, indicating the port area. As *Doulos* came closer, her company on deck surveyed the possibilities, trying to decide upon the most likely berth. When they caught sight of several tiny figures on the pier waving excitedly, they knew they had found the spot. Squinting and straining their eyes, they could eventually identify Bob Clement and the other *Doulos* people who had gone ahead to Tampico to prepare for the ship's visit.

No matter how often the ship came into port, for most people there would be an irresistible fascination in watching the ship navigate those last few metres of water, come alongside the quay, tie up and lower the gangway for local officials to mount. Along with this would come the friendly exchange of greetings and news with the advance preparation team standing down on the quayside. Gradually the excitement would fade and people would begin to melt away, going back to work or to other occupations. An hour or two would pass before the ship's company was finally cleared for going ashore or receiving visitors on board.

A young Indian named Chacko Thomas had the job of co-ordinating conferences on *Doulos*. Having previously worked on *Logos*, he had had enough experience with various cultures to give him a fair amount of confidence as he stood before his first Mexican audience. Still, it was with pleasure that he spotted a familiar song on the music sheet provided for the conference. The song was not only familiar but even a favourite of his, one he had often sung with Spanish Christians during the ship's time in Spain. As he opened his mouth and started to sing in a full, rich tone, he got his first lesson in Mexican culture: the Mexicans had kept the words but changed the tune! He was to learn that Latin America might share a language with Spain — at least to some degree — but Latin American countries were definitely their own entities with their own cultures, outlooks and ways of doing things.

Among the Mexicans affected by the ship's visit was a homeless man. Rex Worth tells his story:

> On the dockside was a tramp in a terrible state, filthy, with long straggly hair down to his shoulders. Johannes, our first engineer, befriended him (while the rest of us all walked past him), won his confidence, took him on board and fed him. Later Johannes was able to persuade him to have a shower. That was no easy task. The man's boots hadn't been off for at least two or three years. Johannes had to get the snips out of the engine room and cut the boots off. The man's toenails had curled up around inside. Johannes shaved him, cut his hair and gave him a 'new' suit of clothes from Charlie [our on-ship used clothing 'boutique'].
>
> The man, he learned, had once been an officer in the Mexican navy. When we sailed away, he had a home with a Christian family and a job as a watchman.

When the ship pulled out of Tampico at the end of her three-week stay, her deck railings were again lined with crew and staff, this time waving and shouting messages to their new-found friends standing tearfully on the shore.

The first port in Latin America had been an exhilarating experience, packed full of activity. The ship's crew and staff had taken part in meetings on board and ashore. They had talked with local people, visited them in their homes, taken part in their church services. It had been an eye-opener to see how Mexicans lived, to experience their culture and to be taken to their hearts in personal friendships.

But now the ship was sailing on and leaving behind . . . what? Friendships that would probably fade with the passage of time? People whose lives had been touched by God in a life-changing way? Or people whose interest in God would diminish when the stimulus of the ship was gone? The tramp on the quayside who'd been given a second chance at life, would he continue in his new relationship with God?

Or Ramón Martínez, head of the dock workers' union, who could hardly stop talking to his friends about his discovery that a person could have his past wiped clean in God's eyes and be able to know God in a direct, personal way. Had he experienced a real and lasting change in his life or was it just an emotional high that would eventually be dulled by the realities of daily life?

What was real and what was just an emotional flash in the pan, heady but without substance? Those on board *Doulos* wondered, but there was no way they would ever know, except as news of someone here or there happened to trickle back to them. Local churches had promised to care for individuals who had shown an interest in spiritual things. Would they follow through on their promises?

Some news did trickle through to Veracruz, the next port of call. A local pastor who had come to wave good-bye to *Doulos* in Tampico had got into conversation with a man standing beside him and discovered that the man was searching for God. There on the quayside as the ship sailed into the distance, this man met God. He too was unable to contain his joy and enthusiasm and within days had led fifteen other people into a similar experience of God.

One of the tiny local churches reported that it had gained twenty-two new members as a result of the *Doulos* visit, a real boost for this struggling church.

[When *Doulos* revisited Tampico three years later, a beaming Ramón Martínez was there to meet her and offer his expertise and influence in obtaining fuel and other supplies when the crew experienced difficulties. And local Christians informed ship people that four churches had sprung up as a result of that first *Doulos* visit.]

The events of Tampico, however, were soon forced into the background by the onslaught of new experiences in Veracruz.

'Did you hear there's a Russian ship in port?' exclaimed one of the *Doulos* workers.

Rose Scott, a dark-haired young British woman, looked up eagerly as she heard the question. Immediately she jumped up and sped out on deck to confirm the report. Yes, there was the ship. Excitement swept over her.

Rose's interest in Russians dated back seven years to a stirring account she had heard a Russian Christian give about life under communism. Rose had become so interested that she had studied Russian without knowing how she would ever use it. Was this now an opportunity?

That evening, with a degree of trepidation, she accompanied the captain and a couple of other *Doulos* men to see if they could get aboard the Russian ship. They were well aware of the fact that Russian ships were always strongly guarded by a formidable commissar who made sure no dangerous ideological elements crept aboard to contaminate the minds of faithful communist seamen.

To their surprise and delight, Rose and her companions were allowed up the gangway and soon joined by a handful of seamen. At first the Russians kept their distance, simply making polite conversation. Rose countered by talking about *Doulos*, saying it was a ship for international understanding and peace. Those were words the Russians understood. Their slogans were full of them. One of the mates thawed out enough to let the *Doulos* visitors at least enter his ship briefly. And that was that.

On their way out, the *Doulos* visitors met a Russian who volunteered the information that almost all the crew had gone to a concert in the central square of Veracruz. As the *Doulos* party thanked him, one of them inconspicuously slipped him a Christian leaflet, which he surreptitiously stuck into his pocket.

'Well, let's go to the square, shall we?' suggested one of the *Doulos* people when they were out of earshot.

They found the seamen at the square and the *Doulos* men were soon in their element passing out Christian leaflets in Russian to the seamen. Rose, however, felt isolated and frustrated. As a woman, she could hardly approach these men and start talking Russian. That would undoubtedly put wrong ideas in their minds. So she prayed, 'Lord, help me find a woman. And please let her be by herself.' That last item was not as easy as it sounded because Russians always stuck together in groups.

Suddenly Rose spotted her. A woman all alone. Rose walked up to her and started speaking Russian. The woman was startled but apparently pleased. Rose soon discovered she was the ship's librarian.

'You must come and visit me on the ship,' the Russian woman said. 'Come tomorrow.'

At that moment a group of six or seven other Russian women descended upon the two, abruptly ending all personal conversation. Still, an invitation to visit had been given and Rose was not going to let that opportunity pass by.

Accordingly, the next afternoon, accompanied by three *Doulos* men, she presented herself at the gangway.

'What are you doing here?' demanded the watchman.

'We have an invitation to visit the librarian,' answered Rose.

'Oh, come on up. She was just looking for you.'

Rose and her party were escorted to the librarian, who graciously gave them a tour of the ship, introducing them to various crewmen here and there. Rose expressed her group's pleasure and presented individuals with small gifts: a Russian Bible, a New Testament or at least a Christian leaflet.

'Such a miracle!' exclaimed Rose later. 'We never even saw the commissar. Yet that evening when we once again returned to the ship, we were refused entrance. "No foreigners allowed," they told us.'

For Dale Rhoton, the port of Veracruz holds a special set of memories. George Miley was again away from the ship, leaving Dale in charge. The ship had been sailing with temporary deck officers who would come for one voyage only, just long enough to take the ship to the next port. That was hardly an ideal set-up, but at least it worked while the ship was in Europe. Latin America was a different story. Fortunately, the ship had a British captain for the next three months and an American first mate who planned to stay long-term. But the second and third mates were returning to the United States when the ship headed south from Mexico.

The captain began to get nervous.

'We have to have mates,' he reminded Dale. 'Who's coming to take on the jobs?'

'Well,' Dale replied, 'there are a couple of possible replacements: Roger Emtage and George Booth.'

'Oh, Emtage and Booth!' Irritation crept into the captain's voice. 'I keep hearing those names. You can forget about them. They're not going to come. Neither of them. Roger Emtage is sitting for his master's ticket in Great Britain. It's his first try. No one gets his master's on the first try. He has said he'll stay and try again if he fails. That will take months.

'Then there's George Booth from South Africa. *South Africa!* Just talk to men on other ships in port here. They'll tell you that they never have a South African officer join the ship in Mexico. Why? Because Mexico won't let a South African into the country. That's why. You might as well give up on him. Who else have you got in mind?'

'That's all, I'm afraid,' admitted Dale reluctantly. 'We'll have to pray that they both make it.'

'Uh . . . !' muttered the captain, shaking his head in frustration.

But pray they did, the entire ship's company.

38
Roger Emtage passed his exam and arranged his flight to *Doulos* in Veracruz.

George Booth and his family took a giant step of faith and began selling their furniture and other possessions. Late one Sunday night as they returned from church, the phone began to ring. Someone on *Doulos* asked if George could come in two weeks.

'Well, we could try.'

The *Doulos* caller explained that George needed to work through an airline that flew both to South Africa and Mexico, suggesting that Varig might be the best one. George should contact the airline which in turn would contact its Mexican office to work out a special dispensation for seamen to enter the country without a visa in order to join a ship. George followed through as instructed. The next day the Mexican office of Varig telexed back that they had never heard of a ship called *Doulos* and they knew of no such agent as ours in Veracruz.

Eventually that problem was cleared up after someone on *Doulos* got to work on it.

George continues the story:

> Meanwhile, we were praying and selling our possessions. We worked on a visa for Brazil because we had to stay two nights there en route. When we resigned from our jobs,

the people we were working with said we were crazy. When we started selling all our things and we hadn't even got permission to enter Mexico, our family and friends thought we were crazy. The permission still hadn't come through by Thursday, the day before we were supposed to fly. That night we swept out our empty house. We didn't know what to do with the pan or broom, so we threw them away. Then we went to stay with my in-laws.

On Friday morning I didn't even bother to phone the Varig office to find out if we had received the permission. I just drove into town to be at the office when it opened at 8:30. As I crossed the square, the lady in the Varig office saw me coming and picked up a white piece of paper. The telex had come through that morning. That afternoon we flew to Mexico even though we still had no visa. All we had was a telex in English saying we were to come. We didn't know if this was going to be enough or not.

As we neared Mexico City, we began to get nervous. Our connecting flight to Veracruz was the last one of the day. It was due to take off at 9:20 that evening, but at 9:20 we were still in the air over Mexico City.

When we finally landed, there were long lines behind the immigration desk. We were just about to join one when a man ran up to me and said, 'Are you Mr. Booth?'

I said 'Yes.'

He said, 'Come with me.'

So Carolyn and our little one-year-old daughter and I ran behind the man. We were taken to an immigration desk where there was no line. Two men were waiting for us. They never even looked at our passports; they just opened them to blank pages and stamped them. We ran through Customs. They tried to open our suitcases, but our

40

man shouted something at them in Spanish and they simply waved us through. We ran through a gate and handed our suitcases to another man who disappeared with them. Our escort grabbed two boarding passes, gave them to us, pushed us up a flight of stairs and said good-bye. We weren't with him more than three minutes. We got up to the top of the stairs, walked down a little corridor and stepped on board a plane. As we stepped inside, they closed the door.

We sat down. I leaned forward and tapped the man in front of me on the shoulder and asked, 'Does this plane go to Veracruz?'

He said, 'Yes.'

We took off and twenty minutes later we were in Veracruz.

A short time later George walked up the gangway of *Doulos*. And discovered that his first step of faith was nothing compared with what lay ahead of him.

The previous captain had planned to stay long-term but had left just the day before, unable to cope with the ship's unorthodox way of operating. The chief officer was an older man who didn't have his master's certificate, so the second officer had just been promoted to master. Roger Emtage had yet to arrive; he came a week later and became second mate. George signed on as first.

Officer uncertainties were only one of the problems. The ship was very old and still obviously in need of a lot of work. Doubts began to swamp George. They weren't helped by the fact that most of the crew were amateurs with no sea experience at all. However, George decided that in running a ship experience often doesn't count as much as enthusiasm. There was plenty of that he found, and a willingness to work.

Meanwhile the programme of the ship continued. The well-known evangelist Luis Palau held an evangelistic campaign in Veracruz in conjunction with the ship's visit. Normally Mexico at that time did not allow public evangelistic meetings; all religious functions had to take place within church walls. Yet exceptions were somehow made for the Luis Palau meetings ashore and the *Doulos* conferences on board. The two groups worked together, sharing publicity, reaching out to people, telling them of the hope God offers, and guiding them towards local Christians who could give support and encouragement long after *Doulos* had moved on.

On the ship Em Namuco, an outgoing Filipino, was responsible for a series of family-day programmes. He didn't know what to expect for the first one, but hoped for an attendance of three hundred, which would fill the main lounge. To his amazement, seven hundred people streamed in, packing every available inch of the room, even after children had been invited to come to the front and sit on the floor. A crowd can be exhilarating, but there can also be too much of a good thing, Em decided. With so many people in the room, walking into it was like meeting the blast of heat one encountered in the engine room. Overwhelming!

That was only a small part of Em's worries. The other *Doulos* workers who were scheduled to help with the two-hour programme had for one reason or another failed to appear. Em was left alone with the crowd. He improvised for an hour and then breathed a sigh of relief when the time came for a 45-minute film. That would occupy the adults. However, it would bore the children who would then wriggle and fret and distract the parents.

42 Something would have to be done. He shuffled the audience around, moving the children to one side where he proceeded to entertain them till the film finished. When it finally did, the programme was ended. Em was completely exhausted.

The measure of his success, however, was the fact that he had to push people out to clear the way for the next group to come in. The visitors were reluctant to leave. On the following days Em often spotted the same people attending again and again, some as many as five times.

Fortunately, in future meetings Em was given a team of two or three people to work with him and relieve him of some of the load. When asked how things were going, he joked, 'Well, Sunday was my best day.'

'Oh?'

'Yes, that's when we had the high winds. The storm kept everyone away. I had a most relaxing day'

Em, with his love of people and outgoing personality was to become one of the ship's best-loved leaders among Latin Americans. Whenever the ship returned to a port, one of the first questions was, 'Is Em Namuco on board?'

He would often compère meetings, introducing himself to the audience as a truly international person. 'I am from the Philippines,' he would say, 'but my shoes are from England, my shirt is from the United States and my tie from

Thailand. My guitar I got in Japan but it was made in Taiwan and now I will sing you a song from India.'

Another aspect of *Doulos'* ministry was showing films. Immanuel Böker, a German with engineering training, was responsible for this. On one occasion he took a team to an inland town, there he discovered that all the Catholics lived on the left side of the main road. On the right were the Protestants. Apparently the two never came together or ventured into each other's territory to mix and mingle.

That presented Immanuel with a dilemma. Where should he show the film? The pastor of the Protestant church advised, 'If you don't want to get stoned, you'd better show it on our side.' Put that way, the problem was easily solved. The Protestants saw the film.

The Catholics objected. Why did they have to miss out on the film? Another visit to the town followed and about 400 Catholics turned out to watch the film.

Not that all was sweetness and light. To begin with, getting permission to show the film was fraught with hassle. Then there was a power failure. When that was restored, the projector decided not to run. Then there were some young children throwing rocks, whether with the intention to disturb or simply out of boredom, the team couldn't guess. Eventually, however, everything worked out. Afterwards the team were able to talk with people in a more personal way.

A 22-year-old Mexican who accompanied the team as translator was so impressed with the experience that he decided he wanted to form a small music group and go around from village to village with music and films.

Eventually the *Doulos* visit in Veracruz drew to an end. *Doulos* would be leaving her first Latin American country and sailing down to Colombia. Before she could leave Mexico, though, a major problem had to be resolved.

The world was in the throes of an oil crisis. No fuel had arrived in Veracruz for weeks and stocks were down to nothing. Ships were leaving and steaming up the coast to other ports in search of fuel.

Meanwhile, *Doulos* was ready to go to Colombia. As a matter of fact, she had to leave immediately if she was to make Barranquilla in time for the opening reception with its numerous VIPs in attendance. *Doulos* workers had already made preparations for sailing. The bookshop had been packed away for the week-long voyage. Departure paperwork had been taken care of. There was only one thing left to do: take on fuel for the voyage.

The ship was moved to the bunker berth where fuel pipe connections were located, but her officers were informed that there was no fuel available. George Miley, back on board as director, discussed the situation with his first engineer, Rex Worth, asking him to work out how far the ship could go with the fuel she had. Would there be enough to sail? Could the ship, if necessary, stop somewhere en route to tank up?

Rex went down to his cabin and worked out how far the ship could go. When he had finished, he turned to his wife and said, 'Ros, this is ridiculous. *Doulos* is the Lord's ship. If he wants the ship to go, he's got to supply the fuel. I think we should pray about this.'

The two of them did pray, telling God this was his ship

and if he didn't provide, they would have to stay right where they were.

They were not the only ones praying. The ship's leaders held a crisis meeting to discuss, pray and decide what should be done. As there was nothing else they could do about the situation, they went to the dining-room for lunch. While they were eating, two men approached the ship. Without consulting anyone, they walked over to the fuel connection pipes and began to hook up the hoses. Fuel began pouring into the ship.

45

'We were the only ship to take fuel,' commented Rex later. 'As we were taking it, my job was to check the specifications and take samples to make sure we had the right fuel coming in. Well, the first one I took was a pale yellow. I took three other samples and was amazed to find they were all different colours. Where the fuel had come from, no one seemed to know. Nor why there was a difference in colour. All I can say is, I've never seen anything like it in my career before or since, but we had no problem at all with the fuel.'

*Doulos* steamed out past the other ships at anchor waiting for fuel. On board was all the fuel she needed to get her to Colombia. An interesting footnote is that the shipping agent never reported the taking on of fuel nor was *Doulos* ever billed for it.

# 4

## Permits, Problems and More Problems

David Greenlee, a tall, thin young American had been sent ahead to Colombia by *Doulos* leaders to do advance preparation, or line-up, as it was called. His specific job was to clear each aspect of the ship's proposed visit with local officials and to get written permits. In some ways he was an ideal choice for the assignment. Though from the United States, he had grown up in Colombia, spoke Spanish fluently and knew his way around the country.

But he had some disadvantages as well. For one thing, at twenty-one he was very young for such a responsibility. Even more of a drawback was the fact that he had never done anything remotely like this and had not the faintest idea how to proceed. An experienced line-up person should have been with him and had intended to be. Unfortunately, Colombia had not shown itself particularly enthusiastic about granting visas to Sri Lankans, so George Barathan was still sitting in Mexico.

Someone did eventually come out from *Doulos* for a short while to give David directions and get him started. Together the two men went to survey the berth situation and agreed that the only suitable location in Barranquilla for *Doulos* was at Las Flores, a wooden berth where tug boats were tied up and confiscated drug-running boats were kept. Though well outside town, Las Flores was much better than the main port area with its tight security inside the port gates and the rough area outside them. Unfortunately, though, the man in charge of the Las Flores berth categorically refused to make it available.

But *Doulos* had to berth there, David realized. No other **47** place was suitable. Eventually he decided to go over the manager's head. Flying up to the capital city of Bogotá, he succeeded in getting an appointment with the assistant director of the national port authority, who listened attentively and responded quite positively.

'Come back tomorrow and I'll confirm it,' he told David.

On the following morning David entered the port authority office with a spring in his step. He looked around cheerfully and then suddenly come to an abrupt halt. Sitting in one of the chairs was the local Barranquilla manager who had categorically denied his request.

'Well, Mr. Greenlee, so we meet again,' said the man, immediately recognizing David. 'What are you doing here?'

'Well, uh . . .' stammered David, 'I thought I'd come up to Bogotá and see if I could find some solution to the berth problem.'

'Over my dead body!'

The man looked David straight in the eyes as he said the words. The venom in his voice was unmistakable.

David's heart plummeted. In the awkward silence that followed his hopes were further dashed when the assistant director said apologetically, 'Well, as you can see, there's no way we can do this for you. It's impossible.'

David walked out of the office embarrassed, discouraged and not a little scared. Another failure chalked up to his account. How could he possibly accomplish what *Doulos* leaders expected of him?

David mentally ran through the other items on his list. One thing he needed was a permit to sell books. He had already received an official refusal for that. Then he needed clearance from Immigration. A long, complicated procedure had been explained to him, but his attempts to follow it were obviously leading nowhere. And finally, he had to get a permit for foreign exchange so that money from book sales could be sent back to Europe to pay bills. But foreign exchange was impossible, he'd been told, unless he first obtained a permit to sell the books. And that took him back to his first point.

It was nearing the end of January and the ship was due to arrive on February 8. The pressure was mounting and David didn't know what to do about it.

One day he was introduced to an older Christian widow. As he told her his troubles, she said, 'Maybe I can help you. I know some people in government; we went to school together.'

She arranged an appointment for David with the minister of government, one of the most important men in government at that time. The minister was warm and friendly, offering to write a couple of letters for David. Those letters changed the situation dramatically. Shortly after they were sent, David was startled to get a phone call inviting him to talk with the deputy foreign minister of Colombia. The minister sent David on to the visa department where officials were suddenly most co-operative and the immigration problem was speedily resolved.

Another call came from the head of Customs who received David and seemed to want to help him, but couldn't find a way to resolve a legal complication.

Only a couple of weeks remained before the ship's arrival and still there was no berth, no permit to sell books and no foreign exchange. David spent the entire weekend fasting and praying. Along with his faith went a practical streak which prompted him to call the line-up team that was trying to arrange the programme for the ship's visit in the port city of Barranquilla.

49

'Frank,' he said to the team leader, 'the ship is supposed to leave Veracruz on Tuesday. If we don't get the break-through on permits by Monday, I think we should call the ship and advise them to cancel the visit to Colombia.'

Frank agreed.

On Monday morning David had set up an appointment with the president of the port authority. At 8am he promptly presented himself at the president's office and waited.

After a while the young receptionist inquired politely, 'Are you waiting for the president of the port authority?'

'Yes.'

'He's not here.'

'Hasn't he come in yet?'

'Oh yes, he's come in.'

'Well, I'll just wait here for him then.'

'But he's not here.'

'I thought you told me he'd come in,' objected David.

'Yes, but he's got a back door.'

'You mean he's gone?' David's voice combined incredulity and consternation. 'Is he coming back?'

'No, he's got meetings elsewhere. He'll be gone for the day.'

A moment of silence followed while David digested that information.

Then the receptionist said a rather unusual thing. 'Sir, you're not being very smart.'

'Why do you say that?'

'You're talking to the wrong people.'

'What do you mean? You don't even know what I'm here for.'

'Of course I do. I know what's going on.'

(Thus David added a very important item to his store of knowledge: secretaries and receptionists were quite important and usually knew what was going on.)

The receptionist continued, 'The president of the port authority is just a political appointee. He won't help you. You need to talk to Dr. Luis Pedrosa.'

'Why? Who's he?'

'He's the technical director. He'll help you.'

'Well,' murmured David pensively, 'What to do?' Looking up at the receptionist he asked, 'Is he available?'

'Let me call,' she offered.

'Send him down' was the reply.

Tired and discouraged, David made his way to Dr. Pedrosa's office.

'What can I do for you?' asked Dr. Pedrosa.

'Well, here's the situation.' David described the ship and his problem trying to secure a berth. 'We wanted to use the Las Flores berth, but that's been denied to us. I wonder if there isn't some way to work out a system for the main port.'

'Can you come back in about an hour?'

Taking his cue, David left the office, found a place to sit and pulled out a copy of *Time* magazine to read. Exactly one hour later he again presented himself at the office.

Dr. Pedrosa greeted David and handed him a paper, saying, 'Here's a copy of the telex I've just sent.'

'Oh, what's that?' asked David bewildered.

'Well, read it.'

David read words to this effect, 'To the Las Flores authority: I hereby authorize the stay of the ship *Doulos* February 8–24, 1979.'

David stared at the words incredulously.

'Is that satisfactory?' queried the man.

David didn't walk out of that office; he floated!

A few days earlier David had decided to have one last attempt to get a permit for bookselling. He had gone down to Customs to try to see the top man. In the waiting room he had stood, leaning against a wall and thinking, *What in the world are we going to do?*

A young woman had approached him and asked, 'Can I help you?'

'I don't know,' replied David, unsure how to respond. 'What do you do?'

'I work for Customs. I'm a lawyer.'

She led David into her office and David explained his problem.

51

'No,' she said thoughtfully, 'you're going about it the wrong way. What you need to do is this. . . .' And she proceeded to tell him how to write a letter to Customs.

David followed her advice and submitted the letter.

That had been several days before. When David now left Dr. Pedrosa's office with permission for the berth, he proceeded on to Customs to see if there was any progress with regard to bookselling permission.

'Has there by any chance been a response to my letter?' he asked with fear and trembling.

'Why, yes, we just got something in.'

There was complete authorization and a copy of the telegram which had already been sent to Barranquilla.

With that in hand, David rushed over to foreign exchange. By then, the working day was drawing to a close. Everyone had already left the central bank except the top man in charge of foreign exchange. He let David in and David explained the situation.

'Well, that's a little difficult,' replied the bank official. 'Normally it takes two to three weeks for approval to go through.'

'What should I do?'

'Do you have a letter drawn up?'

'No.'

'Do you know how to type?'

David nodded.

'My secretary has gone,' continued the official, 'but you can go over there and type up the letter. You have about fifteen minutes to get it logged in downstairs. Come back and tell me what the number is and I'll see that it's out by tomorrow evening.'

That evening down in Barranquilla the line-up team was with a group of Christians praying when the phone rang. It was David. When the news was passed on, there was a loud whoop of joy.

On Monday morning David had had nothing, absolutely nothing. On Tuesday evening he flew to Barranquilla with all the permits in writing.

The ship had a great time in Barranquilla. The lounge was filled time and again with ladies' conferences. Pastors came from all over the country to the pastors' conference. Long, long queues of people visited the book exhibition. And many other activities took place as well.

David's experience was in many ways typical of what went on in advance preparation for the ship in port after port. Local officials had never encountered a ship remotely like *Doulos*. It didn't fit neatly into any of their categories and they didn't know how to react. Often the temptation was to play safe, backing off from responsibility, protesting that there was nothing they could do.

Most of the workers on the ship were young adults in their late teens or early twenties. From this resource pool the line-up teams were drawn. Young, inexperienced people were sent to face high government officials and work their way through the complex maze of arranging for a ship's visit.

Obtaining a berth, visas, permits to sell books and change currency and taking care of numerous other technical details were only part of a line-up team's job. A programme had to be arranged as well. And that required drawing together the local Christian leaders, discussing the needs of the community and working out how *Doulos* could best be used in ministering to those needs.

Each line-up experience was different. Just when things were going well, the unexpected had a way of popping up and throwing plans out of kilter. Or what appeared to be a routine and easy path was suddenly blocked by a padlocked gate. Line-up people were continually made aware of their dependency upon God.

George Barathan was no exception.

When Colombia had failed to grant him a visa so that he could help David with the line-up preparations there, George was sent to Trinidad. English was the official language of Trinidad, the southernmost island of the West Indies seven miles off the coast of Venezuela. Its population was 40% East Indian, 45% black and 5% mixed cosmopolitan minorities.

With his dark skin, George, a Sri Lankan, blended well into the racial mixtures there. And with three months to prepare for the ship's visit, he was under little time-pressure. The outlook was good and there was no reason to anticipate any unusual problems. Of course, the ship was totally unknown in that part of the world, but that was a problem George had handled on several occasions before in other line-ups.

Basically confident, though feeling a few familiar tingles of apprehension in facing a new line-up situation, George landed in Trinidad. Immediately he ran up against suspicion. Everywhere. Among church leaders, among government officials and among the general public.

In the previous year in a neighbouring country an event had occurred that had shocked the world — an event so heinous, so incredible, so tragic that people were still trying to make sense of it. A cult had moved en masse into the jungles of Guyana and set up living quarters at a place they named Jonestown. Suddenly one day its members — about five hundred men, women and children — had followed their spiritual leader, Jim Jones, into a mass suicide.

*If such a thing could happen in Guyana, could it also happen in our country?* wondered Trinidadians. They had already had their own unpleasant experiences with a variety of cults and strange religions imported by foreigners. One such group even brought in a ship.

And now another unknown religious ship was appearing on the horizon. No wonder they were suspicious.

Undaunted, George set out to contact Christian leaders. His first difficulty was in locating them. No one seemed to have any kind of list. Finally George came across a man who had compiled a list, but he was reluctant to hand it over to someone he did not know.

'Give me a week or two to think it over and pray about it,' he told George.

At the end of that time he gave the list to George and George and a co-worker began to visit the pastors and Christian leaders one by one. He explained to them that *Doulos* people believed the same basic elements of Christianity that all main line churches believed; they were not cultists in any sense of the word. Furthermore, he continued, the ship had the respect of internationally known

Christian leaders. He showed written endorsements from several.

Questions. Answers. Probing. Much time was spent in relationship building. The doors of churches began opening to George and his co-worker to show a film strip about *Doulos* and tell what the ship was all about. Christians began to get excited.

In mid February a *Doulos* Information Breakfast was held and a hundred pastors and Christian leaders from different denominations came together to pray for the ship's visit. Several churches requested *Doulos* teams to come and work with them during the visit. Bookings for conferences aboard began to fill up — over one thousand for a youth conference; 236 for a pastors' conference, etc. Sixty-three volunteers wanted to come and help in practical work on the ship while she was in port. For a small island, the response was overwhelming.

Meanwhile, there was also the official side of the visit to attend to. That seemed to be moving along. Customs presented no problems. A good berth was promised, as well as a suitable venue for the *Doulos* cultural event, International Night. The Ministry of Education was ready to sponsor the visit. Everything was falling neatly into place — except that all was contingent on permission from the Ministry of National Security. And the Ministry of National Security remained silent in spite of all the line-up men's attempts to get action.

Time continued to pass. Nothing happened on this front. The *Doulos* programme in Venezuela came to an end and the ship sailed for Barbados to drop off fifty people and some books for an exhibition. It was to be only a brief stop en route to Trinidad. Still no word came from National Security. Ship leaders conferred and decided to make an alternative plan if the Trinidad permission did not materialize. Finally, on March 23, the day the ship was due to arrive in Trinidad, word came from the ministry. The answer was, 'No, the ship cannot come to Trinidad.'

*Doulos* hastily set up a short programme in Barbados while George and his co-worker prepared an appeal, presenting a petition signed by the heads of different Christian denominations in Trinidad. Again the decision was negative. No visit, no programme. Even dry-docking, booked three months earlier, was forbidden.

On the next day one thousand applicants were expected for a youth conference on board, many travelling long distances. *What a mess to be straightened out!* thought George. Fortunately, through radio and newspapers the team was able to announce the cancellation of the ship's visit. George's morale was hardly lifted when he passed a newsstand and saw headlines screaming, 'Floating Jonestown Banned'.

Nor did it ease the pressure to get a phone call from *Doulos* saying that the ship's safety certificate would run out on 29 March, less than a week away.

In order to get the necessary maintenance done and pass inspection, George knew that the ship had to be put into dry-dock for a week or two. That was an annual procedure for all passenger ships. In dry-dock the water would be pumped out of the enclosed dock, leaving the ship resting on huge blocks. The hull of the ship would be cleaned of encrustation, given a stringent inspection, and repaired as necessary. Only then would the Passenger Ship Safety Certificate be renewed and the ship be able to continue sailing.

58     While renewal of the safety certificate was the most pressing matter to be dealt with, dry-dock was necessary for other maintenance work as well, work that could not be carried out while the ship was in operation. Dry-dock would mean an intensive period of work under rough conditions (no running water, no use of toilets, no air-conditioning, no power apart from a very limited amount brought in by electrical cables from ashore) and all non-involved crew and staff would have to move ashore to be out of the way.

George was informed that *Doulos* officers had checked out the only other dry-dock facilities nearby — in Curaçao, Martinique and Venezuela — and learned that they were all fully booked for the next three weeks. That meant there was no choice. The ship *had* to go to Trinidad, at least for dry-dock.

The line-up team quickly drafted another letter and submitted it to the ministry. In the letter they reminded the ministry that dry-dock had been booked for three months. In view of the fact that the ship's safety certificate would run out in three or four days, it seemed rather unfair of the ministry to wait and cancel dry-dock at the last minute.

The line-up men prayed. On *Doulos* people met for prayer. And everyone held his breath.

The answer came back. *Doulos* could come but only with necessary crew and only for dry-dock. There would be no programme.

A sigh of relief escaped George's lips.

*Doulos*, however, was landed with a major challenge: finding immediate accommodation in Barbados for over two hundred people who could not sail to Trinidad. Hotels were out of the question; there was no money for that. School premises vacated for holidays, private homes, churches, camp sites opened up. When *Doulos* sailed the next day, everyone left behind had somewhere to sleep (although sixty single women were hard pressed to count their blessings later when torrential rains washed out three of their twenty tents.)

The arrangements took care of physical needs, but did nothing to address the question in everyone's mind. *Why? We prayed and prayed. Why didn't God answer? We know he can. We've seen him do it. So why didn't he?*

'Maybe it's because he wanted us to visit Barbados instead,' suggested some people.

Perhaps. Perhaps not. Workers on *Doulos* had to face the fact that they might never know the reason why. But they knew God did not let them down. He had his reasons. They trusted him because they knew what he was like.

Hardest hit of all, perhaps, was George. Plagued with guilt feelings, he asked himself, *What did I do wrong?* He felt defeated, discouraged. The reversal of the decision about dry-dock lifted his spirits a little, but they plunged again when he thought about the staff left behind on Barbados. In the end, he told himself and God, 'I can only do so much.

I've done what I could. Many people have been praying. It's in your hands now, Lord.'

Relief flooded in. That is, until the next time he was sent on line-up. *Will I be able to get Doulos in this time?* he wondered. A wave of apprehension engulfed him.

60 On that line-up, however, all went well and his confidence returned.

A line-up team had already spent many weeks preparing for the ship's next port of call after Trinidad. A two-week voyage would take the ship down to Buenos Aires, Argentina. The plan was for the ship to spend one and a half months in Argentina and then gradually make her way northward, calling at several ports along the way.

A young Canadian, Bob Clement, was leader of the line-up team in Argentina. Here's the story as he told it:

> It seemed totally impossible to get into any offices whatsoever. At that particular time, there was a military regime and all government buildings were heavily guarded. One of the great miracles God did in helping us to get a foot in the door was introducing us to the American naval attaché in Buenos Aires, who was a Christian. He was sick the Sunday I visited his church, but I met his wife and was invited back to their house. Initially very cold, he soon began to warm up, though he felt it was very unprofessional of us to put the Argentine government in this difficult situation by requiring the permissions so quickly. Ordinarily the Argentine government does not function quickly, he said, but he was willing to help us.
>
> I remember walking past some of the government

buildings. You couldn't even stand in front of them; the guards would move you on in case you were planning to blow a building up or sabotage it in some way. Just getting into a lobby would be a major accomplishment, we realized: impossible unless we had contacts who were willing to see us.

My first appointment with a high government official came through the American attaché. I was frisked as I walked up to the government building and then I was allowed through the door. Again I was frisked and my papers were checked. I walked to the foyer desk area where they again checked my papers, asking me who I wanted to see and whether I had an appointment. Then they phoned to verify my appointment. Someone was sent down from that office to escort me from the foyer. We had to log in before we could even enter the elevators. We logged in the time, who we were, what we were going to do. When we came out of the elevator, we had to log in again at another desk before we could proceed to the office.

After we had our interview, we had to do the same things in reverse.

One of our challenges in Argentina was Customs, involving a lot of paperwork and bureaucracy. We had a customs agent who was a Christian but we also needed a customs broker. We settled for the one recommended to us: Lucifer and Sons. They said confidently, 'Tell us what you need and we'll get all the paperwork done.'

They went to work, but as we proceeded, they discovered that the only way we could get the permission we needed was to get the head of Customs, an admiral, to give his okay.

We were under a tremendous amount of tension with

the ship sailing closer to Argentina every minute. The owner of Lucifer and Sons, when he heard we had to get permission from this admiral, lost his cool and threw all the papers at me, saying, 'The admiral doesn't say yes to anything. You'll never get his permission. It's a waste of time even to try.'

Interestingly enough, just a week before, God had led me to make an appointment with the head of Customs, so I already had a prearranged appointment set up for the next day. The customs agent and the broker went with us. While we were waiting outside his office, we decided to have a word of prayer. Before we could start, however, the doors opened and we were ushered into a massive office. The admiral never smiled once, never nodded, never gave any indication of his thoughts. He just sat there while I tried to explain the whole thing in Spanish and ask for his permission. When I finished, he said, 'I'll let you know in twenty-four hours.'

That was all. Yet in my heart I knew we had it.

The ship was almost in port when twenty-four hours later he did give his approval. After that, we still had to get twenty-six signatures from Customs. One of their requirements was that we bring a list of the entire inventory of books on the ship, a task that would require a colossal amount of work, but even so, this was a major miracle in our eyes.

Meanwhile we had decided to invite the president of Argentina to open the book exhibition. We had submitted the letters, contacted the right people and everything else we had to do. Then we waited to hear from the president and get an interview. We were hoping this would help with publicity and open some other doors for us.

Soon after we submitted the letter, our office in Buenos Aires was raided. Men came in and took samples of everything. They wouldn't let on who they were. That really shook up our team in the office, but they co-operated and gave the intruders everything they wanted.

Next, we got an invitation. Luis, a mature, godly man who was our main local contact, and I were summoned to a building which he told me was the secret police headquarters. Many Argentinians had gone in there and never come out, he said. He was very nervous.

Again, coming to the doorway, we were frisked. We had to give them our passports and all our documents. That was before we could even get through the doors. We were checked again when we got through the double doors. Everything was taken from us and we were ushered into a waiting room. All around us we knew was one-way glass. We could feel it. That was an incredibly difficult moment. I knew Luis was absolutely petrified. I was a visitor and hadn't heard the stories going around about missing people, but Luis was very aware of what was going on.

Sitting there, we sensed that eyes were looking at us and ears were listening to our conversation. We were given a card with the number thirteen on it. I laughed nervously and said to Luis, 'You know, this is really fortunate. We got number thirteen, but we don't have to worry because it's not Friday.'

Luis looked at me, white as a sheet. He said, 'In Argentina Friday isn't the unlucky day; it's Wednesday.'

This was Wednesday.

We were taken upstairs to an office and seated on a couch. In the wall we could see metal bars where handcuffs could be fastened as people were interrogated. We were interrogated — without handcuffs, though — as they tried to find out what we were about, what the purpose of the ship's visit was, and so forth. They knew absolutely everything. It was incredible how much they'd been able to find out about us and the ship ministry.

Finally they let us go, which was an incredible relief. They gave us back our documents and we left the building. I don't think I've ever seen Luis happier.

The president didn't come to the opening ceremony, so we went through all that in vain.

Another of our problems was that the cost of everything in Argentina at that time was astronomical. To cover Buenos Aires with advertising would have been totally out of the question as far as our budget was concerned. The ship could come to the city and pass unnoticed, for all intents and purposes. We really needed a break. We contacted everybody we could. We gave the word out to the radio, newspapers, television. No one seemed interested.

Bob and one of his team went to a local advertising agency to explore the possibility of paid advertisements. After they had explained about the ship and discussed various advertising strategies, the agent suggested a budget of $30,000 for basic but adequate advertisement.

Caught in a dilemma between the steep financial cost and the ineffectiveness of a ship visit without adequate advertisement, the line-up team contacted ship's leaders for guidance.

The reply came back, 'You put in too many zeros. Surely you meant $3,000, not $30,000. Please confirm.'

The ship had never spent $30,000 for advertising. The ship didn't *have* $30,000 to spend in that way. *Doulos* would have to go without paid advertisement, depending on local churches to spread the news.

The ship's leaders had second thoughts when they came into Buenos Aires and realized that the vast majority of its citizens were completely unaware of the presence of *Doulos* in their port. Some kind of advertising was absolutely necessary. But how could they do it?

'What about spot advertisements on television?' suggested someone. 'Very short ones. Just a few seconds long but appearing several times throughout the day.'

'That would certainly get the word out,' agreed the leaders. 'It's worth investigating.'

The situation was presented to the ship's family during their weekly evening of prayer and a day or two later a delegation went to the television studio to make inquiries. The more the possibilities were explored, the more excited the delegation became — until the price was announced. Thousands of dollars for one minute of television time! *Thousands of dollars!* Never could the inexperienced *Doulos* delegation have imagined television time would be so astronomically expensive.

All attempts to negotiate a reduction in charges were brushed aside as out of the question. Somewhat embarrassed at their naiveté, the delegation made their exit and returned to the ship to face *Doulos* workers who had been at the prayer evening and wanted to hear how God had answered their prayers.

Bob takes up the story of what happened a few days later:

Suddenly we got a call from someone representing a television programme called *Monica Presenta,* the most watched programme in all Argentina and Uruguay as well. They came and made a programme on the ship seven minutes long. It represented probably about $180,000 worth of free publicity. Absolutely everybody in the country stopped everything to watch this show.

It gave us a tremendous lot of prestige and opened many doors for us. Consequently, every radio station and newspaper got in on the act. It was a great answer to prayer.

Almost every line-up presented challenges of one kind or another for the young and largely inexperienced men and women who had to deal face to face with high-ranking officials. Always they were under the pressure of fast-shrinking time limits. Constantly they found themselves in situations out of their depth, pressing for permits or concessions that seemed humanly impossible to obtain. Any of these line-up people could identify with Bob in this incident he recounted.

We were in a prayer meeting a few nights before the ship was supposed to arrive in Buenos Aires. The pastor was very keen on prayer. He had a big blackboard up front.

'Let's write down all the things we need to pray for,' he said.

'Okay,' I said, 'the first thing we need to do is pray that we get permission for the ship to come.'

I'll never forget the look on his face. He just turned around from the blackboard and said, 'You mean you don't even have permission yet?'

It was a great prayer meeting.

Even when permits have been obtained and all technical arrangements worked out, a line-up person tended to hold his breath until the ship actually arrived, was tied up and cleared by Immigration and Customs, as Marian MacIver's experience indicates. In 1980, when the ship had toured Latin America and returned to Europe, she was leader of the line-up team sent to prepare her own home city of Glasgow, Scotland for the *Doulos* visit. It was only her second line-up experience. Here's her version of what happened:

> We had a great time as a team. It was a laugh a minute with dear brother Ronnie Lappin. Of course, we had to learn each other's little idiosyncrasies, one of which was getting the tea right for Ronnie. It had to be a certain colour, achieved by waving the tea bag over hot water a certain number of times and adding a carefully measured amount of milk. And certainly not any of that instant stuff! It had to be real milk, which one of us female line-up team members had to go and acquire somewhere.
>
> The line-up went very well in Glasgow until the ship was due to arrive. The official opening reception was arranged for Friday at 5:45 pm. We had received acceptances from 350 dignitaries of the local civic and Christian communities. The Lord Mayor was coming as guest of honour. There would be representatives of some twenty-five to thirty embassies. The minister of the largest church in Glasgow was also coming.
>
> The ship could only come into Glasgow at high tide on the River Clyde. That was at 5:00 any morning or evening. The ship was due to come in on a Thursday evening to give plenty of time for it to be set up for the reception on Friday evening.

At 5:00 on Thursday evening we couldn't even see the water because of the fog. There was no way that the ship could come in. The agent told me to come again at 5:00 on Friday morning and they would try then to bring in the ship. Our team of three duly appeared on the quayside on a January morning in the freezing cold and sat in our little Volkswagen beetle with its heater that didn't work.

Again we couldn't even see the water. No ship had come in that morning. As soon as the agent opened his doors, we were on his doorstep asking if there was any way the ship could be brought in before 4:00 that afternoon.

'Miss MacIver,' the shipping agent said to me, 'would you please look out of the window? Do you see the building across the street?'

'No.'

'Do you think, as responsible human beings, we can bring a ship in when one cannot see in front of one's face for more than ten yards?'

'No.'

At eleven o'clock we turned up again.

'We can see the building across the road,' I announced. 'Is there any way . . . ?'

'Miss MacIver, yes, I can see the building across the road, but the tide is not going to be high enough until 5:00.'

So we went away, but we were praying, as you might well imagine.

At 1:00 we went back and said, 'You know there are 350 people expected, don't you? Do we have to go on the radio at this late stage and tell them the ship is not coming?'

'Miss MacIver,' he said, 'I have just been on to the port manager down the river. I don't know who you've been in touch with, but he is willing to bring the ship in at 4:30, which means it will berth at 5:15.'

We drove down to the river at 4:30. We stood on the river bank willing the ship along, with our hands and scarves waving to everyone. We then jumped into our 'beetle' and rushed to the quayside. Already there were dignitaries there waiting to get on the ship.

The ship berthed at 5:15 and people walked up the gangway at 5:45. Doulos staff had set the tables and got everything ready while the ship was sailing. I heard one Christian leader remark, 'This is the first time I've ever turned up for a church meeting before the church was there.'

Marian's account was only half of the story of the dramatic arrival of *Doulos*. Captain Isaacson relates the other half:

We were already late coming into Glasgow when we came up to the place where we were going to dock. The pilot on board said, 'Hard aport.'

We turned our ship to the left and sailed in, going fairly fast. The quayside was dead ahead of us.

'Stop! Stop the engine!' ordered the pilot.

We pulled the telegraph to stop position. The engine room answered, but the engine didn't stop. We kept going ahead. It seemed we were going faster than we should have been. The quayside ahead was built of solid concrete; it wasn't something that would give way like an empty box.

By this time the pilot was screaming, 'I told you we wanted full astern!'

'The telegraph says full astern,' I pointed out, 'but nothing is happening down in the engine. We're still going fast ahead.'

There was a malfunction in the engine. Finally they got the engine stopped, but then they couldn't get it into reverse. It was horrible. We were getting closer and closer to the quayside.

George Booth, our chief mate, was standing by forward and I said, 'George, how far are we from the quayside ahead of us?'

He named a figure. It was hardly a ship's length.

The pilot had walked from the front of the bridge and was leaning against the back wall. He didn't faint, but he started to slide down, mumbling all the while to himself.

In the meantime, I and another mate were praying as I've done so often since then, 'Lord, take over. This is your ship. Stop her. Stop her.'

The ship came to a dead stop within eighteen yards of the quayside. The engines had nothing to do with it. The ship then moved away from the quayside to our left. Then all on its own it moved ahead up alongside where the people were standing and waiting for our arrival. I said weakly to George, 'Get the lines out,' and we tied to.

Believe it or not, the pilot was still slumped in the back. I don't care to tell you some of the words he was using.

# 5

## *All in a Day's Work: the Life of a Deck Officer*

Captain, engineers, deck officers . . . all were an essential part of shipboard life. There had been a constant turnover of officers on *Doulos*, but when George Booth had come aboard in Mexico, he was committed to stay and ready to plunge into the work, On his first morning he donned a boiler suit, the sailor's workclothes, and made his way forward to the fo'c'sle to meet his deck-hands and get on with his job. The boatswain, who serves as foreman for the deck workers, spotted him and sauntered over.

'Oh, you're a new guy,' he said brightly in heavily accented English. 'Okay, I give you some work.'

'Oh no,' countered George, 'I'll give you some work!'

There was plenty of work for everyone to do. Even the most cursory look around had been enough to convince George of that. As he later said, 'The ship was a wreck! It had been neglected by Costa Lines during their last months of ownership and was derelict! Deck workers were just chipping paint around the edges, superficially. There were still blocks that were frozen on bits and pieces. And shackles all over the ship! The ship used to click, clank, click, clank as it rolled around. The first thing I did was to remove those tons of top weight.'

72

George went to work with a will, rising to the challenge.

Three months after he joined the ship sailed into Argentina for its first visit there and the ship's director paid him a visit.

'George,' he said, 'we'd like you to take over as captain for a little while till Carl gets back.'

George groaned. He knew the situation. The temporary master had returned home from Argentina. Carl Isaacson, the chief mate, at sixty-three years of age had just gone to the United States to work for his master's certificate. Roger Emtage, the mate who had successfully sat his master's exam in England, had left. Apart from George Booth there was only one deck officer, an American who had just obtained his second mate qualification.

Captaincy was a promotion, of course, but it was a promotion George did not want at that time. 'I raved and shouted,' he recounted, 'because I didn't want to be master. I'd just got my certificate. It was like getting a brand new driver's licence and being set in the middle of rush hour traffic in New York and told, "Well, you can drive a car now. Off you go!" Even if you are qualified, you don't feel able to do the job. I sensed the responsibility in being master and backed off from the whole idea, Yet I knew there was no one else available. It was obvious God had put me into the situation and he would see me through it. In my weakness he would make his strength perfect.'

George accepted the captaincy, but as the job didn't involve much work in port, he continued to do a mate's job as well. One day he worked down in the water tank. At coffee break time he emerged, covered with cement dust, and made his way to the duty mess, a special dining-room reserved for crew in their dirty work clothes.

At the same time an Argentinian officer in fancy white dress uniform strode up the gangway with a form in triplicate to be signed by the captain. The gangway watch-man obligingly escorted him to the captain . . . down in the duty mess.

The officer in his crisp, spotless uniform walked in and looked around uncertainly at the group of men coated with white chalky dust.

'The captain is in here?' he asked incredulously.

'Yes, there he is.' The watchman pointed out a man lounging on a paint-spattered folding chair with a big mug of tea in one hand and a sandwich in the other.

Too sceptical to inquire of George himself, the officer turned back to the watchman and asked, 'Are you *sure* he's the captain?'

George suppressed the urge to quip, 'Sure, I'm the captain now,' and point to someone else, saying, 'and tonight it's his turn.' Instead, he stood to his feet and said in a matter-of-fact voice, 'Yes, I'm the captain. I'll go and wash my hands and sign the papers.'

When the officer had left with the signed papers, the crew doubled up with laughter. They couldn't resist going over to the porthole to watch the man go down the gangway. They'll swear he had his cap off and was scratch-ing his head as he left.

George's captaincy lasted six months, after which he welcomed Captain Carl Isaacson with open arms and resumed his former duties as chief mate. Whenever Carl needed a break, George would fill in for him. Otherwise, they developed a good working relationship as captain and chief mate.

One morning in Barbados after George had been on the ship for well over a year, he was awakened about 3:00 am by a loud banging on his door. Instantly alert, he climbed out of bed, pulled on some clothes and went to open his door. The night watchman, a young Venezuelan, stood there with blood on his face and wild-looking hair, half of it clipped short while the other half hung long.

Breathlessly he exclaimed, 'There's a madman on the ship!'

'A madman!' repeated George, somewhat taken aback.

'Yeah, there's a madman!'

'Okay, well . . . uh . . .' George stalled while his mind raced. 'Let's go and get someone else to come with us.'

They hurried downstairs and came across one of the Brazilian crewmen, a huge young man who'd been rechristened Number Three Derrick because he could pick up anything.

'You come and help us,' commanded George.

The three of them raced upstairs onto deck with Number Three Derrick lagging behind anxiously while prodding the others forward.

George relented. 'Oh, go on back to bed,' he told the young Brazilian, and added jokingly, 'You're more a problem then a solution.'

George and the watchman searched the decks and eventually located the intruder up on the fo'c'sle where he was perching on the bow like a bird. George hastily looked about and found a big stick, which he appropriated, and the two men cautiously approached the intruder, never taking their eyes off of him.

Suddenly the man jumped up and dived over the bow railing into the water below. George and the watchman rushed to the railing and peered over. The man was swimming around the ship, back past the stern and on around toward the gangway. George and the watchman raced for the gangways to secure them and make sure he didn't come up.

That was the last they saw of the intruder. He had obviously been high on drugs, totally 'spaced out'. The watchman had been sitting on deck at the top of the gangway when the man came up and started punching him in the face.

'That was the only time I know that we voluntarily hired night-watchmen,' commented George. 'If anyone was going to beat up Barbadians, we wanted it to be a Barbadian!'

In the early summer of 1980, *Doulos* dry-docked in Curaçao in the Netherlands Antilles. Before leaving Venezuela where the ship had been for a month, many of the staff who would not be involved in the dry-dock were sent ashore in teams to work in the villages. When dry-dock was finished, the depopulated ship returned to Venezuela to pick up these people.

After a couple of weeks on shore, the land teams were eager to welcome back their floating home. The team members gathered early in the morning to be on hand to watch the ship sail in at 10.00 am. When word came to them that the ship had been delayed, they milled around restlessly all day. Finally about 5:00 pm the ship arrived, but it went to anchor instead of coming alongside.

That was too much for the *Doulos* people on shore. They had been waiting all day to go aboard. They took their disappointment to the line-up people who were equally disappointed. A lively discussion ensued, ending with the line-up team calling the ship to say, 'We'd like to send out a launch with *Doulos* people so they can get on the ship.'

'No, don't come,' was the unequivocal answer from the ship. 'The water's choppy here. It's going to get rough and be very difficult to get onto the gangway from the launch.'

'Well, we'll see what we can do.'

'No,' George Booth told them emphatically, 'don't do it, please.'

But the launch came anyway with a couple of dozen *Doulos* staff huddled around inside its tiny lounge area. Up and down the little vessel bounced in the waves, lurching this way and that. As it neared *Doulos*, it slowed almost to a halt, waiting for the ship to swing round to a position offering the launch more protection from the elements. Soon afterwards, the little boat came alongside the *Doulos* gangway which had been put down for customs men who were experienced at jumping on and off.

The gangway on *Doulos* has since been changed, but at that time it used to stick out on the side of the ship, resting on little metal blocks that swung in and out on two small pins. Rope hung from the blocks for securing the gangway when it was pulled up and stowed along the side of the ship. The ropes, not being in use now, hung down.

As the launch reached the gangway, the launch hand grabbed one of these ropes to tie up his bucking craft. Every time the boat rose on a swell, the man pulled the rope tighter.

Inside the launch several of the *Doulos* women rose and made their way with great difficulty to the doorway and out on deck. It was only a few steps to the gangway, but the boat was bucking like a wild horse. The women held hands tightly for safety and the first one readied herself for a flying leap to the bottom of the gangway.

Meanwhile, George had taken some deck-hands to the stern to put out a line for the launch. When the deck-hands saw what was happening by the gangway, they leaned over the rails and shouted desperately at the launch hand to free the rope so it wouldn't pull out the block. A *Doulos* deck-hand appeared with a big knife and started to rush down the gangway to cut the rope. Just as he did, the launch jerked down on a swell and the metal block was torn out from its pins. Flying as from a catapult, it struck the launch hand on the side of his head. He immediately collapsed unconscious on the railing of the launch.

A *Doulos* nurse in the launch quickly made her way to him. What she saw appalled her. His skull was obviously crushed. A towel appeared from somewhere and she covered the man's head. Someone else held the man's body while she steadied his head. A *Doulos* man took firm hold of her legs to keep her from being swept off the launch as it swung around and headed back to shore.

The man was rushed to hospital. The shocked people on *Doulos* could not believe what had just happened.

Everywhere on the ship little groups of people gathered, talking in hushed voices and praying that God would not let the man die.

George Booth went down to his cabin, sick to his stomach and screaming inside himself, 'This is not what I've come to serve the Lord for, to see people die like this.'

The next day word came that the man had died that morning, never having regained consciousness.

The police held an inquiry, questioned *Doulos* people and totally cleared the ship of all blame. The ship's leaders learned, however, that the man had left behind a common-law wife and a small child. Even though *Doulos* was not legally to blame, they felt a sense of responsibility toward the family. Before the leaders could act on it, however, some lawyers approached the woman and talked her into suing the ship.

That placed *Doulos* in a dilemma, as the lawyers well knew it would. If the case went to court, *Doulos* would certainly win, but until then the ship would be required to remain in port. That could take how long? Weeks? Even months?

Since ship leaders wanted to compensate the woman anyway, they decided to settle out of court, without admitting guilt. A couple of very capable lawyers from a local church offered their advice and services. In the end *Doulos* leaders paid the woman what they considered a reasonable amount, small by US or European standards but a large sum to Venezuelans.

A very subdued ship's company sailed from Venezuela. Death, that formless spectre hovering menacingly on a far distant horizon, had suddenly swooped in among them and confronted them with an awareness of their own vulnerability. Yet they realized they had a loving friend to put his strong, safe, comforting arms around them. Did the man who died know that loving friend? Did the woman he left behind?

The question was to haunt *Doulos* workers for months to come.

But life had to go on.

George plunged back into his work, though after that experience he remained very nervous of launches coming to the ship. He had been on the ship for a year and a half by this time, and the ship was still a mess in his eyes. He had made a lot of changes, but there was just so much still to be done that he couldn't get around to doing all of it. The cosmetic aspect was sacrificed to the urgent need of tackling basic problems.

The current problem was the promenade deck. Water had been leaking through the wooden deck to the steel beneath it. For a considerable time George had had some of his men working caulking the deck. Regular washing down of decks, which is a standard part of keeping a ship in order, had been suspended.

That's why the deck looked so messy when Ebbo and Hardy surveyed it one Saturday afternoon. Adding to the mess was the accommodation ladder lying in the alleyway. Usually it was attached to the side of the ship, but it had been removed for the ship's recent passage through the Panama Canal.

For Chief Steward Ebbo Buurma and Purser Hardy Erne, seeing the mess was like putting a torch to the heap of their frustrations. Physically strong, practical, experienced seamen, they had the ability to tackle some of the neglected areas, but they lacked the qualifications on paper to give them the authority. But this, at least, was a situation they could do something about. The main decks ought to be washed at least once a week. Such sloppy neglect!

Being men of action, they immediately found the nearest hose, hooked it up and began to spray a jet of water over the deck.

Just at that moment George Booth came on the scene. And exploded!

'What are you doing here?' he shouted furiously. 'You're ruining my new fire hose.'

'Just look at that deck!' they shot back contemptuously.

Ebbo and Hardy saw the mess on the deck, but George saw his brand-new fire hose being filled with salt water. Remains of salt in the hose would cause it to start deteriorating. That was certainly not desirable for fire hoses vital to the ship's safety.

*My fire hose*, steamed George to himself, *and they were using it without permission. If the mess on deck bothered them, they could have at least asked me about it. I would have told them to go and get the wash hose instead of ruining my new fire hose!*

George glared at the two men and they glared back. Angry words spewed out. George was so irate he was ready to go for them, big as they were in contrast to his slighter frame. Fortunately another deck-hand came along and stood between them.

George turned and stormed down to his cabin where he barked at his wife, 'Carolyn, start packing. I'm going home!'

Still fuming, he left the cabin and made his way up to Dale's office. He knocked on the door and burst in without waiting for an answer. George Miley was seated there, obviously discussing some matter with Dale.

'I've got to go!' George Booth exclaimed heatedly. 'I can't stand it! Hardy and Ebbo!' He spat out the words in disdain. 'I can't take another minute of those guys!'

'What's the matter?' asked Dale in his characteristically calm voice.

'The fire hose! They put salt water in my fire hose!'

'Tell me about it.'

George told him. They talked for about ten minutes and George slowly calmed down. Reason reasserted itself as he realized it wasn't just the fire hose that was troubling him; it was an accumulation of irritations and frustrations. He realized too that Hardy and Ebbo had acted because they were concerned about the state of the ship. Sure, they had made a mistake, but everyone makes mistakes.

'Okay,' he said finally, 'I'll give it another go. One more week. . . .'

Apparently Dale talked to Ebbo and Hardy as well, because a few days later Ebbo went to George and said, 'Come. We've got to talk about this.'

'Yeah,' agreed George, 'we've got to talk about this.'

Years later George commented, 'That wasn't the last incident for us, but their attitude toward me began to change as they saw I was sticking with the ship and my attitude improved as I began to see we were winning the battle in bringing the ship into shape. We started to understand each other. Within a year we were all laughing together over these things. From then on, a deep and mutual bond developed between us. Hardy has since left, but Ebbo remains with OM and I feel very close to him today. I think it is because of the sparks that flew in those early days.'

82

In Kingston, Jamaica, at the end of 1981, the challenge came from ashore, at least the human aspect of it did. The exhaust pipe from one of the *Doulos* generators was quite noisy, sounding like the panting of a monstrous beast. Jamaica at that time had suffered a terrible recession with much political violence and guerrilla warfare. The once lovely waterfront had been devastated. The international hotel was half closed down because people were afraid to go there.

In the midst of this less than idyllic situation, *Doulos* leaders received a threatening letter, followed by another and another: 'If you don't shut off your generator at night, I'm going to send my men around with their machine guns.'

What should they do? Take the letters seriously or shrug them off as the work of a crank? The matter was discussed in the planning meeting, the regular business meeting of the ship's leaders. Chris Papworth, an Englishman who had moved into the position of purser, voiced his strong opinion that the letters should be taken seriously; someone should go and talk with the sender. Chris was landed with the job, which he accepted on condition that George, temporarily captain again, would go with him.

Off they went, in their sharpest uniforms, to a nearby block of flats and up to the penthouse. They were ushered into a huge room furnished in flashy modern decor and seated in a couple of oversized arm chairs at one end of the room. The master would come shortly when he had finished his shower, the maid informed them.

Several minutes passed as George and Chris sat silently, studying the contents of the room. Finally an harmless-looking little black man shuffled into the room and took a seat at considerable distance.

'We've come because we understand you've written some letters. We would like to clear up the matter and apologize,' spoke up Chris.

The black man began to talk, but Chris and George couldn't hear him clearly. They strained to catch the words, saying, 'What?' and 'Pardon?' so often they became embarrassed. The man's grunting noises made him very difficult to understand. Well into the conversation, realization dawned on the *Doulos* officers. The man was talking through his throat. He'd had a tracheotomy.

What he was trying to say was that he was very sorry for what he had done. He had come back from the countryside one night and found the power was off and the apartment like a furnace. He had opened the balcony windows so he could go out on the balcony and sleep where the breeze blowing across the harbour would offer some relief.

Only he couldn't sleep. The *Doulos* generator kept puff puffing away at well above an acceptable decibel level. He had been hot and tired and thoroughly aggravated.

And now he was very apologetic.

Chris and George stared at him in disbelief. What an anticlimax! But it was a welcome end to the problem.

George developed the habit of rising early each morning to be in his office by 5:30. In the pre-dawn stillness he would spend time alone with God in personal devotions. By 7:00 he was ready to make plans for the day's work programme.

At exactly 7:15 one morning he felt a vibration in his office.

*Where in the world is that coming from?* was his first thought. *An engine? The generator? Or maybe a pump?*

As he listened carefully, he realized there was something strange about the vibration as if something was out of sync.

Reaching for the phone on his desk, he called the engine room. 'Did you just start up something down there?' he asked.

No they hadn't. They were busy looking for the source of the vibration as well. That meant the vibration was throughout the ship.

George jumped up and ran outside to look over the railing. Maybe the ship was bumping against the quayside or surging in the wake of a passing ship. Or perhaps an anchor was being dropped nearby.

He could see nothing amiss. Nothing at all.

As suddenly as it had begun the vibration died down. It had lasted only a few minutes.

The next day at exactly the same time it started up again. George again phoned the engine room and rushed out on deck. Nothing. He was baffled.

On the third day he decided to position himself outside the galley near the main entrance to the engine room and wait for the mysterious vibration to start. As soon as it did, he rushed aft to see if it was coming from anywhere in that region. Nothing there.

Then he rushed up to the poop deck. And there he found it.

Marion Isaacson, the captain's attractive wife and charming hostess for the ship, had started a Weight Watcher's Club with some of the women on board. Every morning they met to do aerobic exercises. In unison they would all jump in the air and land again on deck, totally unaware of the effect on the ship.

'I think they were embarrassed,' George commented in telling me the story 'when I said I had been looking for the source of the noise for several days. At any rate, I noticed that the aerobics class took place on the quayside after that.'

In June of 1982 the Latin American tours of *Doulos* drew to an end. The last port was Vitoria, Brazil. One of the last tasks before leaving a country is to search the ship carefully from bow to stern for stowaways. It's a job that deck officers and their men take seriously, because a stowaway can become stateless and the ship ends up owning him. Some commercial ships are sailing around the world with people who have been aboard for as long as five years. These ships have to post a huge bond every time they come into port in case the stowaway disappears.

These stowaways never go ashore. Their own countries

deny their existence as they are not the kind of people they particularly want back. Desperate captains have been known to set them adrift on rafts in the middle of the ocean under cover of darkness, knowing that no one will miss them.

86    The search on *Doulos* turned up one stowaway, who was promptly deposited on the quayside. About 2.30 pm the ship set sail amid much crying, shouting of messages, waving of streamers and singing back and forth between the ship's company and the crowd ashore. After the mid-afternoon tea break, one of the welders made his way down to the dry stores where he was building the base for a refrigerator. A Brazilian worker was already there, chipping away at old paint. The welder looked at him puzzled; the man said nothing but just kept on chipping. Several of the new recruits couldn't speak much English, so the welder simply shrugged and went on with his work, assuming George Booth had sent a man to help him prepare the steel plates he was welding.

All afternoon they worked, till the welder finally announced, 'Time for supper. Let's go and have something to eat.'

In the dining-room some of the Latin Americans saw the Brazilian and began to raise questions among themselves. They recognized him because he had been hanging around the ship in the last port, trying to get recruited. A silent type, somewhat unkempt in appearance, he hadn't seemed to fit in. They took their misgivings to Decio, a middle-aged Brazilian in the *Doulos* leadership.

Decio, in turn, went to Em Namuco, the Filipino

personnel manager, described the man in question and demanded, 'Do you know him?'

'Well, vaguely,' replied Em.

'He said you invited him to join the ship.'

'Well, I didn't invite anybody,' responded Em, somewhat irritated at being questioned like this. 'Why?'

'He's on board.'

'He's *what?*'

Alarm bells began ringing in Em's head, a phenomenon that spread to other leaders as they heard the news. An emergency session was held. After much discussion, a plan of action was decided upon.

They played along with the stowaway's charade and assigned him a cabin. When he entered it for the night, a watchman was posted outside to make sure he didn't decide to sneak off and hide somewhere.

The Brazilian authorities were contacted. The man had no ID, so the authorities could have refused to take him, but they were gracious and said, 'Yes, we'll take him back.' The captain gave orders to change course and head toward Natal, just up the coast a bit further north. The ship sailed through the night and anchored off the port coast at 6:30 am. Arrangements were made for a launch to come out to *Doulos*.

When the launch had almost reached the ship, George's men knocked on the stowaway's door and called out, 'Time to get up and get dressed.'

He jumped out of bed and got dressed.

'Come on upstairs,' said the deck-hands. 'There's something at the gangway you ought to see!' And they helpfully picked up his things and ushered him up stairs.

When they reached the gangway, the launch was waiting. The stowaway looked at it in surprise.

'Off you go, mate,' said George in a tone that brooked no dissent. 'It's for you. Have a nice ride.'

The young man hesitated, looked around, then shrugged his shoulders and climbed down into the launch. George and his deck-hands, along with a sprinkling of other *Doulos* people who happened to be out on deck that early, stood and watched the launch fade into the distance. Then George and his men turned and made their way inside the ship.

Time for breakfast and another day's work.

# 6

## A Major Attraction

George Verwer's original concept of an OM ship was fanned into flame partly by the thought of the many tons of books that could be transported to India for distribution and sale there. *Logos* only partially fulfilled that dream. She did indeed carry tons of books, but transportation of them was not the intent. Rather they were used on board to stock a large bookshop that offered a wide variety of books suitable for families: educational books, cookery books, children's books, novels and many other kinds of good literature. It also offered an extensive selection of Christian books, not only the best-selling Bibles and attendant study material, but also books covering a wide range of practical topics such as sexual relationships, family life or how to cope with tragedy and grief.

The bookshop was the major attraction which drew crowds of visitors to the ship in each port. Visitors from every walk of life: high officials in government and the socially élite as well as the common worker or even the very poor whose purchases came at great personal sacrifice. Professionals, students, children, entire families. Christians, Hindus, Muslims, Buddhists, atheists. They all came to look over a selection of books often far beyond anything they could find in their own local bookshops. And they bought!

A not uncommon sight was people walking off the ship with a big armload or even a large cardboard box filled with books.

When *Doulos* was being considered for purchase, one of the main concerns was space for an even larger bookshop than *Logos* offered, one that could display three to four thousand titles for easy viewing. The upper deck aft on *Doulos*, just a little less than half the length of a football field, had seemed ideal.

Chosen for the job of manager was Mike Stachura, a rather stocky Polish American who had interrupted his doctoral studies a few years earlier to join *Logos* in Indonesia. Having studied social science rather than business or even literature, Mike was acutely aware of the challenge that lay ahead for him.

Nevertheless, he had been fired with enthusiasm as he drove with his wife Jorie and their two young children through the snow-laden Alps to join the newly acquired ship in Genoa. Eagerly he had toured the vessel with his family, examining every nook and cranny. A night or two later he slipped out alone to survey his future realm with a sense of wonder and anticipation. In the darkness broken by pools of light he saw a tiny swimming pool and a few scattered deck chairs. Otherwise, the deck lay deserted and still.

*What will it look like when the book exhibition is here?* he had wondered. At this stage there were no plans to guide his imagination; the only point of reference was his memory of the bookshop on *Logos* cramped into a much smaller space. He walked around the deck several times, praying that one million people would some day be able to walk there and receive God's word.

In the weeks that followed he had tried to work out a design for cabinets to fill the generous deck space. Frequently he got together with one of the deck officers to discuss ideas. Various publishers were glad to supply him with suggestions. One idea was to lay down little railway tracks from the centre of the exhibition outward like wings. On them would be big display units which could be rolled out in port. When the ship went to sea, they could be pulled back to the centre and tied down.

The thought of laying down tracks fired none of the ship's leaders with enthusiasm. However, an idea was born: cabinets that could be brought together, covered with canvas and tied down while at sea. The design that emerged was for a cabinet which was larger at the base, providing space for storage and making it untippable. Above the base display shelves were located, and there the unit tapered backwards to become slim at the top.

A Dutch carpenter offered to make the cabinets in his workshop in Holland and another carpenter was sent out from the ship to help him. Months of work produced two hundred and fifty units of shelving, worth thousands of dollars. Mike's heart soared when he saw them. They were not only functional; they were beautiful. A few weeks later they were in place on the *Doulos* after deck, filled with books and ready for business.

When the ship sailed into France at the beginning of her ministry, word came that there could be no book sales aboard the ship because French law forbade the sale of books from a ship. People could come on board and look at the book display but they had to go down to a tent on the quayside to make their purchases.

*Well*, the book exhibition staff consoled themselves as they put up with the inconvenience, *this is an exception. We won't have to go through this again.*

But they were wrong. In the next port, Bilbao, Spain, books could not be sold on the ship either. *Doulos* was not even allowed to come alongside but had to lie at anchor. A circus tent was hired and the books and cabinets transported by barge to the tent. Making matters more difficult was the pouring rain. Bookshop staff soon got the feeling they were spending half their time ferrying books back and forth.

It became obvious that *Doulos* leaders had not anticipated the complexities of obtaining permits nor the difficult logistics involved. The ship was in the next country, Portugal, for a week before permission to sell was obtained. All the books had to contain a government stamp, entered by hand, before they could be sold. The books, however, had been bought on a sale-or-return basis so they could be stamped only as they were sold. The bookshop staff had to keep track of them on a daily basis.

Actually that was not so bad because the ship was not exactly inundated with visitors. Mike began to wonder if the book exhibition was so large that overcrowding would never occur. At least, that was his question before the ship sailed into Málaga at the southern tip of Spain in 1978. August was holiday time and the line-up team had done an excellent job. Late each afternoon, as the intense heat of the midday sun began to wane, the queue of visitors to the ship would begin to grow until sometimes there were a thousand people waiting to board. *Doulos* people stared in awe.

The bookshop staff had no time to stare; they were kept too busy serving the visitors, keeping up the book stocks on display . . . and trying to cope with tiny globules of black pitch which began appearing on deck, cabinets, books and people. These bits of pitch had first been observed as the staff was setting up the exhibition when the ship arrived in port. Workers soon discovered that the pitch was dropping from the roof.

Back in Germany where the roof had been erected over the deck, a special construction of wood had been built and covered with skin-like material which was secured over a layer of pitch. In Germany this had worked fine. The difference in temperature between a German spring and a Spanish summer, however, is considerable. From between each of the planks in the extensive roof a black goo had begun to ooze.

At the official opening ceremony of the book exhibition, Mike and his staff tried to keep the guest of honour moving around so that he wouldn't have a chance to notice black spots on the books. Then the inevitable happened. A drop landed on the man's shoulder. Exhibition staff gulped in consternation. Acutely embarrassed, they didn't know what to do and ended up doing nothing.

The oozing continued. Staff cleaned off hundreds of books and tried to cover them with plastic for protection.

On board at the time was a missionary airline pilot, a

little older and a lot more experienced than most of the *Doulos* people. He knew a great deal about practical work and proved helpful in doing many sorts of things for the book exhibition. When the problem with the oozing pitch arose, he remarked, 'I notice that you have fibreglass boats. Do you also have fibreglass patching?'

94

A check with the captain and chief officer yielded a positive answer.

'Well,' said the pilot, 'I think I can fix those leaks with fibreglass patches. Once you put the patch on, the pitch will never come through.'

Other technical workers on the ship were sceptical, convinced the patches wouldn't hold. But the pilot was allowed to go ahead and try. Each night at about eleven or twelve o'clock, after the temperature had dropped appreciably, he would begin work and continue until five or six in the morning. Working with one assistant, he patched every single one of the joists and joints throughout the roof, putting up perhaps a thousand patches.

The roof never leaked again.

The visit of *Doulos* to Portsmouth, Virginia in 1978 was the first time either OM ship had ever been to the United States. The line-up team soon realized that obtaining book-selling permits in Europe was a breeze compared to working through the complexities of US law. While the ship was still in England, Mike flew over to the States to assist the line-up team. He was informed that for every single book he had to supply information about the author, his/her nationality, the original publisher and whether it was published both in the United States and Great Britain. Everything had to be done by hand, so he knew this was going to be a long drawn-out process.

He immediately dashed off a letter to *Doulos* telling the staff to send him a book list post-haste and waited impatiently for its arrival, impatiently and in vain. The list didn't arrive. Mike finally did the best he could, trying to recall as many titles as he could and checking them out in catalogues. That method had severe limitations.

Not until *Doulos* arrived in Portsmouth did Mike finally get a copy of the book list so that he could complete the task. The pressure on him was overwhelming. The following morning the official opening of the book exhibition was to be held. Prominent dignitaries were coming for the event. Yet because of the book situation the ship had still not cleared Customs. The customs broker was by this stage almost tearing her hair out.

The exhibition staff worked furiously. Finally, at midnight Mike accompanied the customs broker and the customs inspector around the book exhibition. As they went around to each set of shelves, they saw that some books had their faces turned out towards the customer. Those books would remain on the shelves. The ones with their backs to the customer were those which had not received clearance and therefore could not be sold; they would be removed before the public was admitted.

At 12:15 am permission to sell was granted. The official opening ceremony took place as planned.

Mike learned later that the book list he'd requested had been sent to one of the OM offices to forward. A new secretary had picked up the big brown envelope, weighed it in her hand and concluded it would be too expensive to send airmail. She sent it surface-mail. Two months later Mike was contacted by the customs broker to inform him of the arrival of the list and suggest that perhaps in future he might like to handle things differently.

One of the special visitors in Portsmouth was a man named Gus Vandermeulen, who worked for a large company in marketing and purchasing and was very interested in inventory management. Gus had once visited *Logos* in Africa and had plied the book exhibition manager there with many questions. One of them was, 'How do you keep track of all those books and currencies and such things?'

At his own expense, Gus travelled across half a continent to visit *Doulos*. He spent his time on board asking Mike question after question.

'Why don't you have a computer?' he asked. 'You really ought to have one.'

When Gus returned home he contacted friends at Taylor University, a Christian college and paid for them to go down to Mexico to visit *Doulos* and do a feasibility study. Then he and some others raised money for a group at Taylor to set up a computer system for the ship. A couple of years later a computer was donated to *Doulos* and Taylor assumed responsibility for providing programmers, analysts and operators for three years.

The computer was to prove a headache as well as a blessing. When it arrived at the end of 1980, three problems promptly presented themselves: 1) how to balance the disks (which in those days were the size of long-play 33 rpm records); 2) how to keep the computer area cool; and 3) how to keep the computer from getting knocked out by spikes in the unpredictable electrical system on the ship. Eventually a separate generator and alternator were set up just for the computer and it was given its own air-conditioning system apart from the rest of the ship. The computer became like a little queen in the aft part of the ship. Everybody had to care for it.

Was it worth the trouble? That was the question on a lot of minds.

Mike tells how the matter was settled:

> The first trip down to Argentina we didn't yet have the computer. Bob Clement, our line-up man, called us and said, 'You have to have a cargo manifest.'
>
> 'We've never had a cargo manifest,' we objected.
>
> 'You've never been in Argentina. You must have a complete inventory of every book in every language when you arrive.'
>
> Well, we didn't. We couldn't do it on the voyage because the sea was too turbulent. When we got into the port, Bob insisted, 'Look, you've got to have it. They're going to be here asking for it.'
>
> Our forty book exhibition people worked all through the day, all through the night and into the next morning until 2:00 in the afternoon. We worked about thirty-six hours on this until everything had finally been counted by hand and typed up. It was all done on a manual typewriter as there were no word processors. Everything had been calculated in our special *Doulos* pricing units and put into dollars. When we took it to Customs, the official said, 'No,

98

this is not good enough. We do not accept accounting in dollars. Go back and recount.'

'We can just take the dollar totals and convert them into pesos,' I pointed out.

'No, you cannot do that. You must show on every book the value in pesos, multiply it times your stock and then show us the peso value on all of your nine thousand titles.'

We went back and spent another day and a half calculating all this. The whole ship was praying for bookselling permission because we had just sailed half way around the world to get down to Argentina. We kept praying and praying. The day after a night of prayer on the ship, we had a businessmen's reception scheduled. Just before it began, the government informed us, 'You have now complied with all of our requirements. You can sell books.'

I calculated that we had had forty people working about seventy-two hours each. That meant we put in just short of three thousand man hours to put that list together. I think that was the point when I went to George Miley and Dale Rhoton and declared, 'This we will never do again. We must have a computer.'

Two years later when we came again to Argentina, we did have a computer. The difference in just one week was over $50,000 in sales because we could open on the day we arrived; we had our inventory in hand and could give them the list. When I look back, I think Argentina was a turning point in moving from a small business into a multi-million dollar operation.

One of the challenges of the ship was trying to figure out how the bookshop would be received by different booksellers in the ports. *Doulos* was often welcomed with open arms because it was expected to do a great deal for the book industry. But when long queues of people came to the ship to buy books, the attitudes of some sellers changed. What *Doulos* experienced was that in most places, while it was true there might be a lull in local booksales immediately after the ship left, an interest in books had been stirred which eventually caused sales to climb higher than they had been before the ship's visit.

The bookshop staff tried to develop good relationships with local dealers and do whatever they could to improve local sales. They began buying more and more from local distributors and inviting local publishers on board for book fairs. They promoted local bookshops in various ways, particularly Christian ones struggling for existence in a secular climate. They gave out bookmarks, leaflets and posters advertising these bookstore and giving their addresses. Even so, tensions occasionally arose and had to be worked out on a personal level.

Publishers occasionally made observations or offered advice. Often this proved quite helpful. Other times it proved . . . well, interesting. When a publisher in Spain heard that the ship was going to Guayaquil, Ecuador, he shuddered and commented, 'A horrible place. The only place you can sell books is in Quito. People in Guayaquil don't read books.'

But in Guayaquil *Doulos* broke all her sales records for a port. At one point, a line of visitors two miles long stretched from the ship all the way through the port past the banana boats and out to the port gate. People would come and buy a big book, usually an atlas, and use it as a base to support a stack of other books. People tried to buy the bookshop's plastic book tubs (large enough to hold fifty pounds of books) so they would have something to carry books in. Stronger plastic bags had to be found to pack books in at the sales registers. No one bought just one book; people were buying forty and fifty at one go.

Peru, the next country on the *Doulos* itinerary, was very poor compared with oil-rich Ecuador. Port security was very tight and it became questionable whether the general public would be allowed in at all. In the end they were, but the police at the gate would let them walk in only far enough to board a bus and be ferried about four hundred yards to the ship.

The system functioned fairly well until the weekend arrived bringing crowds of visitors. Then it became impossible to get everyone on buses. On Sunday, the crowd was backed up for hours outside the port gate. The bus kept conveying people back and forth but made little impression in the crowds, while pressure built up at the gate to near-riotous conditions. At this point the police and guards announced that they were leaving.

'All right,' *Doulos* leaders agreed, 'close the gates and we'll close the ship.'

The police left and the *Doulos* crowd-control men left. Mike was in the dining-room eating supper when he looked out toward the port gates and saw to his consternation that they were wide open and people were rushing through. Whenever the gates had been opened up to this point, crowds had rushed in, crushing people and trampling over them. Having heard reports of what happened at

South American football games when people rioted, Mike had visions of what was about to take place before his eyes.

'Oh, Lord,' he breathed in a quick prayer, 'have mercy or someone is going to get killed.'

Suddenly the crowd did something no one had been able to get them to do before. They formed a queue and walked the four hundred yards to *Doulos* in an orderly manner. No one ran. They all moved over to one side of the road to make space for the container trucks that were going back and forth continually. Without a single person from the ship or the police to direct them, they walked calmly to the ship.

Mike's response was to say, 'Thank you, Lord, for your guardian angel,' and to make sure the bookshop was still in operation for the visitors.

In some countries shoplifting became a major problem. In one country the problem was so bad that the bookshop staff reluctantly concluded they would have to conduct a search of everyone leaving the exhibition. One of their most effective security men was undoubtedly Albert, a very dark African who was partial to wearing suits. In this particular country, he really stood out. Even more so when he put on silver reflective glasses that hid his eyes as he strolled around the book exhibition with his hands behind his back. When he spotted a group of children or teenagers looking as if they might be up to something, he would silently move up behind them and stand there looking at them through those inscrutable glasses of his. Eventually someone from the group would turn around and see him and emit a scream. Dropping their books, the group would take wildly to their heels.

Another favourite among the security detail was a man who'd once served with the Canadian special forces. Dressed in khaki trousers, a khaki shirt with epaulettes, black jackboots and a red beret, he would stand at the exit of the exhibition with arms crossed. As people filed out, he would indicate one and say, 'You! I want to look at your books.'

People would freeze. He had no weapon but he had a big belt that looked as if he did. By this time searching everyone had given way to spot checks and the Canadian had an uncanny ability to pick out just the right people.

There were other ways of dealing with offenders. One *Doulos* man took a young thief aside and spent a long time talking with him and the young person ended up committing his life to the Lord.

The bookshop personnel at the top of the gangway used a manual counter to record the number of visitors each day. And, of course, a record was kept of the number of books sold each day. But in some ports a count was also kept of thieves caught. Some days the number went as high as twenty. In one port security apparently missed a few. Ship members walking outside the port gates were startled to see street vendors hawking *Doulos* books at cut-rate prices.

Most of the million people visiting *Doulos* each year, though, were honest and genuinely interested in the ship and what was going on. By far the largest category of visitors was families, most of whom were not Christians. The book exhibition was adapted to meet their needs, enlarging sections on family issues and books for children. Christian books were intermingled with the secular books.

During the first visit to Colombia Dale Rhoton strolled up to the bookshop one afternoon to see how things were going. As he wandered among the book displays, he noticed a Roman Catholic nun enveloped in the traditional flowing black habit. Dale watched idly as she picked up a book and began looking through it. Glancing up momentarily, she became aware of Dale's eyes upon her. Startled and embarrassed she quickly thrust the book back onto the shelf and picked up another.

Dale moved on in his observation tour, but a little later he caught sight of the woman again and noticed she had a stack of books under her arm. His curiosity aroused he manoeuvred his way close behind her and managed to get an unobtrusive look at the book titles. He stared in disbelief. Clearly and unmistakably some of those books were about sexual relationships.

*What in the world . . . ?* he thought. And then reason came to his rescue. The Sister undoubtedly was involved in counselling and *Doulos* offered her a wealth of resource material built on Christian values.

Mike and his staff worked with six or seven book publishers in Spain, becoming for some of them their biggest distributors in Latin America. To order several hundred or even a thousand copies of a single title was nothing unusual for *Doulos*. Computer books, science and technology books in Spanish were heavily stocked. Many of these were not available inside the countries *Doulos* visited. On occasions, educational authorities purchased large quantities to use as textbooks.

A Christian publisher once donated $50,000 worth of

outstanding Bible commentaries and other hardcover study
books for pastors' libraries. The bookshop was able to offer
these for little more than the cost of shipping. Ten books
for ten dollars. The books went like hot cakes at pastors'
conferences as pastors seized a once-in-a-lifetime opportunity to develop a personal library. The experience spurred
the bookshop to make a practise of putting together a
packet of valuable books for pastors and Christian leaders,
a packet often subsidized by publishers.

Problems had a way of springing up in all sorts of
unexpected places. One of these was in relationships between people working on the ship. Mike tells about one of
these tempestuous relationships:

> I think if there was any real difficulty in the beginning, it
> was because we were all so strong-headed. We had one of
> the most aggressive leadership teams I've ever seen. We all
> wanted so badly for each of our ministry sections to go
> well. We had some big clashes. I remember the chief officer
> and I used to battle about every two weeks. George Booth
> was as strong willed and as sharp-tongued as I was. One
> time he decided he was going to wash down one side of
> the ship, including the decks. The book exhibition was
> about to open. When I pointed this out, he said, 'Nope,
> the people can't come up now. They'll have to wait outside
> for another half hour. We are washing the decks.'
>
> 'No, they're not going to wait,' I stated emphatically.
> 'We've officially declared that the book exhibition opens
> at ten o'clock. You'll have to wash decks another time.'
>
> Here were the chief officer and the book exhibition

manager standing toe to toe. The chief officer lost that one. He backed down.

Another time he announced, 'Everybody has got to get off the ship. In fifteen minutes we're moving.'

The book exhibition was full of people. I protested, 'We can't get them off in fifteen minutes.'

He replied, 'Well, the port has told us to shift *Doulos* forward so they can bring in another ship.'

That time he won. We got the visitors all off in fifteen minutes. We told them if they wanted to stay on board for the next three hours while we did this interesting manoeuvre, they were welcome. Otherwise, they could get off right now. There was definitely a 'right now' preference as they quickly left the ship.

One of the special experiences we went through was learning how to work with our teams. The deck department and the book exhibition would constantly fight. *Who's going to load the books? We'll do it. No, they'll do it.* Finally, George and I realized that if we fought, the effects would go through our departments. So the two of us began sending notes to each other. I would slip one underneath his cabin door: 'George, I've been an idiot, a hard-headed Polack. Please forgive me. You were right.' He would come back and say, 'I'm sorry. My words have been too strong. Let's work on this together.' We forged a strong friendship. It was iron sharpening iron, but it taught us the need to go quickly to each other for forgiveness. In the end the deck department and the book exhibition were two of the groups that worked closest together.

Dedicating himself to developing the book exhibition, Mike discovered almost too late, took its toll in another important area: his relationship with his wife and children.

When it comes to the family, if anyone could do it wrong, I did it. When we joined *Doulos*, we had Joel, who was eight, and Crystal, who was two; Jorie was expecting Carolyn. Jorie reminds me of one period when for six weeks she did not get off the ship. I was working the hours of both book exhibition shifts, starting usually at nine o'clock and going until midnight. I can't remember taking a full day off in the first two years. I would take half days off, but I always found it difficult to take a weekend day off because of crowd control, since weekends were the busy time. For a whole year the only place I went to worship was on the ship because I wouldn't go ashore. It was extremely tough for my wife. As I look back now, I wonder how I could have been so insensitive. Jorie tells me there are ports I can remember vividly because of ministry, but she doesn't even know what it looked like on land.

By the third year we had finally changed some things. We had a much stronger team on the book exhibition. I realized I couldn't do everything myself. I had the energy, but I saw what it was doing to Jorie and the children. The Lord began to balance us out. Jorie and I started doing more ministry together. Jorie got involved with a music group. We began to take days off. Our marriage has more than survived; it has thrived, but I think a lot of it had to do with the dedication of my wife.

When I talk with young ship leaders now, I like to start by talking with their wives to find out what pace the husband is living at. I give it to the husbands straight and strong, 'You must keep a day off schedule. You *must* have time when you go off the ship with your family.'

A third relationship problem developed out of Mike's dedication in service for God:

> Early in the book exhibition days — and maybe this is the downside of the heavy work demands of the ship ministry — I got myself into a stage where spiritually I was not listening very carefully either to the Lord or to leaders on the ship. I was not reading my Bible. I was not going to prayer meetings. I had come to the very strange conviction that it was wrong for me to be sitting in a prayer meeting on Thursday night when all my staff was upstairs working. So I'd work every prayer meeting night just to identify with the team. Frank Dietz, who was ship director at that time, came to me one day and said, 'Mike, some of us leaders have noticed that you aren't there in the prayer meeting.'
>
> 'Yes, that's right.' I answered and explained my reasoning.
>
> 'Well, Mike,' he replied, 'I just want you to know we miss you. We miss your voice. We miss your presence. We think it's not to the benefit of the ship's community or to you. The shift working this week on the exhibition won't be there next week. They'll be in prayer meeting. If you as their leader are missing all the time, your ability to lead in prayer will be very limited.'
>
> That was a turning-point in my life. It put the prayer meeting right back in perspective and I've never lost that.

Working hard for God, Mike concluded, was good but in itself it wasn't good enough. Relationships were more important. Relationships with his family, his co-workers and his God.

# 7

## *All in the Family*

In 1980 the port area of Callao, Peru, lay bathed in Sunday morning calm, its customary noise and bustle temporarily laid aside. Aboard *Doulos* was a little more life, but not much. The dining-room was sparsely populated, mostly by *Doulos* workers who planned to go ashore on teams to various churches. Many of the ship's company had apparently taken advantage of the opportunity to sleep late, as the Sunday worship service on board did not begin until mid-morning.

For the watchman sitting at the top of the gangway, the biggest challenge was to ward off boredom. He had little to occupy his attention nor did he anticipate much change in the situation for awhile. He was wrong.

About nine o'clock a long black limousine with tinted windows pulled up at the foot of the gangway. One of the doors flew open and out stepped a well-built man who was obviously a security guard. He ran up the gangway, his eyes constantly scanning the area around him.

A second man was helped out of the car by the chauffeur. He too began to climb the gangway, going at a much more sedate pace. As the watchman sprang up to greet him, he reached out to shake hands and introduced himself, 'I'm Fernando Belaúnde Terry, the president of Peru.'

The watchman gaped and said nothing. His mind was paralyzed. What does one say in a situation like that?

'Wait a minute,' he finally managed, and ducked inside the ship to phone down to Frank Dietz who was acting director for a few weeks while Dale was away.

Frank shot out of bed and rang around to various leaders, telling officers to put on their uniforms. The only place to entertain the president was a small staff lounge near the information desk. Em Namuco went to check it out and discovered the ship's children congregated there for Sunday School. He quickly got his wife to put through a call to Mike Stachura, the book exhibition manager, arranging for him to give the president a tour of the exhibition while Em prepared the staff lounge. Hasty arrangements were made for the children to meet elsewhere. Em straightened up the room and noticed that several of the chairs were quite scruffy-looking. *I'd better find some nicer-looking ones to replace these*, he thought. That done, he started the coffee machine.

Mike Stachura, in relating the incident to the ship's company at the end of the port, said,

> I was sound asleep on a Sunday morning when I got a call from Marilyn Namuco saying, 'Mike, come to the book exhibition quick. The president of the country is here.'
>
> So often in previous ports we have been told when people want to jump the queue that they are the son of the president or the prime minister's relatives. Sometimes it's true, but most times it isn't. I'm extremely sceptical of all these statements. I fired back something like, 'The president of *what* is here?'

Frank took the phone and said, 'Mike, the president of Peru is at the book exhibition. Get here *now*!'

I don't think I have ever dressed so fast in my life.

George Booth continues the story:

We opened the book exhibition early for him and showed him around. He was quite chatty. Spoke fluent English. He knew all about the ship, apparently having read up on it, and he wanted to buy books on the book exhibition. He didn't buy many, but made a careful selection. Didn't touch them himself. Just pointed them out and his man loaded up. Frank told him not to worry about the bill.

We had such a good rapport that on Monday the black limousine appeared again at the gangway and the president's man came up with an invitation for a group of us to visit him at the palace.

On the designated day, George unfortunately cut his hand with a grinder. 'But I'm not missing out on this,' he assured everyone, and went with his finger encased in a large white bandage.

At the palace the group, vacillating between bubbly excitement and subdued awe, was led into an ornate waiting room with rich wood panelling and decorative green ceramic tiles. After a short-time, they were ushered into another ornately-panelled room and seated at a beautiful square polished table which easily accommodated the twenty or thirty people in the party. The president chatted sociably for a quarter of an hour or so with the group. Then came a lull in the conversation. The *Doulos* people began to wonder if this was the signal for them to be on their way. One of them looked around the room, glanced up at the ceiling and asked respectfully, 'Sir, with your interest in architecture, how would you describe this place?'

That started the president talking enthusiastically. He ended up giving the *Doulos* group a personal tour of his residence for the next half hour and then posed for some photos.

For days afterward the privileged ones who had been invited to the presidential palace inundated all willing — and probably not so willing — listeners with a breathless account of the experience.

For workers on board life was full of unexpected experiences, many of them exciting, others decidedly less so. With around three hundred people from thirty to forty countries, the ship offered opportunities for deep, rich friendships among people from vastly different backgrounds. But those same differences that added spice to friendships also presented a potential minefield for relational explosions. People committed to loving each other and working together in God's service found themselves confronted with frictions, tensions, disappointments, disillusionment.

There was the time that Humberto Aragão, a Brazilian, dashed down to his cabin to get dressed for a meeting in which he was a speaker. Of course, he needed a suit and tie for the occasion. He quickly shed his clothes and put on his suit. But the tie! He couldn't find the tie he wanted. Frantically he rummaged through his drawers and closet. The tie appeared to have vanished into thin air. Time was running out, so he grabbed whatever was at hand and flew up to the meeting room.

His cabinmate was already there, standing at the front talking to the audience about showing love to one another. Humberto paused in the doorway, his eyes riveted on the speaker. Not on his face but on the tie he was wearing. Humberto's tie. The one he had been searching for.

Loving was not the word to describe Humberto's flaring emotions at that moment.

Relationship problems continually arose, but the ship's company was repeatedly challenged to face the problems and work through them rather than let them fester unattended or even unacknowledged.

Humberto had cause to remember that on one occasion when the Brazilians got together to enjoy themselves with typical Latin abandon. This time their fun took the form of opening the bathroom door and throwing a bucket of icy cold water on Humberto as he was taking a shower. Not to be outdone, Humberto bided his time until one of his Brazilian friends was in the shower. Armed with a bucket of cold water, Humberto opened the door and threw it in.

Unfortunately, the man in the shower was not his Brazilian friend. It was his Venezuelan cabinmate. And the cabinmate was livid! He rushed out of the bathroom, strode across the cabin to close the door and turned to face Humberto with fire in his eyes. Humberto responded by removing his shirt. They eyed each other warily. One of them made a grab for the other and soon they were rolling on the floor. Humberto eventually succeeded in pinning down the Venezuelan and drew back his fist for a telling blow. The Venezuelan squirmed to protect himself.

The threatened blow never came. Instead, Humberto looked down at the Venezuelan and said, 'Why are we doing this? You're my brother and I love you. We need to talk. Okay?'

Not exactly in the best position to bargain, the Venezuelan agreed.

They talked. They prayed. They embraced one another. And, in the course of time, they became the best of friends.

Some of the greatest tensions were work-related, often exacerbated by other factors as well. On Mike Hack's first voyage after joining the ship in Germany in 1981 the ship ran into a force ten gale, a distinctly unpleasant introduction to ship life for the new recruit. Mike, a husky twenty-two-year-old Canadian, discovered that, strong as he might appear from the outside, on the heaving decks his insides turned to something he'd rather not describe or even think about.

'Oh, Lord,' he moaned, 'I knew you wanted me to go to India. Now I'm sure of it. Maybe I could just jump off the side of this ship, and the water would be calm again. A whale would get hold of me and take me to India and spit me up on the beach.'

For Mike it was a difficult experience which was to be repeated on every voyage to some degree. Seasickness, however, was no excuse to avoid work. Mike was expected to carry on as usual. Each voyage was an ordeal, but he managed to stagger through, doing his work as best he could.

Which apparently was not good enough. The boat-swain, who'd probably never felt seasick in his life, misinterpreted Mike's inadequate work output. 'You're a big strong guy,' he admonished Mike. 'You can do better than that.'

To add a little oomph to his words, he assigned Mike to the bilges for a couple of weeks. That meant crawling around in a dirty hole, chipping off rust and cleaning up masses of sludge.

Mike later confessed:

> I didn't know what I'd done wrong. I didn't understand what was going on, but I was beginning to get mad. I thought, *Everyone else gets to work up in the fresh air and here I am at sea stuck in the bilges*.
>
> I had a big air hammer with a chisel on the end. I got hold of this thing and began to drill and hammer away at the rust. I was really angry. I remember drilling and drilling for about an hour straight with that hammer. I never stopped. Rust was flying everywhere. The noise of these hammers, of course, is deafening and carries through the whole ship. There I was, under the baggage locker, drilling away and pretending that the rust was the boatswain's head. I kept drilling away in anger, thinking everything was unfair.
>
> I stopped for a second to change positions and heard the guttural sounds of a throat being cleared. There behind me stood Captain Isaacson in his spotless white uniform, look-ing at me.
>
> 'What's your name, son?' he asked in his deep voice. 'I've never seen anyone work so hard on this ship. Good for you! Good for you!'

I was shocked. I'd never met the captain face to face. And now I felt guilty because the reason I was working so hard was because I was mad at the ship's leaders. Yet here I was getting praised for my hard work.

I had to repent.

Mike was learning fast.

Humberto, too, had work-related problems. Before coming on the ship he had been a supervisor in the chemical department of a Brazilian company. His job was to control the quality of steel for the company. He left this very good position to embark on 'missions'. In his mind's eye he saw himself singing and preaching powerfully in all sorts of places, even though he had had no experience of preaching before this time.

The reality was a bit different. On the ship he was assigned to the galley.

'I had to peel onions!' he exclaimed in recounting his experience and remembering his indignation.

One day Humberto's boss told him to clean under the refrigerator which sat eight or ten inches off the floor. Humberto immediately rebelled. His mother always did that sort of work at home. Not him. It was women's work and he had absolutely no desire to do it.

When his boss insisted, Humberto stormed out angrily, saying, 'I'm going to my cabin. I don't want to work here any more. If they want to send me home, I'll go.'

Down in his cabin he began to read his Bible. He came to I Corinthians 13, the great chapter about love. As he read it, he thought, *Wow! How can I preach the love of Jesus if I have no love for my brother, if I don't want to do anything that humbles me? Other people here are professionals, yet they're not earning money on the ship. Why shouldn't I also be ready to sacrifice?*

'So I went back,' he continued, 'and asked forgiveness for the first time. That was painful, but I could see from that moment on how much the Lord changed my life in different ways. Anyway, I got my cleaning things and went off to do my job. When I look back now, I think that was one of my best experiences.'

Unfortunately not every situation had such a neat ending. After six months on the ship Ruth Whitehead, a British woman, was put in charge of a pantry shift with twenty young women working under her.

It really got difficult at times. We had such a range of nationalities there. It always seemed as if the Europeans, particularly the German women, were so efficient and so good at doing this kind of work. Some of the Asians, on the other hand, had come from homes with servants and had never done anything for themselves. Suddenly they were asked to serve tables.

It was difficult to know where the balance lay. The Europeans would complain that the Asians were not setting the tables properly. What do you do? Do you chase after all the Asians and try to tell them to place the knife and fork just so or do you try to teach the European women that it probably doesn't matter all that much? It's not so important that we get it right. It's more important to accept each other and not be critical.

One day a Chinese worker got a letter from her home church. It was right at the beginning of work. All she wanted to do was to sit down and pray over the letter. I think it really was something serious, as some of the Asians came from incredibly difficult backgrounds.

Anyway, this Chinese girl just wanted to sit down and pray. The other women were upset that she was not working, because that put an extra load on them.

I finally told the woman she should work because it wasn't fair to the others if she didn't. She got upset with me for showing such a lack of compassion for her situation. She felt I was totally unspiritual in telling her to work instead of praying.

In the end, I asked her if she could pray while she was working. She finally did that, but she had tears in her eyes.

And then there were the children on board. Sometimes they were an irritation to adult workers on board, particularly to those unaccustomed to children, but mostly the children were a joy. Some of the *Doulos* workers came from dysfunctional families and were fascinated to watch the interaction within healthy families. Others were first generation Christians and had never seen a Christian family close up. For them it was a learning experience.

Children almost invariably loved ship life where there was usually someone available to play with them and 'aunts' and 'uncles' ready to shower them with attention — sometimes more attention than was wanted. There were drawbacks as well. Children found it confusing when too many adults tried to tell them what they should or should not do. And parents sometimes found the idea of raising a family in a 'goldfish bowl' atmosphere rather daunting and reacted with frustration when *Doulos* people (or visitors) lavished sweets on the children or interfered with parental discipline.

Overall, though, parents generally recognized there was much benefit in ship life for their children. They saw the opportunities to learn to relate well to other children and to adults from a wide variety of backgrounds, the advantage of a superior education with individual attention in the small classrooms and exposure to the wide world ashore, the privilege of having good role models offered by crew and staff.

Yes, there were advantages to life aboard and the Shafer family became especially thankful for one of them: the legal requirement that the ship have a doctor aboard.

One Sunday evening after supper another American family dropped by the Shafers' cabin to visit. As the adults talked, their two toddlers played with each other. Sammy, the visitor, was having the time of his life riding around on a little car. In the course of his driving, he accidentally ran over thirteen-month-old David's finger.

Instead of crying, David caught his breath. The adults waited for the inevitable expulsion of air and ensuing howl. It didn't come.

The visiting mother broke the silence. 'He's not breathing,' she said with a trace of panic in her voice. 'He's not breathing.'

One of the adults picked him up, patted him and shook him. Nothing happened. The child began to turn an ashen gray colour.

Gary, his father, swooped him up and rushed out to the doctor's cabin. Fortunately, she was there and immediately began artificial respiration. No success. Then she and Gary together began doing a combination of artificial respiration and heart massage. For what seemed an interminable period of time they kept at it. Just as the doctor was at the point of going up to the ship's hospital for a shot of adrenaline, David finally drew in a breath. Another followed. He was breathing normally again.

The doctor felt they should take him ashore to the hospital for a further check-up. That was not so easy as it sounds. The ship was at anchor in the middle of a river, which meant that they must go ashore by launch. Long queues of people were standing and waiting for their turn at the launch.

In an emergency, though, there was no problem about jumping the queue. All the way to the hospital — and it took about forty minutes — the doctor and nurse took turns holding David in their arms and checking his pulse, which was coming and going erratically.

A few days later David was playing on the ship again as if nothing had happened.

During the time around Latin America there were at least fifteen to twenty children of school age on board. Some of the older ones were encouraged to work at little jobs around the ship to earn extra pocket money. A banking system was set up for them so that they could save money instead of spending it as soon as it came to hand. The big goal of the ten-to-twelve-year-old gang was to save up to buy Playmobil as soon as the ship reached Germany.

Sometimes the children came up with their own creative ideas. Ten-year-old Sharon Rhoton and her friend Karen

Poynor liked to help out in the coffee bar aboard ship. Instead of getting paid in money, however, they were paid in confectionary because the ship had got them for a good price and was heavily stocked.

Some of the confectionary undoubtedly went directly into the girls' stomachs, but a considerable amount was squirrelled away in their cabin drawers. In Maracaibo, Venezuela, it all came out when they got the idea of setting up a stand just outside the port gate. For days they offered glasses of lemonade and confectionary at bargain prices (undercutting the *Doulos* Coffee Bar!).

When the ship reached Bremen, Germany, they were among the ones who excitedly went shopping and returned laden with enough boxes of Playmobil to keep them happily occupied for years to come.

Even when times were tight, the ship's leaders agreed that the children must not be penalized. Adults could forego their pocket money until there was a little more in the kitty, but the children should always in any port have access to the money they had put in the '*Doulos* Bank'.

That occasionally led to some interesting situations. At one time Roger Malstead's everyday shoes were worn and torn beyond repair. Yet the financial situation at the time was too tight for pocket money to be granted. His son Raymond, proudly withdrew the necessary money from his account and took his dad out to buy him a pair of shoes!

Some of the children were new to ship life, but others were old hands, having lived for years on *Logos*. One of the latter was Rebecca Poynor. As she approached ado-

120

lescence, she began to yearn for a larger circle of friends her age. There were no teenage girls on the ship for her to socialize with and share those confidences so important to developing teenagers. She faced an agonizing dilemma. She desperately longed to live ashore and attend a normal school surrounded by other children her age. Yet she knew God wanted her parents on the ship as her father was a highly-valued engineer. To ask that he leave the ship to accommodate her wishes was something she wouldn't even consider. As the family discussed the situation, they decided to try a boarding school. They had heard there was a good Canadian one about a three-hour drive from the ship's headquarters that had recently been set up in Germany.

An OM worker in Germany hastily made arrangements and within three weeks Rebecca was packed and ready to go. So hurried were the arrangements that the Poynor family had not had a chance to learn much about the school beyond its good reputation. They did not even know its proper name.

On the day before Rebecca was to fly to Germany most of the engineers went ashore in Rio de Janeiro. During their outing they met a Canadian couple, talked with them for awhile and invited them back to the ship for a visit later in the evening.

Unfortunately the couple got lost on the way to the ship and did not arrive until around eleven o'clock at night. However, Mike and Carol Ann Poynor were still up and about and invited them into the cabin for a cup of coffee.

In the course of conversation the Canadians commented on a couple of packed suitcases standing in the cabin. 'Someone going away?' they asked sociably.

'Ah, yes, our daughter Rebecca is headed for boarding school in Germany tomorrow. Actually, we feel somewhat uneasy about the situation. You see, we don't really know much about the school . . .'

The Canadian couple, it turned out, had grown up next door to the Jantz family who started the boarding school. They could tell Mike and Carol Ann the name of the school and just about everything about it — a great comfort because it was six weeks before a letter got to the parents from Rebecca.

In Puerto Montt, Chile, a group of young men from *Doulos* had an experience they are not likely to forget. They were part of an intensive training programme and one of the requirements was participation in a strenuous hike. Much of Chile is arid desert, but Puerto Montt, located in the south, is in a fertile area. Its most distinctive landmark is the snowy peak of Mount Osorno, a dormant volcano rising up behind the city. It was on this mountain that Mike Koch, in charge of the physical aspect of the training, decided the men should take their hike.

Three or four days after they set out Mike's wife Rita went to Dale Rhoton and expressed deep concern.

'I think we should do something,' she said. 'They were due back yesterday. The ship is to sail tomorrow. What if they miss it?'

Soft-spoken, diminutive Rita was not one to get alarmed

at the slightest disturbance, so her words were taken seriously. Besides, Dale's seventeen-year-old son John was also part of the expedition. Dale and his wife went with Rita to the local police station.

'Oh, there's no cause for alarm,' the police told them breezily. 'The Chilean navy has a training camp in the snow up near the top of the mountain. All the paths are very well marked. There's no way your people could get lost.'

'But you don't understand,' Rita insisted. 'My husband wouldn't have kept to the trails. The purpose of the expedition was to rough it.'

The policeman couldn't or wouldn't see her point of view. There was nothing to do but wait.

Just as Rita had anticipated, Mike and his men had indeed left the trails and set out across the side of the mountain. It had been rough going, working their way down the terrain thick with undergrowth and strewn with rocky cliffs. At one point they made their descent via a small waterfall and got thoroughly soaked in the process.

All this, however, was nothing compared with what they faced as they reached lower ground. They found themselves in a cane jungle so thick that they could only work their way through with machetes. At times the going was painfully slow. To make matters worse, the food supply gave out.

Cold, wet, hungry, exhausted, they were in no way cheered when one of those in front shouted, 'Hey, come here and see what I found!' Drawn by curiosity, they went to look. And stopped to stare in horror. There on the ground, stretched out before them, lay the complete skeleton of a man!

Suddenly the group found renewed strength to attack those canes vigorously.

Hours later the dense growth began to thin out, and they were able to move faster. But it was with a heartfelt sigh of relief that they finally reached the nearest town and phoned *Doulos*.

124

And it was with a heartfelt sigh of relief that Rita and the Rhotons welcomed the men back on board.

That same day the ship weighed anchor and set out on a voyage of several days to the next port.

The port before Buenos Aires was Mar del Plata, which could be called the 'Riviera' of Argentina. With a population of about five hundred thousand in the early 1980s, it would swell to accommodate over two million during the summer holiday time. The great city of Buenos Aires would become like a ghost town as its inhabitants flocked southward to Mar del Plata.

*Doulos* leaders saw the place as an irresistible opportunity to reach great numbers of people. Accordingly, six weeks of the summer season starting in mid-January, 1981 were blocked off on the ship's schedule. A line-up man was sent to lay the groundwork. He soon discovered that ship berths were extremely limited. The only one suitable for *Doulos* was the place where passenger ships docked, just inside the breakwater and outside the naval base. He was assured it would be possible to obtain this berth for *Doulos*.

A little over a week before the ship was due to arrive, a bombshell was dropped into the line-up preparations. The port captain decided that *Doulos* could not have the passenger berth after all; the demand for it was simply too great. He had already had to refuse some passenger ships.

There was no other berth capable of receiving *Doulos*. This was serious! Six weeks had been scheduled for Mar del Plata. Six weeks! Where else could the ship go? All other major ports had been scheduled for later dates and plans could not be reshuffled at this point in time. Yet to sit idle for six weeks would not only drive the ship crew and staff wild with restlessness, but would also be financially disastrous.

After much discussion, the ship's leaders decided that a delegation should go to Puerto Belgrano. Located near Bahía Blanca where the *Doulos* visit was drawing to a close, Puerto Belgrano was the biggest naval facility in Argentina. Captain Carl Isaacson went as part of the delegation.

Bob Clement, who was also part of the delegation of four, described the occasion:

> Carl was older and white-haired. With gold braid on his white dress uniform, he looked very distinguished. Anyone who had a uniform in Argentina at that time was saluted, respected, feared. Carl was just great to have along.
>
> We were ushered into a massive office and warmly greeted by the admiral. We explained the project and our problem. 'We really need that berth,' we told him, 'but the man there won't give it to us.'
>
> 'Just a second,' said the admiral. He got up, went to the phone and put through a call to the port captain. Whatever the other man may have said, it didn't seem to impress the admiral.

Nevertheless, when the conversation was finished, the admiral turned back to us. 'I've just talked to my man and I'm sorry. It's not possible for you to have that berth.'

Just at that point Carl — and only he could have done this — said in his deep booming voice, 'Well, Admiral, I just want you to know that this is not our ship. This is God's ship. If he wants the ship in that berth, then we'll get it.'

The admiral's jaw dropped. I wanted to crawl under the table. This is not the public relations way of doing things. You don't talk to the head of the navy that way.

After the admiral had put his jaw back, he said, 'I'll call the port captain and get back to you.'

The delegation left, convinced they'd never get the berth. The discussion in the car on the way back to the ship grew quite heated as argument raged about the diplomatic thing to do or say on such an occasion. When they arrived back at the ship, there was nothing to do but report the news and wait.

Actually, there was something that could be done and the *Doulos* family took up the challenge. Mike Hack tells about it:

We prayed and fasted and had prayer meetings. The night before we were to sail we were having our regular weekly prayer night. By eleven o'clock in the evening there were about two hundred still at the prayer meeting. The lounge was full. Someone began to sing a song. We all stood up and joined in. We sang and sang. Nobody was leading the meeting for about an hour. There was such a spirit of praise and power and faith. I *knew*, and everybody else too, we just knew we were going to get in. We were going to Mar del Plata the next day.

Eagerly the line-up team waited for the phone call that would determine the future of the ship for the next six weeks. So much importance was attached to the call, that those on board were forbidden to use the ship's phone to make calls. It had to be left free for *the* call. Ronnie Lappin, one of the line-up men, hovered continuously in the area.

Shortly after midnight of the prayer meeting night, the phone rang in the ship's programme office. An aide to the admiral identified himself. He wanted to speak to the captain.

'I'll take the call,' said Ronnie, 'and pass on the information to the captain, since I speak Spanish.'

Everything was arranged, he was told. *Doulos* could now go to Mar del Plata for the six-week period.

A day later as the ship was steaming into Mar del Plata, the pilot who had come aboard to help take in the ship asked conversationally, 'How long is the ship staying in Mar del Plata?'

'Six weeks,' responded the captain.

'Six days!' exclaimed the pilot, thinking he must have misunderstood the captain. 'You can't stay that long. No ship ever stays six days!'

'I didn't say six days. I said six weeks,' boomed the captain. 'This is God's ship. We prayed to get six weeks and we're going to stay six weeks.'

The pilot had no answer to that.

*Doulos* remained at the Mar del Plata passenger berth for the entire six weeks and carried out a lively and fruitful programme.

Yes, there were problems. Yes, there were struggles, stresses and strains. But there were also moments that made it all worthwhile, glimpses of God at work, an exhilarating awareness that all on board were involved in what he was doing. One of those moments occurred in Rio de Janeiro in 1981 where a special meeting had been arranged for wives of the local Lions Club members. Somehow, among all the well-dressed, cultured ladies another woman slipped in, obviously a 'gate-crasher' rather than an invited guest. She was dirty, unkempt, smelly and completely out of place. Oblivious to quizzical glances from the rest of the audience, she took a seat and listened intently to everything that was said by the *Doulos* people up front. As she did so, she began to catch a glimmer of the hope these people were offering, meaning for her dismal life, something that could come only from experiencing God's love. At the end of the meeting she prayed with a local believer, asking God to come into her life and give it meaning.

Then she told her story. Day in, day out, she would roam the streets, picking up bits of paper and selling them for a pittance. This she would take to the market and buy the cheapest food she could find to take home and feed to her hungry children. She had no husband. Life was hard and depressing. In her desperation as she left home that morning, she had even toyed with the idea of committing suicide. On the bus into the city she overheard a conversation between two women seated in front of her. They were discussing a visit they'd made to *Doulos*.

*Maybe I should go there*, thought the woman. *I might be able to find someone there to talk with.*

And that's how she came to the ship and met God.

Two years later, when *Doulos* revisited Rio de Janeiro, a worker who had been in that meeting encountered the woman again. She was still working hard, but with a glowing face she told about her happiness in knowing God and having friends in one of the local churches. The hard work was still there, but her life now had meaning. It made all the difference in the world.

# 8

# *Training for Ministry — More or Less*

'I liked your songs,' a young Argentinian man commented. He was referring to the songs a music group had just presented in a meeting on board. Humberto Aragão had been one of the singers and after the music had spoken briefly about a personal experience he had had of God.

The Argentinian, after a few moments of conversation, came diffidently to the concern weighing heavily upon him.

'I'm thinking about committing suicide,' he said. 'I have epilepsy and can't keep a job. Whenever I have an attack, I get fired. I have a wife and an eight-month-old child, but I have no job, no food to give them, no home. We have to sleep at the railway station.

'My wife is young. She's only twenty. If I die, she can get another husband who will be able to take care of her and my child. It's better for me to die.'

*Now what do I say to that?* wondered Humberto. He himself was young, single and inexperienced. *God is good. He is faithful. He can take care of you* seemed hollow words.

'Can you wait a few minutes for me?' he asked the Argentinian. 'I'll be right back.'

He rushed down to his cabin, closed the door and started to cry out to God, 'Lord, I don't see any answer for this man. I don't have enough faith to tell him you'll meet his needs. I don't know what to do. I have nothing here to give him. Even if I could give him some food and clothing, where would he live? What shall I do?'

After a few minutes, with his questions still unanswered, he went back upstairs.

'What are you planning to do now?' he asked the man, not knowing what else to say.

'If I leave here without any answers, I'll kill myself.'

'Okay,' said Humberto, an idea taking shape in his mind. 'I'll help you. I'll get a knife for you so you can kill yourself now. If you want to kill yourself, it's because you don't see any other solution. Have you tried Jesus?'

'No.'

'Well, why don't you try him before you kill yourself? If he can't help you, I'll give you the knife myself. He's the only way I can see for you. I don't have any answers for you. But I know one thing. Once I was a bad man and Jesus changed me into what I am today. Why don't you give him a chance?'

'Do you think it will work?'

'It worked in my life. Why not in yours? At least, it's worth a try.'

The Argentinian decided to trust his life into Jesus' hands. The two prayed together an intense, emotional prayer.

Two other young men who had also been in the meeting approached them at this point, saying, 'Humberto, can we talk with you?'

'Not now. I'm praying with this young man.'

'Well, can we join you?'

'I guess so, if you want.'

They prayed with Humberto and his new-found friend. When they had finished, the two men offered to take the homeless man and his family to a small hotel for a couple of days, all expenses paid.

132

Two days? A help, of course, but hardly an overwhelming answer to their prayers. At least, it bought them time.

The next day a ladies' conference took place on board. One of the ladies got into conversation with Humberto afterwards. In the course of the chat, she commented, 'My husband and I have a small house at the back of our home. We're both old now. We'd like to have someone living in that little house. Do you know anyone who really needs a place to live?'

Humberto told her about the epileptic husband and father.

'Well, send him to my house.'

A men's conference took place the following day. After the meeting one of the guests asked Humberto, 'Do you know anyone looking for a job? I have a shoe shop and I'd like to have a Christian working with me. Someone who needs a job.'

Amazed, Humberto replied, 'I certainly do.' He pulled out a piece of paper, jotted down a name and address and handed it to the man. 'Go to this hotel,' he said, 'and ask this man to go with you. He has just trusted his life to Jesus and he could use someone to encourage him and help him understand what it means to trust Jesus.'

'Great. I'll take care of him. He can go with me to my church.'

In two days God had fully answered prayer. Humberto could hardly believe it. He felt humble yet excited to have been involved in what God had done.

One evening when he had been on the ship for several months Humberto made his way to the dining-room after it had been cleared from dinner. The ship was at sea and seemed very quiet after the hectic pace of life in port. Humberto found himself a table back in a deserted area where he could be alone to think over things and pray. *I've been singing and singing and singing in meetings*, he thought, *and I've enjoyed it. But now I've gone through my repertoire again and again. I'm getting tired of singing the same old songs. I'm getting tired of singing, period. I'd like to do something else. What I'd really like to do is to preach.*

'Lord,' he prayed, 'will you give me an opportunity to preach?'

He decided to write to his parents and ask them to pray about this too. He had just poured out his heart to them when he looked up to see Captain Isaacson approaching his table.

After the customary exchange of greetings, the captain said, 'You know, Humberto, in the Azores, where we're going now, the people speak your language. I'm scheduled for a prison meeting there. Why don't you come along with us. I'll be giving my testimony and you can sing.'

*Sing? Again?*

'Oh well,' agreed Humberto somewhat reluctantly, 'Yes, I'll sing.' His voice picked up confidence. 'It'll be a pleasure.'

The captain eyed him speculatively. 'Then,' he continued, 'you can also prepare a message. A thirty-minute message.'

134

'*What?*' Humberto could hardly believe what he was hearing.

'Well, you speak the language. It would be easier for you than for me.'

Suddenly Humberto got cold feet. He hesitated and as he did so, his glance fell on the letter he had just written. He saw the words, 'Pray for me because I want an opportunity to preach. . . .'

'Yes,' he told the captain, 'I'll do it.'

He immediately gathered his things from the table and went down to his cabin to start preparing. He went to the library to read up on how to prepare a sermon. He went around to different leaders, asking them, 'How do you prepare your messages? Please help me because I have to preach.'

He had one week to prepare and he was apprehensive. He'd heard that some of the men in the prison were really dangerous. There were some who'd been in prison for many years and would likely die there. *I need to preach something with substance,* he thought. But he didn't know how. He read a lot of books that week, trying to take in as much as he could.

He memorized Bible verses. He prepared a draft of his message. He preached it to the mirror in his cabin.

The time for the meeting relentlessly approached. Humberto was so nervous his knees shook as he sang his song. The captain told how he had met God and then he introduced Humberto, saying, 'This is Humberto from Brazil. He's working with us on the ship and he's going to give you a message from the Lord.'

135

Humberto went forward to stand in front of the prisoners. He put his hand into his pocket for his notes and a searing flame of panic shot through him. They were not there! He hastily felt in his other pockets. Nothing! And everything he needed was in those notes!

He silently breathed one of the most fervent prayers of his life and started to preach. As he did, the words came to his mind. At the end of the sermon, he gave an invitation for those who would like to know God in a personal way to come and pray with him. Of the thirty prisoners in the meeting, twenty-five responded.

'I cried more than they did,' he commented as he recalled the incident, 'because I saw how the Lord could use me even when I forgot my notes. He put the words together. He made me remember the things he had taught me from the Bible. That day determined my future ministry in preaching and pastoral care.'

Humberto's experience was typical. Occasionally there were seminars to train ship people in preaching and other ministry skills, but to a large extent, they were simply 'thrown in at the deep end' and given the incentive to learn to swim in a real life situation. Certainly mistakes were made and some people were made painfully aware that they were stumbling around in an area for which they had no gifting whatever. Others discovered, to their amazement, that they had gifts and abilities they had never suspected.

Preaching was by no means the only ability needed in the ministry aspect of the ship. People discovered gifts in other areas of public speaking: sharing a testimony, presenting what the ship was and did, compèring. Others realized they could relate well to children and hold their attention in school meetings.

Some with musical ability saw how God could use them, not only to entertain and bring enjoyment into people's lives, but also to bring home to people in a powerful way a message from God.

George Booth, the South African deck officer, was another one who was thrown in at the deep end in preaching. He found he did well in speaking to Christians in a church meeting, but preaching to a secular audience in the open air was an entirely different thing. Ray Lentzsch, a highly effective open-air evangelist with the ship, sometimes took George with him. George would pass out evangelistic leaflets while Ray preached. But one day that all changed.

'He just plonked me on the soap box and told me to go for it,' George recalled. 'I remember going from Genesis to Revelation trying to explain God. I tried to convince people there was a God and that they were sinners and God would come to their rescue. I went on and on, while realizing I was not getting through to the people. I decided then and there that I was not an evangelistic preacher at all. I couldn't do that sort of thing. My calling was to encourage Christians.'

Some time after that experience, Mickey Walker came aboard. He too was an open-air evangelist. His big thing was using the sketch board to attract attention and clarify concepts. That required a certain adeptness at painting which George also figured was 'not his thing'.

Mickey began working on preparing a manual for training the people on board in evangelism skills. To make the manual more interesting, he wanted to sprinkle cartoons throughout it. He asked an artist on board to do these cartoons. The result was hours of work on the part of the artist to produce life-like drawings — beautiful, but not in the remotest way resembling cartoons.

George, however, could do cartooning. He'd never had any formal training for it, but he used to do it for fun sometimes when he was at sea. One day in conversation with Mickey, he happened to casually mention the fact. 'Yeah, I've done a little cartooning,' he commented.

Mickey immediately seized the opportunity. 'Could I give you some ideas and you work them out for me?' he asked eagerly.

George had some time on his hands so he agreed, 'Sure. Give them to me and let's see what I can do.'

An hour and a half later he found Mickey and presented him with all six drawings he had wanted. After that, George was 'totally roped in', as he put it.

His friendship with Mickey developed and he often went out with him for open-air meetings. He shied away, however, from the sketchboard and its accompanying preaching, in spite of Mickey's urging to give it a try. He was too busy on deck to give the time he needed to learn how, he offered as excuse.

That excuse vanished in May 1984 when for the first time he was released from deck duties because there was someone to fill in for him. He spent the week in a training course taught by Mickey and discovered to his delight that he had a talent for the sketchboard, even though he was no great artist.

'After that,' he said, 'I really enjoyed preaching on a soap box. It's like painting a picture, but the colour keeps fading. You have to paint the picture again and again because the crowd keeps moving and changing. You have to keep explaining all over to the new people. With a sketchboard you can not only hold people's attention longer, but you can also recap much more briefly.

'I started thinking up my own drawings and messages. I got into it so much that when Mickey and another evangelism leader went away from the ship for a short while, I took over.'

It was a skill and an enthusiasm he took with him when he finally left the ship to live ashore, first in South Africa and later in New Zealand. He was continually on the watch for interested Christians he could train and take along with him to public places where they could share the message of God's love to needy people.

People may have been thrown in at the deep end on *Doulos*, but there was also considerable teaching and formal training for them at different times. Recruits coming to the ship expecting it to be a Bible College (even though they had been told otherwise) were in for a shock. Eight hours of practical work was required, just as the average person on land faces. Study and ministry were to be fitted into after-work-hours for the most part. All the same, an amazing amount of teaching was packed into these outside-of-work hours.

There was a forty-five minute devotional time most mornings, used for Bible teaching, challenging, giving information. All on board were expected to take part in a small-group Bible study every week, discussing the insights or questions arising from two hours of personal study on a topic. Even the weekly prayer night, beginning at eight o'clock and extending past midnight, provided a wealth of information about the world, as the needs of various countries were presented for prayer. Frequently elective seminars were held on free evenings, giving teaching on a certain subject or offering workshop training in various skills.

The most famous – or infamous, depending upon one's point of view — of the specific training programmes in the early years of *Doulos* was one that might last anywhere from six weeks to six months. The participants were released from their work departments for the duration of the programme. Aptly named Intensive Training [IT] and sometimes nicknamed Intensive Torture, its purpose was to stretch people, to challenge them to extend themselves to the limits of their strengths and abilities . . . and then to do more. The idea was that they would thereby discover unexpected reserves of strength and experience the deep satisfaction of proving to themselves that they could do more than they dreamed.

The idea came from a secular programme, but the ship tried to apply it to both spiritual and physical disciplines. Under the direct supervision of one the ship leaders, the participants in this voluntary programme were challenged to meet an incredibly high set of goals: early morning exercises together, a certain number of pages read from various books, so many letters written, so many teaching cassettes listened to, and so on. On top of this, there were teaching sessions, evangelistic outreaches and sudden calls to fill in around the ship wherever needed either in practical work or participation in meetings. Their motto was, 'Anything, anytime, anywhere,' meaning they could be called upon to do anything at a moment's notice.

Along with these activities, the IT trainees always faced at least one gruelling test of physical endurance, often in the form of an arduous hike. It was this hike that had set the scene for the unforgettable experience of the young men in Puerto Montt.

And it was one of these hikes which almost defeated Pedro Arbalat. A young Spaniard on a six-month IT, he was excited about the spiritual aspects of the programme but could see no point in putting himself through a physical ordeal just to prove to himself that he could do it. Other people might like to do that sort of thing, but he had no interest in it. And he definitely did not want to go on the hike.

He knew he would go. The question was, *how* would he go? Resenting every step?

It was an issue to be settled in his own heart and mind. He decided that faithfulness and obedience to his leaders in this non-moral issue were the paramount values.

The hike took him nearly one hundred kilometres in freezing weather through the snowy mountains of Wales in Great Britain. By the time he got back to the ship, he was so sore he could hardly climb the gangway. Worst of all, he never derived any particular sense of satisfaction from his physical test of endurance. Yet many years later, he looks back on his IT experience — all of it — with deep appreciation. The discipline he learned, he says, and the realization that he could do more than he thought, have changed his life, challenging him to do ever more for the Lord. Even that nightmare of a hike taught him the value of faithful obedience to those in authority even when one does not totally agree. And that, he says, is a valuable asset for him now that he himself is in a position of leadership. It helps him know what to expect from and give to those working under him.

For many of the young people, particularly the young men, IT was the outstanding experience of their entire time on the ship, contributing more than any other single thing to shaping them for their present roles in life.

While there was always a heavy load of practical work to be done and a great deal of training sandwiched in and around it, the main focus of *Doulos* was ministry. All day long the ship was a hive of activity. The bookshop was open, often drawing large numbers of visitors. Conferences and meetings of various kinds kept the lounge occupied much of the time: meetings of schoolchildren; ladies' meetings; receptions for doctors, lawyers or ethnic minorities; family conferences; missions conferences. The list was endless. Often the public address system would call one of the ship's company to the information desk because a newly-made friend had come to talk further.

At the same time, ministry continued ashore. Generally *Doulos* people would go out in teams. Often they went to schools, hospitals or prisons and put on a short cultural programme representing the various home countries of those on the team. They might explain some of the customs of their countries, sing typical songs or even put on a dance with the help of fellow team-members. Usually they would explain why they were on the ship. That gave them the opportunity to explain something of what God meant to them personally. In some situations they could go still further in inviting the audience to ask questions or challenging them to develop their own relationship with God.

When the ship left Brazil for Europe in late 1979, a group of about ninety workers, most of them Latin Americans, was dropped off for a three-month programme in Spain and Portugal. Humberto, under the direction of one of the ship's leaders, led a team of Brazilians in northern Portugal.

In one of the cities where they worked, a medical doctor who was also an aspiring politician, heard about the team of Brazilians from the ship *Doulos*, which was visiting Portugal. This team, he heard, sang Brazilian music and the Portuguese liked Brazilian music.

He visited the team and invited them to go to a local hospital and sing some Brazilian songs for the patients. Not Christian songs. Cultural ones.

Humberto was unwilling to go under those circumstances. 'We would sing at least one Christian song,' he insisted.

'Well . . .' the doctor-politician considered the matter. 'I want you to come anyway,' he decided. 'If you can dance, do that too.'

Humberto had never danced in his life. None of the other Brazilians on his team was particularly experienced in the activity either. But they were musicians, at least to some extent. A hasty bit of practise and they were ready to perform a samba for the patients.

In recounting what happened next, Humberto hastened to explain that his team members were young. They were enthusiastic Brazilians and balance in people-relationships was not their strong point.

As they were going to the hospital, Humberto gave careful instructions. 'Look,' he said, 'we're going to three rooms. In the first one we'll just sing Brazilian songs and dance. In the second one we'll also sing in a very low-key way about Jesus. In the third and last, we'll go all out and sing Christian songs and preach. If they want to kick us out, we'll be finished anyway.'

'Oh no!' objected one of the team members uneasily. 'That won't work. I can just see them kicking us out.'

'Let's try it at least,' countered Humberto. 'After all, our goal is to tell these people about Jesus.'

Everything went well in the first room. The patients were an appreciative audience, applauding the songs and even seeming to like the makeshift dance. The doctor-politician beamed and announced, 'Now I would like to sing a song too.'

That wasn't in the programme but, of course, Humberto nodded for him to proceed. The man needed no encouragement. When he came to the refrain in his song, Humberto pricked up his ears. The doctor was singing, 'When Jesus comes, when Jesus comes.'

That was the only reference to Jesus in the entire song, but it was enough for Humberto. When the song was finished, he turned to the audience and said, 'That was a very nice song, wasn't it? Did you hear the chorus, "When Jesus comes, when Jesus comes. . . . ?" Are you ready for Jesus when he comes?'

The doctor stared at Humberto and opened his mouth to object, but Humberto silenced him by saying to him, 'Yes, that was a very nice song. Can you sing it in the next room too?'

Humberto had already arranged for one of the team members to talk in a low-key way about his own personal experience of God. Because Humberto knew that the young man was a fervent preacher who tended to work up into a grand passion as he spoke, Humberto had also arranged a signal. 'If I give your jacket a tug,' he'd told the young man, 'that means you're going farther than we planned and you're to slow down.'

The young man exercised admirable restraint and the meeting in the second room went well. The doctor objected only mildly to the bit about God.

In the last room, after the cultural contribution, the team began to sing Christian songs while the patients listened in apparent enjoyment.

*So far, so good*, thought Humberto.

The preaching came next, quite openly. That didn't sit well with the doctor-politician at all. He stood up and interrupted, 'That's enough now. We can go now. You weren't invited here to talk about Christianity.'

'Hey, hey!' another voice interrupted him. It came from the director of the hospital, herself a medical doctor, and was addressed to the politician. 'Who are you to say these men must stop? They will continue. I like it.'

Turning to the team, she said, 'Please continue. I think this is the right room for you to preach this message. Go on.'

They needed no further encouragement. The preacher resumed his message. When he had finished, three patients decided to ask Jesus to take charge of the remaining days of their lives and thereafter. The team discovered that 'the remaining days' were indeed few in number. All of the patients in that room were terminally ill with cancer.

'Yes, we were unbalanced,' admits Humberto, looking back. 'Perhaps we were foolish, insensitive. But I learned something. If you are honest with the Lord and sincere in your desire to serve him, he can use you just the same. I was never more sincere in my life than at that time.'

Most of the ship evangelism was organized, at least to some extent, by the programme department on the ship. Sometimes, though, it arose spontaneously.

Mike Hack was in charge of the evangelism teams in Santos, Brazil in 1981. One of the men on the ship came up to him one day and said, 'Hey, Mike, why don't we take a team down to the rough area of town where the seamen, prostitutes, transvestites and drug-pushers hang out.'

The idea appealed to Mike but was enough out of the

ordinary for him to feel he should check it out with the ship's director.

'Look, we'd like to put together a special squad and go for an all-night blitz,' he explained.

The director agreed.

146　　Mike gathered together several married men and a few of the single men, including some Brazilians to translate as necessary. They spent the entire night out among the brothels and bars, dodging brawls and outshouting the blaring music. They'd had the foresight to take a good sound system with them so they could outblast even the discos. Taking turns, they preached through the night. Anyone who showed interest was escorted to the rear of the *Doulos* van for further conversation.

The team had really prayed hard before venturing out. Here's Mike's account of the experience:

> We sensed the presence of the Holy Spirit with us even as we walked around among half-naked women and seamen fighting over them. All sorts of crazy things were going on.
>
> I was in charge of the team, so I kept a watch over the guys to see that everything was all right. On the team were a couple of Venezuelans. I had been hesitant about bringing them along, but they had really wanted to come. Suddenly I realized that these two Venezuelans were missing. I went running through all the whorehouses looking for them. Finally I spotted one of them surrounded by about eight women wearing practically nothing. He was talking to them about Jesus, but I could see his eyes were a bit glazed and he was losing it. The other Venezuelan was standing nearby, looking around.

'Get out of here,' I cried, running up to them. I grabbed the one who was talking — he was a rather short guy — and literally pushed him down the flight of twenty stairs or so. 'Wake up,' I prodded him. 'Let's get out of here.'

That night, among the seamen and prostitutes, eight people came to the Lord and prayed that he would take control of their lives. A lot of Scripture went out as we went around to all the bars speaking to people. I remember one girl came up to me and said, 'What you're doing is very good. We need this. We're so terrible.'

We tried the same thing a couple of weeks later. I took it for granted and didn't pray as I had before. I wasn't on my guard. When I went there, my mind filled with temptation and I couldn't speak as I had before.

Here was another reminder that it was not the ability of the *Doulos* people nor their degree of spiritual attainment. It was *God* who made the work effective.

Sometimes an evangelism team from the ship divided up into pairs to go door-to-door and sell literature or simply talk with people. Often someone fluent in the local language was paired with someone whose grasp of it was not so good.

A young Singaporean woman named Ai Ling was part of a pair who went knocking on doors in Glasgow, Scotland in 1984. At one door they knocked and waited. And waited. They were just about to move on to the next home when they heard a noise inside the house. It sounded as if someone had jumped and landed with a thud. The sound of footsteps followed. Then the door was opened just enough for a distraught face to peer out. It belonged to a woman who appeared to be in her early thirties. Anxiety hovered in her red, puffy eyes.

Ai Ling, being the only one of the *Doulos* pair who was fluent in English, introduced herself and her companion. The woman eyed them silently, but the door remained open. That was enough for Ai Ling. She began talking about the hope that Jesus offers.

The door opened a little wider. Unthinkingly, Ai Ling glanced from the face of the woman to the room behind. Her words faltered as she gazed in shock. A mirror on a nearby wall gave a faithful reflection of what was otherwise out of sight in a corner of the room, a noose hanging from the ceiling and a chair situated below it.

Ai Ling gave herself a mental shake and resumed talking with a great deal more fervour. The woman listened and tears began to stream down her cheeks.

'How could Jesus die for me?' she asked. 'What hope do I have?'

'Our hope is in Jesus himself,' replied Ai Ling. 'He's the only one who can forgive our sins and give us eternal life. Listen to what the Bible says.'

Ai Ling opened her Bible and pointed out a verse, reading it aloud to the woman, "For I know the plans I have for you," declares the Lord, "plans to prosper you and not to harm you, plans to give you hope and a future." '

The woman brushed away her tears and fixed her eyes on Ai Ling's face. A tentative gleam of hope, slipped into her face as Ai Ling talked further.

Her marriage was in tatters, the woman blurted out, and was on the verge of breaking up. On top of that, she was having trouble with her children. How could God help her?

Ai Ling tried to explain to her.

Eventually the woman came to a decision. 'I think I want Jesus.' she said. 'I don't want suicide.'

She prayed with Ai Ling, asking Jesus to forgive her and help her.

Ai Ling had to sail on with the ship when it left port, but she corresponded with the woman, continuing to offer her encouragement and hope.

# 9

## On the Verge of Financial Disaster

Salaverry, Peru, was a sleepy little town with a population of about fifteen hundred, set in the middle of a desert. Whatever fame it might have lay chiefly in its function as port town for the city of Trujillo, some twenty kilometres inland.

*People will never come that distance to visit Doulos*, thought the young American, Norm Przybylski, as he prepared for the ship's arrival in 1982. But people *did* come. In droves. At one point Norm saw a queue more than a kilometre long waiting patiently in the hot, hot sun to come aboard.

It was not until the programme had ended and the ship was moving off that Norm's real problems began. There had been a huge swell the entire ten days *Doulos* was in port. Even inside the port the surge was so horrendous that fifteen of the ship's mooring ropes snapped; the crew had to be continually watching for chafing. An anchor was put out to help stabilize the ship even while it was tied up at the quayside.

When the time came to leave, a tug towed the ship from her berth. Deck-hands began pulling up the anchor chain, which moved freely until the slack had been reined in. Suddenly the chain went taut. During the ship's ten days in port, the anchor had sunk down a good five yards into the black ooze of the sea bed. The windlass motor hauling in the chain was going too fast. When it suddenly hit resistance, the chain snapped and the end flew up into the air, leaving the anchor down in the sea bed.

George Booth was captain at the time and had to decide what to do about the lost anchor. Should he reberth and try to dig it out or proceed to Lima to be in time for the scheduled opening ceremonies? The pilot advised him not to worry about the anchor since they were only going a little way up the Peruvian coast to Lima. The anchor could be recovered and sent up to Lima on a lorry. Since *Doulos* had two other anchors on board, George decided to move on.

151

As line-up man, Norm was dispatched back to Salaverry to recover the anchor. For an entire frustrating week he kept getting the runaround from port officials. No, they didn't have the equipment. No, he couldn't use the crane because another crane somewhere in Peru had been used for something similar and it had toppled into the water. Every request was met with an excuse.

David Greenlee, by this time an experienced line-up person, was sent to help him. They discussed the situation and prayed about what to do.

In port were some fishing trawlers, perhaps forty feet long, with large winches. David and Norm went to the shipping agent to sound out the possibility of obtaining the service of one of the trawlers. The agent pointed out the company that owned the boats and Norm and David strolled over to approach the owner, a tough businessman whom they assessed to be a hard-working, hard-living type of man, the complete antithesis of themselves as young single Christian men. Norm and David told him their predicament, playing up the fact that no one was able to help them.

That apparently was the kind of challenge the owner could not resist. An impossible task? Then he would do it.

152 He called over a man from one of the fishing trawlers and together the group worked out an all-or-nothing contract. If the anchor was retrieved, the trawler men would be paid. If not, then no money. It appeared to be just the kind of agreement to appeal to the company owner.

The anchor was located twenty or thirty yards from the quayside. Although it had sunk deep into the mud and muck, the top was still exposed. A diver was sent down to attach a cable to it and then the winches on the trawler began to pull. The side of the boat dipped way down almost under water from the force of the pull. But the anchor didn't budge.

Negotiations and preparations had taken all morning, so it was early afternoon by the time salvage operations got under-way. The sun was beating down so mercilessly that David put on a heavy sweater to avoid getting burned.

Efforts continued but got nowhere. After three or four hours, the men admitted, 'This is not working. We can't get the thing up. What we need is an underwater pump to blow away some of the muck and loosen the anchor.'

Fortunately, the shipping agent had a pump, but more negotiations were required to handle the additional cost. The fishing boat went to shore and the pump was loaded on.

That item of business concluded, the agent drew David's attention to a lorry standing by, which David and Norm had contracted to transport the anchor to Lima. 'Look, if you want to hold that lorry here, it's going to cost you more money.'

'It's got to stay,' decreed David and handed out enough money to hold it for another hour.

The men on the trawler resumed working and the diver went down, stirring up the muddy water.

By this time the dock workers had finished work and had gathered on shore to watch the fun. David noticed the head of the dock workers' union handling a lot of money and realized what was happening. The men were taking bets on whether or not the anchor would come up.

Now David had just been in touch with the ship and had been assured that everyone was praying at a specific time just before supper. So he walked over to the man who was taking the bets and remarked, 'You may be interested to know that there are 325 people praying right now that the anchor will come up in the next few minutes.'

'Oh, yeah?' queried the man in a surprised tone.

'Yeah.'

David watched with secret amusement the ensuing flurry of financial activity with bills being returned to their original owners.

Shortly before six o'clock the diver emerged from the water and moved out of the way. The trawler started pulling again. Harder and harder. The boat began listing more and more till it seemed the side would go under. All of a sudden there was a loud 'Poof!' and the anchor sprang loose while the trawler rocked wildly. The crowd on shore gave a loud cheer.

The winches pulled the anchor until it broke through the surface of the water. It was then lashed very securely to the side of the boat. No one was taking any chances of having the cable break now that they had the anchor. When the boat reached the pier, a shore crane lifted the anchor up and deposited it in the waiting lorry.

Unfortunately, David had made one serious mistake. He had ordered a lorry but had failed to specify that it should be an *empty* lorry. The lorry sitting on the quayside was probably carrying at least ten to fifteen tons of cargo already. The anchor would add another three tons.

The driver had brought along his uncle to travel with him. As there was no room for two additional people in the truck, it was decided that Norm should return to the ship by bus. David would accompany the anchor. He was assigned the middle seat which meant he had to wrap his long legs around the gear lever all night long.

The coast road was full of hills. As soon as they started up the first one, David groaned and thought, *Oh, no, we're never going to get there.* They did, however, make it to the top, grinding along in first gear the whole way.

Then the driver had to sleep awhile. He hadn't slept before the trip.

All this time David was thinking about the ship, knowing it was due to leave from Lima at midnight the next evening. He became increasingly beside himself with impatience as the journey continued. What would have taken about six hours by car took twenty-seven in the lorry.

Finally, at 11 pm the following night they pulled into the port area. A line of perhaps fifty lorries stretched out from the entry gate.

*Good grief!* groaned David. *We'll never make it.*

'Let's try another gate,' he suggested to the driver.

They did, and were almost devoured by a pack of German shepherd guard dogs.

'Oops! I think we'd better go back to the main gate,' concluded David.

As soon as the lorry took its place in line, David jumped out and hurried to the front of the line to talk with the guard. 'We've got the anchor for *Doulos* in that lorry back there,' he said, pointing.

'Ah, yes,' exclaimed the guard and motioned the lorry to the front of the queue and on inside the port, not even stopping to check it out.

At this point they were still about a mile from the ship. David was so relieved that they had at least got inside the port area, that he reached out and pulled on a horn attached to the outside of the lorry, 'BEEP, beep, beep, BEEP!'

They drove round to the ship. Everything was set up and waiting so they could hook the anchor on immediately. Even the surveyor was there to check that it was a certified anchor and all was as it should be. He approved and away *Doulos* sailed.

The next day as David was talking with Chris Papworth, the purser, he commented, 'It was great to have the surveyor there when we arrived.'

'Actually, he was leaving,' responded the purser. 'When it got to about eleven thirty, we all concluded you weren't going to make it. We had got an exemption and were going to sail with or without the anchor at two in the morning.'

'Oh, thanks, guys. What was I going to do?'

'Well, we knew you'd find your way to the next port.'

[In actual fact, George Booth had discussed the matter with Frank Dietz, who had taken over as director when Dale left. Frank had been rather nonchalant. 'If the anchor doesn't arrive here, we can pick it up in the next port.'

George had firmly countered, 'Oh, no. Between Salaverry and here there is no Customs, but the next port is in Chile. You know South American Customs. The anchor would sit at the border until it rusted into a pile of brown flakes. It would never come through.'

That had given a sense of urgency to the affair.]

Chris went on to explain to David that the surveyor had just been getting into his car to leave when he heard the horn blowing. He got out of his car and said, 'That's them.'

'How do you know?' asked the purser.

'The sound of the horn on that lorry is different. That's the kind of horn the lorries in the north have, not the kind that Lima lorries use.'

If he hadn't heard that horn, the surveyor would have left and the anchor couldn't have been installed and used without his approval. There would have been further delays until the next day. Not a serious problem, of course, but it would have had repercussions for the programme in the next port.

A commercial ship, for whom time is money, might have abandoned the anchor and paid whatever it cost to replace it. For *Doulos* that was not an option. To purchase a new anchor and have it transported out to *Doulos* would have cost thousands of dollars — a large outlay of money even in the best of financial times. However, this was far from the best of financial times for *Doulos*. When she had circled South America the first time, the distributor for a large Spanish-language publishing house had told her leaders, 'You won't sell on the west coast. Ecuador, Peru. They won't buy books. Believe me, I'm telling you out of experience.' That had only increased the amazement of those on board *Doulos* as they saw a mile-long queue of people waiting for entrance to the book exhibition and when they saw visitors leaving with boxes full of books.

But this second time around the continent was a totally different story. The economy of country after country was falling into shambles. In Ecuador the currency devalued 50 per cent while the ship was in the country. *Doulos* book sales plummeted. Income from book sales had been expected to meet a large part of the expenses of the ship, but that money was instead tied up in stock sitting in the book holds of the ship. *Doulos* had continually operated at the heads-barely-above-water level; now there was nothing to fall back on to absorb the loss of book sales. Only the Lord.

Theoretically, every person on the ship, from the captain down, was expected to have a certain amount of financial support from churches, friends and family. That would pay all the expenses of the ship: fuel, accommodation, food, ministry, everything. In actual fact, many ship workers received only a portion of that required amount. The ship was dependent upon book sales and general donations to make up the deficit. There had been some hard times when food became monotonously simple, when money was too scarce to issue pocket money for personal spending, when bargain prices had to be found for equipment and the purchase of everything not absolutely essential must be postponed. Those on board had become adept at finding bargains. And time after time they had been amazed at the Lord's provision in unexpected ways.

158

Like the time in Guayaquil, Ecuador in 1980. The main exports of the country were oil and bananas. Right behind *Doulos* was a huge banana boat loading bananas by the ton. The overseers were so particular that if there was the slightest blemish, the whole stalk would be discarded and simply thrown down on the quayside. When the banana boat finally sailed, mountains of rejected green bananas were left on the wharf. Bulldozers came along to dispose of them by the simple means of shoving them into the water.

When some *Doulos* people realized what was happening, they rushed over to the bulldozer operators.

'Wait! Wait!' they pleaded. 'Can't you delay this operation for an hour or two so that we can get some of the bananas?'

'Sure. No problem.'

'Thanks. We'll try to collect as many as we can.'

The ship's vans were pressed into action, doing relays back and forth, loaded with bananas. Onlookers from *Doulos* exclaimed excitedly, 'The bananas may be green now, but they're going to ripen one of these days and we're going to enjoy ourselves to the fullest.'

Sure enough, the bananas did ripen one day. All at once. All two tons of them!

Then there was the time in Bilbao, Spain. That had been earlier, in 1978. The ship was anchored mid-river and from its decks Chief Engineer Rex Worth could see scrapyards ashore. Curiosity got the better of him and he took a launch over to see what he could find. In one of the yards there were generators like the ones on *Doulos*. One of them had just been overhauled and contained all new parts. Rex and his crew were able to strip them off and for these brand new spare parts they only needed to pay scrap prices. God had many ways of supplying needs.

Another experience of this occurred in Argentina in 1981. The situation there was an economic nightmare at the time. Inflation was incredibly high, so that shops didn't even bother writing the prices on stock as they would have to be changed within a day or two anyway. A retired colonel who had been head of military communications told the *Doulos* purser, Chris Papworth, that he had once sold a house he had got as a ranking military officer. While the paperwork was being processed, there was a devaluation of the Argentinian peso. When he finally got the money from the sale, all he ended up with was enough money to buy a teaset.

With that knowledge of the Argentinian economic situation, Chris was walking back to *Doulos* late one morning when he began to notice that banks were closing their doors. That set off alarm bells in his mind.

On *Doulos* at that very moment was sitting about

$100,000 in Argentinian pesos. It had been saved up from book sales, counted out and set aside to buy fuel which had to be paid for in Argentinian currency. An official had thrown a spanner into the works by pointing out a rule stating that foreign vessels couldn't buy fuel in Argentina. *Doulos* had done it last visit, but that fact hadn't impressed the official. There must be a way around the problem, Chris knew, but they hadn't yet been able to find the right person to help them out.

Seeing the banks closing, Chris immediately ran to a friend who worked in a company that was trying to help *Doulos* get the fuel.

'Tell me what's going on,' Chris asked.

'There's going to be a big devaluation. It's obvious.'

'But we've got all this money for fuel. . . .' Chris objected.

'Don't worry. Come with me.'

They raced from his office to an exchange house. The manager was a friend of Chris's friend.

'The purser from *Doulos* has got a lot of money,' he explained breathlessly. 'Can you help him?'

'I can help him if he's here with the money within the next half hour.'

Chris dashed out, flagged down a taxi and urged the driver to make all haste back to the ship. When they arrived, Chris rushed up the gangway, burst into the finance office, scooped all the money into his briefcase and dashed off without stopping to tell anyone where he was going.

As soon as Chris entered the exchange bureau, the

manager closed the door behind him and changed all the money. Chris walked out with dollars in his pocket. The money was safe. (No danger of robbery in those days. The streets were perfectly safe.)

That afternoon all the banks were closed and remained closed the entire week while dust from the devaluation was settling. But *Doulos* had the full amount of her money and was eventually able to purchase the fuel needed.

Perhaps the most dramatic provision of financial help occurred in Valparaiso, Chile in 1982. The ship had been following the recession which was spreading down the west coast of South America after Mexico admitted to the International Monetary Fund that it had less money than it had been maintaining. The further the ship went down the coast, the more trouble she met and the fewer books she sold.

In Chile ship members found prices had escalated since the previous visit, while *Doulos* book sales were significantly lower this time round. That left *Doulos* with far too little money to pay exorbitant port dues, pilot's fees and other expenses. Her leaders didn't know what to do. With the ship halfway round the continent, it looked as disastrous to turn back as to go forward.

The small team at the ship's headquarters in Mosbach, Germany, agonized over the situation as well. George Miley, staggering under the weight of his responsibility for the ship ministry, sent a telex to OM offices around the world: 'I feel *Doulos* is in a situation needing emergency prayer. The financial situation continues to worsen.

Now [the ship is] in Valparaiso, Chile. Yesterday the banks stopped selling dollars. Ship has only seven days fuel left. Uncertain if they can buy fuel with local money. Chronically overdue bills in Mosbach. Cannot even buy spare parts for lifeboats . . . I sense entire *Doulos* ministry in jeopardy.'

162

Another telex followed a week later: 'Ship can buy fuel in local currency with 20 per cent surcharge. God has given a little breathing space, but we sense we are in financial hole which will take time to dig out of . . . At moment, not enough fuel to leave Chile. We are now in process of taking definite steps to cut ministry back in light of financial realities. . . .'

The next scheduled port of call was Talcahuano, a port that had been cancelled on the first tour of Chile, much to the disappointment of Christians there. Kenny Gan, a Singaporean who had been sent to do line-up there, spent much time in fasting and praying with his team. He tells the situation from his perspective:

> One week before *Doulos* was due in Talcahuano, I went back to the ship in Valparaiso. There was literally no money. We had no money for fuel, no money for the berth or for fees. We just had no money. They had called me up and said, 'Kenny, you've got to cancel Talcahuano.'
>
> I told them, 'No. This would be the second time to do it. I've been fasting and praying for this port for the last few months and I don't believe God wants us not to go there.'
>
> Frank (the ship's director) still thought that we should cancel the port because there was no fuel to get to Talca-

huano or even to pay the port fees so we could leave Valparaiso. The idea was to stay put until we were able to get money some way. Frank called my boss, Bob Clement, to try to convince me. Bob tried, but I insisted, 'Bob, let's just continue to pray. I really believe strongly that the ship will get there. I don't know how, but it will get there.'

The ship's team on *Doulos* decided to approach President Pinochet. Through the navy they had a Christian contact to Pinochet's private secretary. Phoning the contact, they asked what chance there might be of getting an interview with the president. He checked and called back almost immediately, saying, 'I think it might be arranged.'

Ship leaders immediately got together to discuss and plan. If they got an appointment with the president, who should go? What should be asked for? What should they tell him? Their meeting took on an air of unreality and yet excitement. Just suppose the president were to be wonderfully disposed toward *Doulos* and ask, 'What can I do for you?' what should they answer?

'I think we should ask for *everything*,' commented Bob Clement, director of the programme department, in a calm but earnest voice.

'No,' countered Chris, the purser, 'I think we should be more circumspect. We should work out exactly what it is we really need and not act greedy.'

That's the course they finally decided upon.

The people to go, they decided, should be Captain Isaacson in his dress uniform, Program Director Bob Clement in his best suit and tie, and J. J. Jenkins who, as line-up man, was the official link.

The attempt to set up an interview proved successful. Ten to twelve minutes was promised for it.

Bob Clement takes up the story here:

> I remember standing in the foyer of the palace just before we were going to be ushered in to see the president. It was a large room and very elegant. Several people came and told us exactly what to do and what not to do. They said 'When these doors open, you are to proceed one at a time through the corridor and walk straight toward the double doors ahead. As you get close to them, those doors will open and you will be received by the president. When he sits down, you sit down. When he gets up, it means the interview is over.'
>
> The doors opened and we marched through. It felt really awe-inspiring. As we walked into that corridor — and it was quite a long corridor — we saw there were guards. As we passed them, they would click their heels and do whatever they do with their rifles. They stood at attention as we walked through them, which was shocking and scary at the same time.
>
> We walked toward the big double doors that were closed. Just as we came close to them, they opened and we were flooded with the brilliant lights of television and flashes of light bulbs going off. . . . And there, right in front of us was the president in flesh and blood. He had a beautiful uniform on and so much gold braid he looked like a Christmas tree all lit up and with bright lights on. He looked absolutely impressive. It almost took my breath away.
>
> We got over the formalities and sat down and did what you do at this sort of thing. Then it looked like the audience

was up. I knew we had to do something, so I said, 'Mr. President, there's one situation we need cleared up and only you can help us with it. That's the port fees. We desperately need to see these port fees waived. We submitted a letter and haven't heard anything back. Is there any way you could help us?'

The president turned to his right-hand man and said, 'We've waived the fees, haven't we?'

'Yes sir.'

He looked at me and said, 'They've been waived.'

'Well, thank you very much.'

The next thing you know we were ushered out and we were all standing around. It was an incredible moment for us. The president had just waived $180,000 in port fees. I kept asking, 'Did you hear him say what I heard him say — that the fees had been waived?' Everyone concurred.

The fees were indeed waived and with that financial obstacle removed, the ship was able to continue her programme throughout Chile.

But financial pressures continued. In February as *Doulos* left Chile for Argentina, George Miley told his leadership team in Germany: 'Personally, there is no way I can react to our situation other than giving myself to extra, extended periods of prayer. To pray without taking realistic steps is wrong. To take realistic steps and not pray is worse.

'. . . I would like us to begin by coming together for prayer in my office on weekdays, Monday through Friday from 1700 to 1800 [5–6pm]. . . . I feel we should continue this at least until all *Doulos* Spanish book bills are paid.'

And to other OM leaders around the world he wrote: 'We seem to be losing around $2,000 per day in the total ship ministry operation . . . We have paid nothing since 22nd December toward the old bills to the Spanish publishers, to whom we are now three to five months overdue. . . . Ships just barely pay own local expenses with local gifts and book sales and have practically nothing to put toward books so the bills pile up here in Mosbach.'

The most emotional time in the ship's tour of Latin America came as she was preparing to leave Brazil for Europe a few months later. Of course, there were the to-be-expected tears of farewell because *Doulos* was not planning to return to Latin America, but the saddest part was something else.

Because of the financial crisis the ship was facing, her leaders decided they would have to do something they hadn't done before: send home Latin Americans who weren't receiving their full support of one hundred and fifty dollars a month. On board were around three hundred and twenty five workers. Of these, close to a hundred were Latin Americans. Many of them were well into a two-year commitment to the ship ministry; others were just starting.

David Greenlee, newly transferred to the position of personnel director, was given the task of interviewing the Latin Americans, assessing their financial situation and making the decision whether they must go home or could stay. He called them individually into his office to discuss their situation. They could call or telex their pastor or whoever was in charge of their financial support or David himself would call for them. What was needed was a clear and definite assurance that the money would be regularly supplied.

Time and time again someone could go into the office, a valued worker, someone very close to all the ship's members, but who just didn't have the financial support. David would have to tell the person, 'I'm sorry; you're not going to be able to stay on.'

They would go out of the office crying. And, admitted David, 'I would sometimes slip away to cry too. It was very difficult for me because I was so committed to getting Latin Americans involved in missions.'

Two-thirds of the Latin Americans had to return home. There was a steady stream to the airport or bus station. The situation was so serious that when the ship reached Europe, the numbers aboard were streamlined from over three hundred to about two hundred after many Europeans also went home.

Observed David, 'It took *Doulos* years to recover from this serious blow because in cutting down the numbers so drastically, we completely eliminated much of the training. The IT programme, in particular, had been providing a continuous flow of people who had a good level of training, especially in the personal sense of character development, and who would go on to become line-up people or various other middle-level leaders. In Brazil we had been running five IT teams of about eight people each. Suddenly there was none. The flow of up-coming leaders had dried up.'

On 22 June, 1983, *Doulos* left Vitoria, Brazil and limped back to Europe.

# AROUND AFRICA 1986–1987

| 1986 | 1987 |
|------|------|
| Las Palmas (Spain) | South Africa |
| Cape Verde Islands | Kenya |
| Senegal | Tanzania |
| The Gambia | |
| Guinea Bissau | |
| Sierra Leone | |
| Liberia | |
| Côte d'Ivoire (Ivory Coast) | |
| Ghana | |
| Togo | |
| Cameroon | |
| South Africa | |

# 10

# Entering Africa

What now? How could the ship be rescued from its deep financial difficulties? Where would the money come from? Had OM got in to deep water by buying a second ship? Should it be sold?

These were some of the many questions raised as *Doulos* arrived in Europe. Much time was spent in discussion, evaluation, planning and prayer.

In the meantime, *Doulos* was kept in Europe where she was relatively close to the headquarters in Germany and expenses could be better controlled. Much of the ministry was directed toward Christians, as ship members linked in with churches in the ports, encouraging, challenging and stimulating an interest in world missions.

Slowly money began coming in, mostly from donations, as the book exhibition was not a great attraction in countries already richly supplied with books of all kinds. Largely as the result of a single gift, one of the generators on *Doulos* was replaced by another type operating on a cheaper grade of oil which significantly lowered the fuel expenses for the ship.

For two and a half years *Doulos* kept to European waters, but the time eventually came when the ship's leaders, along with the board of directors, decided that the time had come for the ship to move out again. Not back to South America this time, but to Asia, where *Logos* had been working successfully for several years.

To get to Asia, however, *Doulos* must either make the very expensive passage through the Suez Canal or sail around Africa. If South America had been unpredictable, what would Africa hold?

The decision was made in favour of Africa. With excitement that the ship was finally getting underway again, but with a degree of apprehension as well, the ship's company steamed southward along the west coast of Africa.

Senegal presented a new challenge for *Doulos* workers. Not only was this their first visit to an African country, but it was also the first time the ship had visited a Muslim country. What kind of reception would her people get? What could they do of significance there? The official language was French, but many Senegalese spoke only tribal languages. Among the *Doulos* company were few French speakers and no one who knew any of the tribal languages.

Response from Christian missionaries was discouraging. 'None of the teams speak French,' the missionaries pointed out. 'What can they do? It will be a waste of time. More problem than help.'

As usual, a committee of local Christian leaders was formed to plan the visit. The man asked to take responsibility for evangelism had no idea how to go about organizing it. 'What do I do?' he asked helplessly.

Kenny Gan, who was leading the line-up team, sat down with him, took a map of Dakar and waved his hand over the city. 'That's what we want to reach,' he said. 'The whole city of Dakar.'

'You're crazy!' was the reaction, though phrased more politely.

'Let's pray and try what we can.'

When the ship arrived, teams went out into the streets with tracts and Bible correspondence-course applications. The first teams were somewhat apprehensive, not knowing how the Senegalese would react to such open evangelism. They need not have worried. They couldn't give out literature fast enough! Men and women who were over-looked in the scramble to obtain tracts, pressed their way forward to beg for them. Cars and taxis even stopped traffic on occasions to get tracts.

By the time the ship sailed two and a half weeks later, nine hundred and ninety people had signed up for the Bible correspondence-course. Churches reported that their members had become more committed to Christ, more challenged and involved in evangelism. The committee chairman told Kenny that one day a Moroccan had come to his church and asked if someone could study the Bible with him; as a result, the pastor and this Moroccan began doing Bible study together every day. Other people came to the church wanting to buy Bibles and to get more information about the gospel. A missionary in the city began meeting with fifteen new converts, three of whom had already started to attend church.

The ship was set up primarily to minister in spiritual areas, but sometimes that can also be done through meeting physical needs. The ship's doctor held a training seminar, through translation, for nine Senegalese women who travelled a great distance to the ship. These women were being prepared by a mission for leadership in their respective villages. The doctor talked to them about sanitation, safe drinking water, essential health care and infant nutrition. At the end, one of the women told him, 'What you have shared with us may seem very small to you, but to us it is very important.'

172

Nor was ministry directed only toward Senegalese. A couple of Koreans from *Doulos* visited a South Korean cargo ship in port and participated in a Bible study on board it. The Korean seamen were invited to a Sunday afternoon evangelistic meeting on *Doulos*. Several came and made commitments to Christ, including the captain himself. When the cargo ship sailed, her nightly Bible study on board had grown from six members to thirteen.

By the time *Doulos* reached the Gambia, she had visited four countries with four different languages in a little over a month. That meant the bookshop staff had moved book displays from English in Gibraltar to Spanish in the Canary Islands to Portuguese in Cape Verde to French in Senegal. In the Gambia, the shift had to be made back to English.

More difficult than language adjustments however, was the adaptation to new cultures with their new sights, sounds, smells, distinctive thought patterns and different ways of doing things.

According to Assistant Director Mike Stachura, the Gambia, a former British slave-trading colony, was 'hot, sticky, and mosquito-infested. The dust, dirt and poverty of the capital city was something Jorie and I had not seen in our nearly fourteen years of life outside the USA. Streets with gaping holes in the middle and no safety lights around them. The only running water was to be found at several taps at different points along a major street; sometimes they worked. Houses were made of patched-together corrugated steel.'

The country was 90 per cent Muslim and the ship was arriving in the midst of Ramadan, Islam's holy month of fasting. What would await *Doulos'* people in the Gambia?

The best seller proved to be not a single book but a small packet of books containing the New Testament, a Gospel of Mark, several evangelistic booklets or children's tracts and a postcard of the ship. The price? Twelve cents.

That may sound like a give-away, but it was, in fact, the equivalent of an adult worker's hourly wage. Yet four thousand of these packets were sold, many of them towards the end of the two-week visit as people caught 'packet fever'. A local missionary commented that she had never seen such a wide distribution of God's Word in the Gambia in her many years of service there.

The book exhibition was not the only busy place on the ship. Programmes for over six thousand school children kept the main lounge overflowing. The children were entertained by a video tour of the ship, an introduction to some of the crew with a chance to ask questions, music, drama or puppetry and, finally, a sketchboard message. For most of these Muslim children, the concept of a loving, personal God was totally new.

Many of the children also bought a special gospel packet

made up for children. The book exhibition manager met a small boy on the beach who proudly announced that he knew all about *Logos* and *Doulos*; he'd read about them in a bookazine [book in magazine format] he'd got on the ship. He added that he was also reading a little from his New Testament every night before going to sleep.

174

Throughout most of Africa ship members were continually amazed at the great interest in literature. *Doulos* spent only three days in Guinea Bissau, one of the world's poorest countries. Again the challenge was to get the word of God into the hands of the people. On the first day an evangelism team was sent out on the streets to try to sell the packets. The evangelism leader challenged them: 'If you can sell a hundred of them today, you'll be doing very well indeed.'

The first team went out and returned half an hour later. They had sold all their New Testaments before they even got outside the port gate!

On the second day the ship's crew and staff, including volunteers from local churches, mobilized to assemble another four thousand packets to meet the demand. Taxis would stop in the middle of the street for the driver to lean out and yell, 'Hey, I want one of those!' Crowds of people, filing out of the local stadium spotted the evangelism team and rushed toward them to get packets. By the end of the three-day visit nine thousand packets had been sold.

Other book sales, too, were unbelievable. Richard Beaumont, who had become manager of the bookshop, explained, 'When you're in a poor country, you'd expect lower sales, but actually, it goes the other way. When a country is very poor, the people don't have many books available. So when the opportunity arises, they really sacrifice to buy books.'

Visitors to the bookshop spent an average of five hours' wages per person, but taking advantage of the bargain prices of used books donated by Christians in Britain and America, they were also able to get a lot for their money. People in wealthier, developed countries, wallowing in a surfeit of books, have no idea what it means to a literature-starved person to be able to get a precious book or two into his hands, to own it, to read it, to share it with his family and friends. For many in Guinea Bissau, *Doulos* was a treasure ship!

Most people working on the ship came for a two-year period. While some joined at different times throughout the year, most came in October after the annual autumn OM conference in Europe. One of those who joined in Cameroon in October, 1986, was Kathy Newman from Great Britain. She wrote about her first evangelism experience with *Doulos*:

> The day after we arrived in Cameroon, we were introduced to evangelism in Africa. Fifty of us were each given a box of twenty French New Testaments and instructed to sell them on the streets of Douala. The aim was to sell them all. I was horrified. My only other attempt at bookselling was in France where I sold only one book in three summers. I shot a quick prayer to God and set off. Within three hours everyone had sold out. I have always believed theoretically when Jesus said: 'Open your eyes and look at the fields! They are ripe for harvest.' In Cameroon I came

to believe it experientially. The people I talked to in my poor French were hungry for the gospel. It was a real privilege to distribute the word of God to people who were eager to receive it.

176 Selling was not the only way literature was distributed. Some of the *Doulos* crew had a particular interest in Russian seamen. On several occasions a Soviet ship was in port while *Doulos* was there. The crew would seek opportunities to talk with the Russians. One of the favourite ploys was to try to arrange a football match between the crews. The Russian seamen would respond eagerly, but generally the political commissar would step in and cancel arrangements.

In the Gambia, however, the political commissar apparently raised no objection. An enjoyable good-natured game took place, ending in a one-all draw. After the game, to the surprise and delight of the Russians, a gift was presented to each one. They opened the gifts and discovered a Bible and another Christian book in Russian.

A lively conversation erupted among the Russians, utterly unintelligible to the *Doulos* crew. They could only watch and wonder as all the gifts were collected and put in a bag. Would the books be smuggled aboard and passed out to the team later or would they be turned over to the political commissar?

That same evening one of the Russians appeared at the gangway of *Doulos*. 'Do you have more Bibles?' he asked the watchman.

'Yes, of course.'

A few quick arrangements were made. Later that evening

Mats Johansson, carrying a big bag laden with Bibles, New Testaments and cassettes containing gospel messages in Russian, headed out into the darkness and on towards the Russian freighter. The gangway to the ship was flooded with pools of light and well guarded. Mats paused and stood weighing his chances of getting aboard with a bagful of Bibles. Experience had taught him it was impossible. But then a movement caught his eye among the shadows alongside the ship. A hand was sticking out of a porthole, gesturing toward the bag. With a cautious eye on the watchman, Mats sidled toward the ship and hastily stuffed his bag through the porthole. Mission completed, he straightened up and nonchalantly wended his way along the quayside back to his own ship.

How to communicate with people whose language they did not know was continually a challenge to *Doulos* people. Translators were necessary, of course, but translators were not always available. Evangelist Ray Lentzsch, for whom talking about Jesus Christ was the breath of life, found an effective way to communicate a message not only once but time and time again. The secret was audio cassettes.

Immensely popular in Africa, these would be played over and over again. Cars, buses, lorry drivers would pop a cassette into their player as soon as they passed the outskirts of town and got beyond the reach of local radio. Radio reception might fade out but the cassette would continue to come in clear.

Ray saw that and became excited about selling cassettes which he obtained from Gospel Recordings. He would put gospel tapes into a cassette player and shout out the price while the tape was blaring. The price was set just a little higher than the cost of an empty cassette so there would be no temptation to buy the tape and erase it afterwards.

A favourite place to sell in Kenya was among cars queued up waiting to board a ferry for the mainland. If the cars were too far from the cassette player to hear Ray's demonstration clearly, the drivers could put the tape into their own vehicle player for a demonstration. The last three days in Kenya Ray sold an average of a hundred of these a day.

Another way of using the cassettes effectively was with a flip chart. This was a set of colourfully painted illustrations of a story or message. They were assembled like a huge calendar; as soon as one page was finished, it could be flipped over the top and another page would be revealed. The cassette told the story in the local language while a small pip cued the 'preacher' when to turn the page of the flip chart. This proved to be a great crowd-puller in Africa.

Workers on *Doulos*, seeing and hearing of many local people making decisions to follow Jesus Christ, often wondered how deep their commitment went. Undoubtedly some of the professions were superficially made under the sway of emotion, yet occasionally reports came back of people whose lives were clearly changed by their new-found relationship with God. These reports encouraged ship workers to keep pressing on, realizing there must be many more changed lives that they never heard about.

Clarence was one whose story they did eventually hear.

In Liberia, as in other countries, the ship's main lounge was continually used for conferences and meetings of various sorts, but occasionally there would be lulls when the room was free for large blocks of time. A common practise of holding *Welcome on Board* meetings developed. An announcement would be made to visitors in the book-shop that a short programme about the ship would take place shortly in the meeting room; all visitors were warmly welcome.

Clarence had already been to the ship once to buy books, but he was back again for more. When the announcement came booming out on the book exhibition, he thought, *Why not? It sounds interesting.*

He made his way down to the main lounge and found a seat along with a number of other visitors. A short video gave an inside look at the everyday lives of people on the ship: the baker, the doctor, the engineers, and even the children in school. Someone explained what *Doulos* was all about, why people worked on the ship and why it had come to Liberia. This led into a short sketchboard message. On this particular day the message was entitled 'Almost a Christian'. It was about a person who did all the Christian things. He went to church, believed the Bible and tried to live a good life, but he still wasn't really a genuine Christian because he had never asked forgiveness for his sins and turned control of his life over to God.

Clarence was caught up in the message. *Why, that's me!* he thought. *I'm almost a Christian. Almost! How awful!*

That afternoon he prayed to become a real Christian rather than an almost one.

A week or two later the ship sailed away, but by that time Clarence was in contact with one of the local churches. A short while later he entered a Bible school for a two-year course of study. After that was completed, he went to work for the Lord in one of the cities of Liberia.

180

Tragically, civil war erupted in Liberia, sweeping over the country, engulfing its people in indescribable horror, suffering and death. Along with many others, Clarence and his fiancée fled to neighbouring Sierra Leone for refuge.

Five years later, when OM's other ship went to West Africa, one of her staff met Clarence working among Liberian refugees in Sierra Leone. In most of the camps there were churches with pastors and Christian leaders. Clarence was giving evangelism training for Christians and taking them out in the camps to bring a message of hope to people who had lost everything, whose lives no longer held meaning, whose whole world had ruptured into irreparable fragments.

Jonathan Harris was another *Doulos* worker who received a follow-up report on a young man he had talked with. Jonathan was leading a team to sell New Testaments out on the streets of Kenya when a young man bought one and walked off, looking through his new purchase. Suddenly the man hesitated, turned around and walked back to Jonathan.

'If I read this book, will it tell me how to become a Christian?' he asked in a concerned voice.

Realizing it might take the man quite a while to read the New Testament, Jonathan suggested, 'Why don't I just explain to you the main message of the Bible?'

There on the street Jonathan told him the amazing story of what Jesus Christ had done for him. The Kenyan listened eagerly. When he had understood, he prayed asking Jesus to forgive him and take charge of his life.

A few days later Jonathan was paged on the ship and told he had visitors. Going up to the information desk area, he found the Kenyan man and with him, another young man.

'This is my brother,' the new Christian told Jonathan. 'He wants to know about Jesus too.'

Jonathan again explained the good news about Jesus Christ and the brother too committed his life to Christ.

A week later Francis, the first Kenyan was back again, saying, 'This is my neighbour. He wants to know Jesus.' A few months after the ship had left Kenya, Jonathan received a letter from Francis telling how he had been going out into the towns and villages in his area, sharing the gospel and bringing other people to Christ.

*Doulos* workers reached out to local people in many ways. Not all of it was through planned, structured activity. On one occasion in the Gambia Mike Hack and another *Doulos* man were walking along a road when they saw an Arabic school.

'Let's go in and see if we can talk to some of the students or the teachers,' suggested Mike impulsively.

'Never hurts to try.'

They walked through the front door. Approaching someone who looked as if he represented authority, they introduced themselves and told him about the ship. They were warmly welcomed with curiosity and respect.

'Could we teach a class?' they ventured to ask.

'Why, yes, please do,' came the gracious reply.

They were not given a class to teach, though. Instead, the entire school was brought into a large room to hear the visitors. Mike and his colleague found themselves looking into a hundred faces staring inquisitively at them. After telling the students something about the ship, Mike launched into a sketchboard presentation of Jesus Christ. (He and the others in evangelism training had just been studying Islam, looking for meaningful and culturally sensitive ways of presenting the Gospel.)

Students and teachers alike were impressed. 'We've never heard Christianity explained in this way,' they said.

Some time later, eight of the students made their way to *Doulos*. 'We've come to learn more about Jesus Christ,' they announced. Mike and one or two other men spent several hours teaching and explaining.

'You've conquered us,' the students said finally. 'You've shown us that your faith is better than ours.'

That's as far as they went. They were not ready to receive Jesus Christ as Saviour. The words had laid the groundwork, but only the Spirit of God could bring the students to repentance and commitment.

In Sierra Leone British First Officer Richard Prendergast and his wife were strolling along the quayside, chatting and enjoying the sense of release and relaxation that comes from getting off the ship. A young man came up to them and begged, 'Can you give me a shirt?'

Instead of brushing off the young man impatiently, the Prendergasts stopped to talk with him. A sad story came out. The young African had injured his hand in an accident the previous week, leaving it paralysed. With no money, he could not go to a doctor for treatment. And with a paralysed hand, he could not get a job.

Marjorie Prendergast slipped away as the men talked and paid a visit to Charlie, the ship's used clothing 'boutique'. When she returned ashore with a shirt in her hand, Richard was talking with the young man about his greatest need, salvation. He had also given the man an Arabic Bible,

'Would you like me to pray for your hand?' asked Richard as the conversation came to an end.

The man nodded. Richard prayed for the full restoration of the hand, if God pleased. The man thanked him and left.

The next day Richard was paged on the ship's public address system. When he checked in at the Information Desk, he was told a visitor was looking for him. It was the young African, excited and practically incoherent in the story he had to tell. As he had left the ship on the previous day, before he could even reach the port gate, his hand had been completely healed!

'Give praise to God,' Richard told him. 'It's God's doing!'

A few days later Richard visited the man. He and his family were clearly shaken by what had happened. Richard talked further with them about trusting Jesus Christ.

That's as far as the story goes, from Richard's standpoint. But he continued to pray for the man, fully convinced that God was able to water the seed that had been planted in that man's heart and mind.

Work on the ship was hard and, like workers anywhere, *Doulos* people looked forward to their days off. In Ghana two of the young women decided to spend their free day at the beach, stretching out on the sand, soaking up the sun and doing nothing. Just relaxing.

184     They biked down to the beach, found a good location and sat down. Then before doing anything else they prayed for protection. After all, they were two young women alone and they had heard stories. . . . [One story they hadn't yet heard, fortunately for their peace of mind, was that of a *Doulos* man who'd returned to the ship robbed of everything, including his shoes.] After praying, the women carefully placed their bikes at their heads to make sure they didn't disappear and stretched out on the sand. Before long, they both fell asleep.

All of a sudden one of them heard a noise. Voices. Alarmed, she jerked up to a sitting position and looked around apprehensively. Behind a nearby rock she caught sight of a man. The sun glanced off the blade of a long knife in his hand. Her heart stopped beating. *This is it!* she thought. *Here go our bikes and maybe our heads as well!*

Two old men, identifiable as Muslims by their clothes, appeared beside the man with the knife. They were talking loudly in Arabic. The *Doulos* women, wide awake now, watched in silent apprehension as the men approached and started talking to them in Arabic.

'*Doulos! Doulos!*' the women repeated, trying to explain in English that they were from the ship. Obviously they were not getting their point across.

Relief poured in as a family with two small children and a goat appeared, bringing up the rear of the party.

The *Doulos'* women's relief was short-lived, however, as another horrible thought — though decidedly less horrible than the previous one — began to dawn upon them. The goat was to be sacrificed right there in front of them.

The African wife and mother could speak English. She seated herself sociably beside the two *Doulos* women and announced, 'We're going to sacrifice this goat so God will give health and prosperity to our family.'

The men tied the legs of the goat and started cutting with the knife which was not as sharp as the women had imagined. The process took time. The goat wriggled and blood spilled down on the rock.

The *Doulos* women stared in macabre fascination.

'I'm a Christian,' the African mother continued conversationally, 'and I believe God will be pleased with this thing we are doing and will favour us.'

That was the cue for the *Doulos* women. Shifting their attention from the goat, they looked at the African woman and began to tell her about Jesus being God's perfect sacrifice. His blood could bring true prosperity by cleansing people from sins. Eventually the African prayed to take advantage of that greatest sacrifice of all.

In describing the incident, one of the *Doulos* women remarked, 'I think the Lord knew this lady's desire to get to know him. In the place where they were going to sacrifice to him, God revealed his sacrifice for them.'

## 11

## Meeting the African Church

The little church in Sierra Leone had a low roof made of corrugated steel. Someone had apparently taken a one-room house, put an extension on one side and added a roof over the whole structure. The pastor, from his vantage point behind the tiny pulpit at the front of the church, could see his entire congregation, neatly divided by a wall running down the middle of the building. Originally the wall had been an outside wall of the house, containing windows. The glass had been removed, but the window frames remained.

Promptly at ten o'clock on Sunday morning the *Doulos* team showed up as they had been instructed to do. The men were dressed in suits as had also been instructed. Suits. Ten o'clock in the morning. Tropical Africa. They were off to a good start.

A brass band of seven or eight people, located just in front of the pulpit, blared enthusiastically. The singing started, rocking the whole building. People began clapping to the beat and swaying rhythmically from side to side. The team had never been to this church, but they had a feeling the music might go on for a long time. And it did, for at least an hour.

In the building, naturally, there was no air-conditioning. Neither were there any fans. Outside windows were very few and far between. The heat generated by the congregation was stifling for *Doulos* people who were not used to it. Eventually, after an hour of jubilant worship, the time came for the *Doulos* team to make its presentation. That included a personal testimony, a musical item and a presentation of some of the books the team had brought along to sell. This was followed by preaching. Mike Stachura, the ship's assistant director, had been invited to do that.

As soon as the church service was ended, the team members hastily and eagerly made their way outside to set up a book table for the church people.

'Oh, the joy of getting outside!' Mike related later. 'It felt like stepping into a cold shower!'

As they were standing around the book table, selling books and talking with church members, the pastor came up to them. 'We really liked everything you said,' he told them and then continued, 'We're going to have a meal now. After that, we'll have another meeting.'

The *Doulos* team packed up their things and squeezed into a little van. Carloads of people, packed together and hanging out of car windows, drove for an hour out into the bush. The van with the *Doulos* people wove on and off the road, swerving out on the edge to avoid the worst of the deep ruts. At times they were certain the van would get stuck, but it made the trip safely and pulled up in a small village surrounded by nothing but dirt.

And there in the middle of the bush a huge feast was set out. The village had been waiting for two and a half hours for their guests to arrive. That was no problem for them. They were completely relaxed and welcoming.

The foreign visitors by this time were totally drenched with perspiration, their shirts, jackets, dresses clinging to their skin. They sat down to eat an array of food, most of which they had never seen before. Cassava, various types of fruit and so on.

After the meal they were eagerly led to a little chapel no bigger than the average European or American living-room. The building was not quite completed, but local Christians wanted it dedicated by the *Doulos* team. Only when Mike walked in did he realize that he was expected to preach for the dedication. He sent up a silent prayer for help and searched around in his mind for something appropriate. When he stood in the pulpit, he described to the congregation the dedication of Solomon's temple and went through the things Solomon had said at that time.

The Africans were pleased, both the ones from this new church and those from the mother church that had planted this one. They felt the message was right on target.

And so Mike Stachura and most of his team had their first experience of the African church.

Church meetings had always been an important part of the *Doulos* ministry. On any given Sunday there might be anything from ten to fifty meetings arranged for *Doulos* teams. These were set up through the programme depart-ment on the ship. A pastor who wanted a team called in and the programme department put together a team, usu-ally consisting of four or five people.

Generally a fairly experienced person was assigned the leadership of the team. He was given a paper containing all the details: who the speaker would be, if there was one; who else would be on the team; the name and phone number of the church; what was expected from the team; how they would get to the church; and so on. The team leader was then responsible for getting the team together and planing what would be done by whom. There were various possibilities, depending upon what the church would like: music; testimony of how a team member became a Christian, why he had come to the ship or what he had learned while on the ship; a presentation explaining what the ship was all about; a short mime; slides.

Sometimes a church would offer a team only part of a service, just to acquaint the congregation with what the ship was. At other times a team was expected to preach the sermon as well. Often the ship's leaders or guest speakers who were visiting the ship would do the preaching. But there was also ample opportunity for others aboard who showed a gift in the area to develop experience.

The teams went into every kind of church imaginable: Anglican, Baptist, Pentecostal, liberal, conservative, charismatic, non-charismatic. One Sunday a team might be in a vast ornate cathedral with superb acoustics. The next week some of the same people might find themselves in a tiny plain cement-block building where the sounds bounced loudly from one wall to the other.

'We always came to a church meeting with a little bit of fear and trembling because we never knew what to expect,' said Third Engineer Gary Deane. 'The church might be warm and friendly and welcome us with open arms. Or its members might sit in the pews, reserved, passive or even somewhat sceptical. It was always amazing in a church like that to see people melt and at the end of the service come up to shake hands warmly with the team and thank them for the things they had shared.'

For individuals from *Doulos*, this was an incredibly broadening experience. Some came from non-Christian families. Others with Christian backgrounds had never set foot in a church with a different way of worshipping from that of their own church. For these it was an education to see how much variety there could be within the family of God.

A church might be packed out or it might be half empty, as a team involved in film ministry found when they went to a so-called 'coloured' church in South Africa. The array of empty pews was not a very encouraging sight for the visiting team, but they began the service anyway, telling about *Doulos* and why they were working with the ship.

'How many of you would like to be missionaries?' asked the team leader.

'Amen!' came the thunderous response from the congregation.

'That's great!' exclaimed the *Doulos* speaker. 'Because you're going to have the opportunity right now. Look around at all these empty pews. I challenge you to go out and find lost people and bring them in to watch the film.'

The church emptied. Half an hour later it was packed with some of the roughest looking characters imaginable sitting right in the front row. That night two men came to know Jesus Christ as their Saviour.

God used the *Doulos* teams to challenge and encourage local churches, but perhaps the greatest blessings were experienced by the teams themselves. Mike Stachura's assortment of church experiences gives an idea of the deep impression made by African Christians on *Doulos* workers.

In the Ivory Coast a very large Methodist church had contacted the ship and asked that the ship's director himself come to their church. Mike and his wife, Jorie, went along with three other *Doulos* people, including an Italian who spoke French and would serve as translator.

After an hour-long drive following the directions of a church member who had come to escort them, they arrived at the outskirts of a town. A group of men and a marching band blocked the main street.

'Leave your vehicle here and come with us,' the team was instructed.

Andrea, the translator who also doubled as driver, was concerned about the safety of the car.

'No, no, don't worry,' he was assured. 'It's absolutely safe. Leave the keys with this man here and he'll bring it along to the church.'

All this was going on in French, which Mike couldn't understand, but he had no trouble grasping the situation and Andrea's uneasiness.

The band assembled itself into marching order. Mike marvelled at the dress. Men in smart western-style suits. Others in regal Ivory Coast robes. Women in beautiful colourful African gowns.

The team marched behind the band up a dirt road which was obviously Main Street. They went the length of the town and then doubled back, turning off finally toward an enormous church situated in the middle of nowhere. In through huge iron gates they paraded and were met by twenty-four elders in long black ecclesiastical robes. The elders led them into the church and onto a polished marble-like floor. They swept past beautiful pews up to the front of the church beneath a great pipe organ. It was like being in a church in Europe somewhere.

This was one of the many African churches where double or triple translation was needed. Mike spoke in English. Andrea translated into French and a local person turned it into a regional dialect. It took a long time for the sermon, but that was no problem. Everyone had lots of time.

After the service the *Doulos* team put out Christian books they had brought from the ship. To Mike's astonishment, the best sellers were clearly the large French theological tomes of Calvin's Commentary. Everyone seemed to buy them.

In stark contrast, Mike went at another time to a tiny little church in Liberia, among a very low class of society. Not only was the *Doulos* team very international; it also appeared very rich among these people.

The team was given a place of honour at the front of the church. Directly before them, filling the first five or six rows, were nursing mothers, and in Africa it's quite open nursing. Mike found preaching to an audience like that a bit disconcerting.

This was a church where none of the women could read and few of the men could either. All music was done from memory. At one point in the service came the time for the offering, which was taken in the traditional African way. The congregation stood and made its way row by row up to the front, singing, swaying in a rhythmic combination of march and semi-dance. As the worshippers passed by the offering receptacles in front, they tossed in their 'mites' and danced back to their seats.

Gloria, a Peruvian woman with a beautiful voice, stood and sang a song of commitment, after she had explained it in her heavily accented English. Apparently the congregation understood because no sooner had she finished than spontaneously the people stood up and began singing and dancing their way again to the collection receptacle up front.

The pastor evidently sensed Mike's amazement because he leaned over and explained, 'In our culture among the people of this church, if God speaks, if there is a message from the Lord, our people give.'

Mike was deeply touched. Never had he seen that kind of spontaneity in western churches nor the joyousness that was evident in giving the very little that these people had.

During the service Mike noticed little heads outside popping up fleetingly above the window sills, children jumping up to try to see inside. As the service progressed and the temperature in the building rose higher and higher, the back doors were thrown open for ventilation. Immediately the opening was lined with twenty or thirty street children peering in. *A symbol*, Mike thought. *Here is a church in the midst of the poor. The church itself is full but there are many, many more on the outside waiting to hear.*

After the church service the *Doulos* team set up a book table as usual. On it was a big selection of used Christian books donated by Christians in Europe and North America. The books were offered for only a few cents each. Every one of them was sold.

194   Afterwards the team wondered about that. Why would people who couldn't read buy used books? They concluded that the people treasured God's word so much that they would find someone who could read it to them or they might depend on their children who were going to school.

In Ghana Mike and a team were invited to the largest Assembly of God church in the country. The building was large enough to seat about fifteen or twenty hundred people. It was a good solid structure with strong walls, doors, floor, a platform, everything that a church building needed . . . except a roof! The congregation had started building but had been interrupted by a severe famine a couple of years earlier.

When the *Doulos* team arrived, thirty-seven little groups were sitting around on the floor in various places, huddled around chalkboards. These were Sunday School classes working through material sent out by the denomination.

The team had arrived about nine o'clock. The pastor was not there to greet them, so they sat on a tiny bench and observed the Sunday School classes. After a while the pastor arrived but immediately left again.

At ten thirty the church service started. For an hour there was non-stop worship, which was very expressive with people going up and dancing in front. It was nothing extreme, just very African. The first offering was taken and wave after wave of men from one side of the room and women from the other side rose and began wending their way forward in their dance-march, swaying and waving little white handkerchiefs. Their money deposited, they continued the exuberant march back to their seats.

The entire event took twenty minutes. According to Mike's description, 'From row after row they would come flowing up. It was beautiful! A marvelous sense of "We bring the sacrifice of praise." '

All the time the congregation was singing and clapping to the beat until Mike's hands were almost raw.

A short mini-message from the pastor followed. Then a prayer time. The pastor explained that one of the church members had been taken to prison and that's where he, the pastor, had been all morning, trying to get the man released. Apparently the whole thing was a form of harassment of Christians.

At eleven thirty Mike started preaching. At the pastor's insistence, the sermon with translation went on for an hour. After the service, there was the usual *Doulos* book table and interaction with church members. Four hours of church!

The people milling around the church and talking were expecting to go out on evangelism in the afternoon and then come back to the church for the evening service. Mike looked at them in wonder. Four hours of church and he was already exhausted.

'Now you must come to my house,' the pastor informed the team.

196

That was customary in Africa. Every time the *Doulos* team went to church meetings in Africa, they were invited for a meal afterwards. Always.

This meal was at the pastor's house. The pastor and one other man sat with the six team members around a table in a very simple kitchen. The pastor's wife was nowhere to be seen, nor was anyone else.

On the table was rice. Almost all of the meal was rice, mixed with a few bits of ground beef. There were also a few vegetables, and water.

During the meal the pastor got to talking about the famine. (Mike didn't even know there had been a famine!) He told the team what it was like to be a pastor and have people coming every day to his door to ask for food. The pastor would give the family's food to anyone who came. Many, many days there would be one cup of rice to be divided among himself, his wife and his four children. That was all they had to eat.

'How long did that go on?' asked Mike.

'For a year.'

People never stopped coming for food, yet the family never went for long periods without food. They simply believed that since the Bible said to give when someone asked, they should give.

In telling this story, Mike commented, 'It made eating very difficult because we saw we had at least a cup of rice on each of our plates. That made eight cups. We looked at it and realized that wasn't a whole lot of food for us, but it represented more than a week's worth of food for a family of six during the famine.'

One other meal in a pastor's home stands out in Mike's memory. This one was in Cameroon. By this time *Doulos* was nearing the end of her West African tour and her people had gathered enough experience to figure out a few things about eating. One was the fact that the team would always eat with the men or, often, just with the pastor. His wife never appeared except to bring in food. Children never appeared at all.

Mike, his wife Jorie, and the team were led into a small room where they saw a large table set with fish, rice, bananas. A real banquet. Including the pastor, there were seven people to eat it.

Mike and Jorie had cautioned the team not to eat much, not to take seconds and to make sure their plates looked full but weren't. The host, however, was very aggressive in urging them to take more. His wife, too, urged them on, saying, 'You must take seconds.'

'Oh, no, no,' the team demurred. 'Really, we're quite full.'

It was a somewhat tense moment, but the team had already caught a glimpse of a dozen or so children outside. They were the pastor's children and his nephews and nieces. The team had nudged each other and glanced toward the window. Immediately several little heads ducked down out of sight. The *Doulos* people realized that these children couldn't have eaten prior to the team's coming. They were undoubtedly hoping that the visitors would eat very little because whatever was left over, would be their meal.

Looking back over his time in Africa, Mike mused:

That was one of the things we were struck with. The West Africans who had so little gave so generously. They were very quick to offer food or help with transportation.

I remember coming back from church and the driver casually asked my wife, 'Do you like apples?'

Too tired to be alert, Jorie replied, 'Why yes, I like apples.'

Instantly the man pulled over to the side of the road, jumped out of the car and bought a bag of apples from a vendor. Six apples. One for each of us, but none for himself. We realized that an apple in West Africa was a delicacy and must have cost so much.

But that to us symbolized the African Christians. If they had a cup of rice, they shared it with whoever came. Their guest would eat first and their family second. Even though you came from the great white ship, if you wanted an apple, then they would stop and you would have an apple.

I think there were more lessons that I learned from the churches and church meetings in Africa than any place other than India when I first joined *Logos*. Never have I taken so many church meetings as I did during that time in West Africa because I learned so much.

## 12

# Inland Adventures

The evangelism-training team in Togo got off to a slow start. First there was the interminable wait for the *Doulos* vans to be cleared through customs. Then the Christian leader to whom the team had been assigned was late arriving. With all the delay, it was well after four o'clock in the afternoon before the seventeen-member team could head off for a village a couple of hours' drive away.

They started out with some trepidation. This would be a completely new experience for them and they didn't know what to expect. Ten days to be spent in a small village where the population couldn't much exceed five hundred. They knew conditions would be primitive and communication difficult. Villagers would have their own tribal language. Though some of them might know a little French, that wouldn't help the team members much because most of them didn't know French.

Their assignment was to find out as much as they could about the culture and the interests of the people. Then the team was to try to find some kind of communication bridge to be able to share the Gospel.

Having left the ship so late, the team arrived in the village after dark. And dark it was! No lights, no fires, nothing to welcome them. The welcome part, at least, was soon remedied, as it seemed the whole tribe began pouring into the street to meet the visitors and shake hands with them. Unfortunately, the visitors couldn't see anything, neither the villagers nor even themselves because it was pitch dark. They just felt hands coming at them and shook one after another without any idea of the body attached to it.

Finally the team was led to a little house with a dirt floor. Rather a nice little house, if one didn't mind the bats on the ceiling. Mass confusion resulted as the team tried to organize their living quarters by candlelight. The women got the inside of the house while the men slept outside on the verandah. Two of the men settled down in the van.

Hardly had they got into their respective sleeping quarters when the sound of an approaching car broke the stillness of the night. It pulled up outside the house and two men jumped out, identifying themselves as policemen and demanding to know what white people were doing in this village without permission.

Extensive discussion followed. Eventually it was decided that four of the team along with the local Christian leader should accompany the policemen back to the police station located in a village twelve kilometres away. The police were quite uncommunicative, so no one knew what was wrong. That did nothing for the team members' peace of mind.

Edu Leite, a young Brazilian who remained behind in the village, can remember sleeping at the doorway of the house which had no proper door, only a curtain. He had a great night, he says, with all kinds of animals nudging him in the dark. He decided he would sleep easier if he didn't try to identify them, so he just curled up inside his sleeping bag.

Those who went to the police station met an upset mayor, who demanded to know why they hadn't come to see him first as is customary when strangers visit a village. (The local Christian with them knew this custom, of course, but had decided it was too late for a courtesy call when the team finally got to the village. He assumed it could wait until morning.) A thorough grilling followed. The mayor wanted to know who these people were and what they were doing in his village.

By this time it was well into the early hours of the morning and everyone, including the mayor, was tired. He decided to let the *Doulos* people return to the village for the night, but the local Christian should remain at the station.

'In the morning promptly at six o'clock I expect to see the entire team here,' ordered the mayor.

The 'entire team' decided that only those who hadn't been to the station already should go. Accordingly, this group went and presented themselves to the police. The mayor never did show up, but the team was kept sitting outside the police office for hours. No explanation. Once some prisoners were brought in and forced to the floor, bumping against the legs of the *Doulos* people sitting there. The police yelled, beat them and led them off to one of the two cells.

And the team sat, watching and wondering. There was no one to give answers. The police, who could speak

French, wouldn't. The prisoners appeared to know only the tribal language. In time a Baptist missionary who had been contacted came to their rescue and helped to work things out. The team returned to their village and began the process of settling in.

202     There was no running water; all water had to be carried from the village well. Accordingly, Edu and one of the other men grabbed a bucket and set off. A group of local women had gathered around the well. Only women. That little detail didn't register with Edu and his companion. They simply stepped over the low fence enclosing the well and proceeded forward.

The women stopped what they were doing and watched, giggling but not saying a word. When the men tried to fill the bucket, some of the women came and pulled it out of their hands. The men were taken aback and, not knowing how to react, they did nothing. The women filled the bucket. Now was the time for action. Edu reached out to take the bucket back and in doing so set loose a scene. The women began yelling and pushing the men.

*What is this all about?* Edu asked himself in confusion. *Are they going to take our bucket and water away from us?*

A village man walked up to the two white men and rebuked them in headmaster tones, 'Men don't do that sort of thing,' he said, pointing to the water bucket. 'That's for women!'

The second night Edu and two other *Doulos* men slept in the van – or at least, started to do so. They were startled by the deafening sound of drumming, singing, crying, screaming and other assorted noises, all loud. The men in the van couldn't see each other, but they could feel the sudden change of atmosphere in the car. They had no idea what was happening in the village but they were not going to investigate. They were scared, very scared.

'Why don't we pray, Edu?' suggested one of the men. They took turns praying aloud, with Edu last. All the while they were praying they could hear the bustle of villagers coming and going around the car and throughout the village, the sounds of beating drums and of women running and screaming. In the darkness they could see nothing.

When it came tp Edu's turn to pray, he did so at length until he noticed that the noise had quieted down.

'Well, guys,' he commented in relief, 'it's all quiet now.'

No answer. Edu called to them. Still no answer. Both were sound asleep.

For Edu, however, sleep didn't come so easily. Every time he heard a sound, he would jerk back to wakefulness. It was a long night.

Later in the week he learned that the night's events had been part of a mourning ceremony for the oldest woman in the village, who had recently died.

After lunch the next day, the team collapsed on the floor of the house and slept. Edu remembers hearing the familiar voice of Ronnie Lappin, a ship leader, exclaiming jokingly, 'What's happening? They're all sleeping!' Just a dream, decided Edu, knowing Ronnie was back on the ship. He turned over and continued dreaming.

Only it wasn't a dream. Ronnie and several others had dropped in unexpectedly for a short visit just to check that everything was okay.

On the next day, Sunday, the team had charge of the morning service in the one Protestant church in town. It was a depressing experience. They had the feeling they weren't getting through to the people at all. Afterwards the translator admitted he'd had a little difficulty in translating.

What were they doing in the village anyway, they wondered. They felt they were just groping around and accomplishing nothing.

With renewed determination they went out into the village again after lunch, just walking around trying to talk with people and relate to them in any way they could. One of the *Doulos* women tried to imitate the village women's way of carrying a bowl on the head. The onlookers laughed good-naturedly at her clumsy attempts and encouraged her on. Later a dance was held in honour of the woman who had just died and the team watched in fascination.

As time passed, the verandah of the team house became a drawing point for village young people. They would come and stand around and try to talk with team members. One sixteen-year-old boy took a particular fancy to Edu. He knew a very tiny bit of French and Edu's French was about as limited, but somehow they managed to communicate.

One day the boy appeared with a teenage girl at his side. With a huge beaming smile, he went to shake Edu's hand warmly and then pushed the girl toward him.

'Oh,' stammered Edu, somewhat flustered, 'this is your sister, is it?'

'No, she's not my sister.'

'Your friend?' inquired Edu hopefully.

'No, she's not my friend. She's for you.'

'Well. . . .' Edu didn't know what to say, even if he could have said it in French. He hastily marshalled his thoughts and tried haltingly to explain his way out of the situation.

He learned something about the culture and social customs, though. It was unthinkable that a man (or a woman either, as at least one *Doulos* woman discovered through a similar experience) could reach a certain age without having sexual relations.

The team continued with their attempts to learn about the villagers and in some way communicate the gospel. In the church they could find no mature Christians, not even among the leaders. It was in a discouraging state, very much in need of spiritual revival and solid Bible teaching. That, at least, was something they could work on. One of the men on the team began teaching sessions with the elders each evening.

The problem remained, however, of how to share the gospel with non-church people. They decided that a visit to the chief was in order. Edu tells what happened:

> Finally we got an appointment to see the chief. His house was in the middle of the village. We had never been allowed to go near it. Now some of our friends went with us there. The way got narrower and narrower the closer we came. Then an interesting thing happened. At a certain point our friends suddenly stopped and wouldn't go any further with us. All around were animal bones and we could see pots of animals that looked like they had been sacrificed.
>
> The chief was the spiritual leader of the tribe. His hut

was very, very dark. We could feel the presence of evil there. Coming from Brazil, I had seen a lot of spiritism and I saw the same thing here very clearly.

We talked with the chief. It was good to have Paothang [from India; leader of the team] and Margaret [from Papua New Guinea] who came from backgrounds where they could understand what was going on. The chief listened but didn't say much.

Then the chief invited us to a festival they were going to have. Witches and sorcerers from neighbouring tribes were coming together to test their powers and see who could do the biggest miracle.

I really got afraid. When we went home, we decided that the next day we wouldn't do anything. We'd just stay home and pray and fast and ask the Lord to give us wisdom about what to do in the situation. We didn't want to go to the festival, but we didn't know how we could avoid it.

As the time for the festival came close, a messenger arrived and told us that the sorcerers from the different villages refused to come because there was some strong power in the village and nothing would work that day. So the festival could not take place.

We asked to see the chief again because we wanted to explain what this strong power was. We were able to explain the gospel to him. An African Bible school student who had been sent a few days earlier to help the team was able to translate. It was the first time I had ever talked with someone who had never heard of Christ and had no idea at all about Christianity. We talked about 'the spirit of light' and 'the spirit of darkness' and told the chief that he was dealing with the spirit of darkness.

He didn't make a decision but he said he wanted the missionary to come and teach his people about this spirit of light.

After that, our time in the village was wonderful. We had the approval of the chief. I felt that there had been something opposing us in the tribe and now it had left. It became easy to talk and share the gospel.

I'd been on the ship for two and a half years, but for me this was the beginning of learning about God's power. I already knew it in theory, of course. I learned a lot. When we come to a new group of people, we should first be patient and learn about them. We should spend time with the people, doing nothing but walking around with then and letting them show us things. Then we should pray. God is sovereign. He can make a way to share the gospel.

Edu and his team mates were participating in a thirteen-day missionary training programme which had been started on *Doulos* in West Africa. Its objectives were 1) growth in cross-cultural awareness and communication, 2) deepening understanding and appreciation of other cultures, 3) evangelism, and 4) expanded concern for reaching the spiritually needy.

The general schedule was one day of team-orientation, five to seven days on an inland team and the remaining time in classroom training with written homework assignments and supervised practical experience in the port city. Local missionaries were used as much as possible to share their experience.

Edu's team, perhaps, had suffered more disorientation than most teams because of the scantiness of information available beforehand about the country and its customs and official procedures. That undoubtedly contributed to the problem with the police.

Each person on the teams, however, was given some very specific guidance in observing the culture. A page and a half of questions was given to them to find answers for. Such questions as these about clothing:

> What do men wear? Women? Different for married people?
> Who makes the clothes? Same clothing in bed? At work?
> Where are the clothes washed? How are they dried?

or concerning jobs

> Where do the men work? The women?
> What type of work is available?
> What value is placed on work? What do people do for leisure?

and religion:

> What is the dominant religion?
> Where do the people worship? How do they worship?
> Are there sacred places? Where are they?
> What do the people see as their greatest religious needs?
> What is their concept of Christianity and Jesus Christ?

It was a fully packed, challenging, exhausting, exhilarating time of learning. The people involved had to be released from their work departments on the ship for the two weeks, as it was not something that could be done part-time only. Some of the prospective participants found the concept too overwhelming, too threatening and backed off. Others were negative about it for other reasons. But for many of those who took part, the experience was the highlight of their time in West Africa.

Inland teams had a wide variety of experiences. In Liberia Mike Hack [the Canadian who several years earlier as an irate seasick new recruit had been commended by the captain for his hard work] was in charge of organizing the teams. He contacted a Catholic Mother Superior about visiting her leper colony.

'I can bring electricians, carpenters, nurses, all sorts of people,' he told her. 'We'll do whatever you want us to help you with, but we will also preach the gospel and sell Bibles.'

'Fine,' she responded. 'You're welcome.'

The team found a colony of about one hundred Muslim lepers. It was quite an experience living among them, touching them, listening to what they had to say. Because Liberia has an English heritage, many could speak English.

In the mornings the *Doulos* crew worked hard digging ditches and fish ponds, setting out banana plants, building rabbit hutches (suspended over water so that driver ants wouldn't come and kill the rabbits), mending furniture and working in the wards with patients. In addition, they had to build their own fires and cook their own food. The afternoons were spent selling Bibles, doing evangelism and simply visiting people.

The team faced bee stings, ants, a few snakes and similar problems, but they managed to survive it all. They soon ran into problems, though, in a totally different realm: their relations with one another on the team. They just simply didn't seem to be able to get on with each other without bickering. Morale dipped so low that returning to the ship would have been a great temptation if they had had the money to do so.

On the last day things came to a head and were faced openly. Team members responded by asking forgiveness of one another and of God.

An interesting sequel is that on that last day they sold more Bibles and New Testaments than on all the other days put together. When they put their sales money together, they had exactly enough to pay for their trip back to the ship. No more, no less.

While Mike was occupied with the team at the leper colony, his wife and her team of four other dynamic young women were touring the country with some Scripture Union workers, moving from school to school and preaching to around three thousand students.

Their first two and a half days, though, were spent at a Scripture Union girls' camp trying to make friends with the campers, bridge the cultural gap and give spiritual help. Here are some excerpts from a letter Rose Hack wrote:

> The first night we watched a film and I summed up with a challenge to give their lives to Christ and live for him. There was a hush in the room and we could sense that the Holy Spirit was speaking to hearts. That night we got to bed well after midnight. Meetings here are not run by the clock!
>
> The next day we rose wearily at 6 am (yawn!). That day, amongst other things, we led small group Bible studies on temptation and backsliding. During this time we were

growing as a team, learning to pray together and adjusting to the situation. (It was a long walk to the well, but we were becoming such proficient water savers that four of us managed to clean our toothbrushes in half a cup of water!)

That evening the breakthrough came. . . . After the evening meeting Amos asked those who had been challenged or wanted counsel to go to a separate room. Out of the eighty at the camp forty responded! We were up till well after midnight counselling about a whole array of problems. Some of those young people were in situations that would make your hair stand on end! We all felt inadequate to help, but God time and time again gave us Scripture and Biblical principles to share. We saw breakthroughs in many lives.

On Monday, Michelle and I both woke to the gentle growling of our intestines! We foresaw problems and armed ourselves with toilet rolls! That morning the five of us took six school meetings. It was HECTIC!

Time and again I saw my lack of faith. During one meeting we gave a challenge to those who wanted to accept Christ. Afterwards I was busy selling New Testaments. Amos came up and asked what to do with all the people.

'What people?' I asked.

There were over a hundred who had come for counselling. At least sixty-four re-committed their lives to the Lord and another thirty-six made first time decisions for Christ.

Friday, the last day, came. Usually after a week away from the ship I am ready to return, but not this time; we felt our task was only half finished. At 7 am we set up a stall in the local market, wanting to sell the last of our New Testaments. The locals seemed amused to see these foreigners setting up shop between the cigarette seller and (live) chicken vendor! We had novelty value and sold fifty New Testaments. Later as we drove by, it was great to see many sitting by the roadside reading God's word!

212

In Ghana Mike Hack and three married men in the evangelism training programme decided to go on a four- or five-day 'faith trip' out in the jungle. That meant no advance planning and no financial resources. They would trust God to lead them and provide for them.

'But we were a little soft,' Mike admitted afterwards. 'We decided to take a van.'

As they were preaching in one of the villages in the jungle, they came across someone Mike knew, a Ghanaian named Stephen. Mike had met him at a pastors' conference on the ship. Stephen was single, about thirty years of age and pastor of five churches in five different villages, which he visited by foot. For this work he received the equivalent of about one dollar a day to live on. He lived in a tiny one-room mud hut containing a bed, a desk, a candle, a Bible and a concordance. According to Mike, he was 'one of the humblest, most fervent, blessed men' Mike had ever met. 'Humble and quiet yet with a powerful presence.'

The team stayed with him, two of them sleeping on the floor, one in the van and the fourth on top of it.

The next day Stephen took them out to a village to preach. While they were in the village, bus after bus came rumbling past, packed with people beating drums, yelling, banging on the sides of the vehicles and making a deafening racket.

'What's all this, Stephen?' asked the team.

'It's the Disco Christo Church. They're having an all-Africa conference for the denomination.'

'Let's follow them and see what's going on,' suggested Mike.

Stephen was hesitant. 'Well . . . okay,' he agreed somewhat reluctantly.

They jumped into their van and trailed the buses over wretched roads, bouncing along through the jungle until they came to what Mike, who was telling this story, termed the strangest place he had ever seen. Actually, the word he used was 'weird'.

It was a village. Everything was whitewashed and scrupulously clean. Throughout the village were several remarkable structures with names like Solomon's Temple and Ark of the Covenant. Scattered around were sepulchres and statues and evidences of animism.

The patriarch of the cult was carried around the village on a kind of litter supported by poles. The team was told that whenever he took a bath, his followers would carefully conserve the water and drink it to gain a special blessing.

As the *Doulos* team was walking through the village with Stephen, a nicely-dressed man came up and greeted them pleasantly. 'Welcome to our village,' he said in very good English. 'My name is Mr. Hack and I'm pastor of the church here.'

Mike was quite taken aback, but he rose to the occasion. 'Nice to meet you,,' he answered. 'My name is Mr. Hack and I'm the evangelism pastor on *Doulos*.'

They talked amiably for a few minutes. Then the African pastor moved on.

Stephen leaned over and said softly but urgently, 'We should get out of here. It's almost nightfall.'

'Why?' asked Mike. 'I'd like to see if I could get a chance to preach here. Just think. Six thousand people!'

'We should go,' insisted Stephen. 'this place is evil.'

'Okay,' agreed the team, 'we'll follow you. You know more about these things than we do.'

As they were driving away in the van, Stephen remarked, 'This is a strange, deceptive cult. It's full of spiritism and witchcraft and all sorts of evil things. It's best to stay away unless you have a specific reason to be there.'

As they continued to discuss the group, Mike put a question to Stephen. 'Stephen, have you ever seen the supernatural in your ministry? I mean a miracle of some kind?'

'Well, yes,' he replied hesitantly. 'Last week a woman in my church was raised from the dead.'

The team sat there stunned.

'What!!??' exclaimed Mike finally. 'Wow! I've heard stories like this, but I've never actually met up with it face to face. A person raised from the dead! Why didn't you tell us earlier?'

'We decided not to tell anybody. We'll just let the Lord take it and use it the way he wants. In this past week already a lot of people have been saved as a result of Elizabeth's testimony.'

Elizabeth, a twenty-seven-year-old mother, had been sick and failed to wake up one morning. Of course, there was no medical equipment to monitor her brain or heart to verify the death, but the villagers had had a lot of direct experience with death and as far as they were concerned, she was dead.

The family immediately sent for Pastor Stephen. By the time he got there, she had been 'dead' for at least an hour or two. No breathing, No sign of life. Nothing. Her body was turning cold.

In relating the experience, Stephen said, 'I didn't know what to do, so I just prayed and she woke up. I was as surprised as anybody.'

The *Doulos* team sat a moment in silent awe. Then Mike spoke up, 'Stephen, can we meet this person?'

'Why, yes. Tomorrow is Sunday. You can preach at one of my churches. She'll be there.'

The team pondered that. Mike spoke for them, 'I don't know that we should preach. We'd rather hear you. I think you have many things to teach us.'

Richard Prendergast, a *Doulos* officer, ended up preaching, though. Mike sat with the rest of the team at the back of the church. On the men's side, naturally. The women sat on the opposite side. Mike studied them speculatively, trying to figure out which one might be Elizabeth,

After the service Mike asked Stephen, 'Where is Elizabeth? I want to meet her.'

'Oh, I'm so sorry. She went to the capital city for the day to see some relatives. That's why she wasn't here.'

Mike was disappointed about that. Nevertheless, all in all, the team had what they termed 'a really great time'.

Gary Deane, an American engineer, went on a team that worked for a week alongside a pastor and headmaster of a Scripture Union school. The small team stayed at the little farmhouse where the pastor lived with his wife, his fourteen-year-old daughter and his fifteen-year-old son. The prayer life of this man made a deep impression on Gary.

216

But what impressed him even more was something that Gary himself had been struggling to do well, something that was done every evening in the pastor's home. After supper the pastor would relax with the team, drinking a cup of cocoa with them. After a while he would say, 'Let's have a time now with the Lord.' Then he would stand up, walk into the living-room and pick up his Bible. The family would sit around as the father consulted his Scripture Union daily Bible reading guide and said to one of the children, 'Open your Bible to. . . .'

One night, Gary recalls, the passage was about Mary and Martha. Martha was busy preparing the meal while Mary was sitting around listening to Jesus. Martha complained to Jesus, 'Why don't you tell Mary to help me?' The Lord answered, 'Mary has chosen a good thing and it shall not be taken away from her.'

The daughter read the passage. The father asked, 'And now what is the Lord saying to us here?' He went on to explain. As he talked about Martha busy serving, the listeners could see her doing it. The father brought alive the passage so that everyone was captivated by what the Lord had to say. Gary could tell the family was listening, *really* listening.

Gary took it all in. He had been praying for a considerable time about how he could make family devotions a more meaningful and joyful time for his family. He commented, 'God put me on this team and in this man's house to bless me and show me what a true shepherd is. I'd been with pastors and Christian leaders during my short time as a Christian, but I'd never experienced family devotions like this family had. Never in my life.'

Again a *doulos* went out to serve and found himself being served and blessed.

# 13

## *Snapshots*

In Sierra Leone there had been only one berth that could accommodate *Doulos*. Tied up about a hundred yards from it was another ship that had been confiscated several months earlier for gun smuggling. The rumour was that the weapons had been intended for insurgents against Liberia, which at the time was extremely fearful of invasions from neighbouring countries. *Doulos* people found that mildly interesting, but assumed that it had nothing to do with them. A wrong assumption, they were to discover after they had moved on to the next port, Monrovia Liberia. A major concern of the line-up team in Liberia was obtaining easy access for the public to visit the ship. And that had involved dealing with the police.

According to Assistant Director Mike Stachura the standard uniform of the police appeared to be tee-shirts and New York Yankees baseball caps. Only when a badge was pulled out and thrust under one's nose would one realize one was dealing with the police. The public were prohibited by the police from driving their vehicles to the ship. Instead, all visitors had to park and walk a mile and a half to reach it. As they started the walk, they were stopped for a police check. About a hundred yards from the ship they passed a small booth where they were again checked by police and all cameras and umbrellas were confiscated for the duration of their visit.

'We could understand taking the cameras,' commented Mike, 'because they might figure the people could be spies taking photos. That was a concern in a number of ports. But we couldn't understand the umbrella angle. We asked, "Why, why are you taking the umbrellas?" The reason was they figured the umbrellas could be weapons.'

It was the rainy season with torrential downpours. People would walk through mud the first mile and a quarter, sheltered under their umbrellas, until they reached the second checkpoint. There they would be relieved of the umbrellas and have to run the next hundred yards to get into a queue going onto the ship. Everybody would get drenched.

That was bad, but things got worse. The harassment began. One moment the people would be allowed in. The next moment they would be refused entrance. Back and forth it went.

Suddenly on a Saturday as the ship was about to open to the public, *Doulos* leaders were informed that the ship must remain closed.

'Why?' they asked, puzzled.

'We suspect you have weapons on board.'

Two contingents of security men arrived, one in uniform and the other in the usual tee-shirt, baseball cap attire. In all, there were a couple of dozen of them, all armed, mostly with handguns. *Doulos* leaders were never able to figure out who they all were. Police? National security? Port authority?

At any rate, this was clearly a violation of international maritime law, as the ship had already been cleared by Immigration and Customs. *Doulos* leaders hastily got together to decide how to deal with the situation. The captain was seething with anger.

Mike described the captain's protest, 'I don't think there was ever a day I was more impressed with Carl Isaacson because he stood strong and said firmly, "I want to declare that we are protesting this action. This is a violation of international maritime law. You have no search warrant, no documentation to show why you're here. You have no reason to suspect us. We have come as a goodwill ship." '

Brushing aside Captain Isaacson's words, the security men said brusquely, 'We want to search every cabin, every chest of drawers, every compartment on the ship. Your ship cannot be open to anyone until we do that.'

Fearful that the searchers might themselves plant weapons or drugs to justify the search, *Doulos* leaders quickly assembled their own twenty-four man detail to match each security person and keep an eye on what was happening.

The security men went everywhere, absolutely everywhere. Down in one section where the crew was rebuilding the decks, there was a pile of sand for the construction. Security officers made the men dig through the sand to see if there were weapons underneath. After searching a cabin, they would put a big chalk mark on the door. Inside the cabins each cabinet would get a mark. The security men were very belligerent in the beginning and some remained that way till the end, but most of them gradually became quite uncomfortable with what they were doing and began apologizing when they went into women's quarters or into family sections. But of course, their orders were clear; they had to do this.

'It's okay. It's okay,' *Doulos* people would reassure them. 'You can come in. We know you're just doing your job. Here, look,' and they would start opening doors and pulling out drawers to show officials. That only made the security men feel worse.

'The search that was supposed to take all day was done in an hour,' reported Mike. 'Now there's no way they could have searched the whole ship. In the end, certain sections were done so quickly you wondered what they had done. I think what really had happened was that all the fight, the fire had fizzled out. I'm sure they had figured we were going to resist, but we walked with them everywhere. People greeted them. It wasn't the type of thing we were happy about, but there was no hostility, no belligerence.'

In the end, as they reported to the captain and director, they admitted, 'We found nothing.'

'Well, what did you expect to find?' inquired one of the ship leaders.

'You were in Sierra Leone. We heard reports that you had weapons on board your ship.'

In *Doulos* devotions on Monday Mike commented, 'Isn't it interesting? It depends on what you're looking for, doesn't it? You could search all over a peaceful ship and not find a single weapon. Yet when they went down into the bookholds, they didn't find the most powerful weapon we had. The Bible. We have hundreds and thousands of "swords" — "two-edged swords" — that could totally transform this nation. They had no idea of the arsenal down in those holds.'

More literature was distributed in Liberia than in any other part of Africa.

There was no more harassment. Police and *Doulos* people waved to each other and talked. The whole atmosphere was changed. (But they still collected umbrellas.)

That was perhaps the most dramatic event of everyday life on the ship in Africa, but there were many other incidents, impressions, experiences and surprises that added colour. Here are a variety of snapshots that give further glimpses into life aboard *Doulos*.

Bookshop Manager Richard Beaumont and his wife Julie, both New Zealanders, were wondering about their future. What should they do after their time on the ship? Their hearts were very much gripped with a mission vision and Africa was one of the possibilities they wanted to explore.

With that in mind, arrangements were made for them to go to a mission station inland in the Gambia. The country was a small finger about 400 kilometres long in the middle of Senegal, with a river running down the centre of it. Accompanied by a couple of missionary ladies, Richard, his wife and their six-month-old son travelled on a ferry up this river to a small village, arriving at dusk.

'Officially, I should take you now to meet the village chief, but we'll leave it till morning,' one of the ladies told them.

The next morning they got up, breakfasted and went off to visit the village chief. He spoke no English but was very pleased that these two foreigners with their little child had come to visit him.

One of the missionaries translated for them and they did all the proper things. Richard went in to see the chief while the women stayed outside because women were not allowed in the chief's hut. After a preliminary chat, the chief rose to his feet and went out to see Julie and little Matthew.

'You have a beautiful little boy,' remarked the chief through his translator.

Julie smiled and Richard said, 'Thank you.'

'I would like you to give him to me,' continued the chief.

Julie and Richard looked at each other horror-struck. Then they looked at the missionary helplessly. Not fully trusting that avenue, Julie looked back at the chief and said simply, 'But we can't give him to you. We love him.'

The chief paused and thought about that a moment.

'Don't worry,' he reassured her, 'I'll look after him.'

He was completely serious.

What the missionary said to him, Richard and Julie never found out, but they all left soon afterward.

'It reminded me,' commented Richard in telling of the incident, 'that God gave up his son so we could know fulness of life. Confronted with being asked to give up our own son, brought it home in a real and fresh way.'

Within thirty minutes of the meeting with the chief, Richard and Julie were introduced to a mother who had half a dozen children. They were obviously very, very poor. The mother spent fifteen minutes begging Julie, 'Please take one of my children back home where you come from. Please take him. I know wherever you take him and whatever you do with him, he'll get a better life and have more opportunity than he will by staying in this village.'

224    Many, many books were sold during the ship's visit to the Gambia. On these sales a very nominal tax was levied. It fell to Richard as bookshop manager to see that the tax was paid at the end of the visit, once the exhibition had closed and the numbers were added up.

Richard obtained exactly the right amount in local currency and set out as soon as office hours began. The ship was to sail at eleven o'clock that morning, so there was not a lot of leeway. He went to various government offices, stood in queues and got shuffled from one office to another. Finally, he reached the right person just as the man was going out for morning tea.

'Please let me pay the tax now,' begged Richard. 'This is how much it is and here's the money.'

'I'm sorry, sir,' the man replied, 'but we can't take local currency. We have to have a bank cheque. They don't trust us with cash. The bank is just a couple of blocks from here. You can get a cheque there.'

Richard rushed to the bank, jumped the queue and said, 'I need a bank cheque.'

'Okay. It will cost you x amount of money for me to write the cheque.'

The amount was petty but Richard had only the exact amount required for the tax. And eleven o'clock was fast approaching.

'You start writing the check,' he flung back at the teller as he turned and ran out to the street, thinking he would have to rush back to the ship.

Just at that moment a pastor came chugging down the road on his motorbike. He recognized Richard and waved. Richard flagged him down.

'Can you let me have some money, please,' Richard begged breathlessly.

Having got what he needed from the pastor, Richard rushed back to the bank. It seemed to take forever for the man to write out the cheque. As a matter of fact, it took an hour.

Then came the rush back to the tax office to pay before the lunch-hour closedown.

'Here's the cheque,' announced Richard. 'Just put a stamp there and sign it. That's all I want.'

As he hurried back to the ship, he caught sight of its funnel and breathed a sigh of relief. *At least I haven't held them up*, he thought. Entering through the port gate, he could still see the funnel. He could also see, to his horror, that the ship was in the middle of the river, and heading out. As he rounded a corner and came into sight, a great cheer went up from *Doulos* people standing at the deck railing.

The ship had had to leave early because another ship wanted the berth, but the captain ordered a tug for Richard. When it nosed up to the quay, Richard jumped on and away they went to the middle of the river. A rope ladder was hung down the side of the ship as is normal for pilots boarding or disembarking. Richard attached his brief case to a rope to be pulled up, climbed up the ladder and made his way to the bridge.

'I just wanted you to know, Captain, that I'm on board and safe,' he announced.

'I just want to let you know,' boomed back the deep voice of Captain Isaacson, 'we weren't going anywhere without you.'

Guinea Bissau at the time was reportedly one of the five poorest nations in the world. Authorities in Senegal had told *Doulos* people, 'There's no way you will get to stay five days in Guinea Bissau because the country's got no food left. A supply ship that comes in every week is the only source of food for the country. When it arrives, it takes the one and only berth.'

*Doulos* people prayed. They didn't have enough faith for ten days or for seven days but decided they could trust God for five days. And so they set sail.

The pilot lived on a little island at the entrance to the port and *Doulos* crew had to go with the lifeboat to pick him up. Some on *Doulos* wondered if the pilot had even gotten the message that they were coming. They need not have worried. He was packed and waiting when the lifeboat arrived.

Part way down the river leading to the port a tugboat came alongside to escort the ship. And thus Doulos came into Guinea Bissau.

Arrangements were made for the ship to stay one day alongside. After that she would have to go to anchor for

four days to make room for the food ship which understandably had priority. However, the food ship broke
down on its way to Guinea Bissau and didn't arrive until
the end of the fourth day. Authorities then made it
wait another twenty-four hours until *Doulos* was due to
leave.

Here is one of Richard Beaumont's memories of the
country:

> We had Portuguese New Testaments. We offered them
> for the equivalent of a few pennies in the local currency
> so that people could afford them, as we didn't want to
> just give them away. We sold thirteen thousand on the
> streets. They were gobbled right up. The people were
> very, very hungry for them. We were also able to stock
> up the Christian bookshop. They had just ones and twos
> of books scattered around on the shelves. Most Doulos
> people had more personal books in their cabins than that
> bookshop had.
>
> Then we ended up with local money which was
> worthless anywhere else. We found out there was nothing
> in the country to buy with it. The supermarket had long
> since been shut. The stock in other stores was limited to
> buttons, tacky souvenirs and pencil erasers. There was
> nothing for us to buy with our money except mangoes.
> So somebody in his wisdom went out and bought man-
> goes. We had mango jam, mango ice cream, mango
> yogurt, mango tart. We had mangoes frozen, deep fried,
> easy over, any way you wanted them. For about six
> months we had mangoes. I could never look another
> mango in the face.

School carried on as usual for the children of families on board regardless of whether the ship was in port or at sea. The only concession to a voyage was the occasional shifting of a class to a more central location when the motion of the waves exceeded the tolerance level of the children or, as was more often the case, that of the teacher.

Amy Boyd was teacher for the handful of five-to-seven-year-olds. Each day's work was launched with a devotional time, part of which was prayer. The children would suggest various things they wanted to pray for and all the class would join in praying for these things.

At the beginning of a voyage there was always one standard prayer: for safety along the way. The voyage to Cameroon, however, was special. For months all the voyages had been short ones, but this one was to be a full week. It would be the first long voyage for some of the children.

A special voyage called for a special prayer.

'Let's pray that we see whales,' suggested one child.

'Oh, yes!' agreed the other children enthusiastically. They had seen porpoises and smaller creatures at sea, but whales? Never. The thought was exciting.

Every day the children prayed faithfully that they would see whales. Two or three times the bridge announced over the public address system, 'There's a whale on the starboard side' or 'on the port side'. The class would jump up out of their seats, dash through the door and head for the outside deck.

Too late. The whale had already disappeared in the

distance or submerged, not to be seen again. The most the children saw was a fin disappearing into the water.

Each day the children prayed. Each day passed without any of them seeing a whale. Eventually the ship pulled into Walvis Bay, South Africa, and the voyage was ended. No whales.

The children didn't give up. All through the week spent in Walvis Bay they prayed to see whales on the next voyage. The teacher began to grow tired of the subject, but one of the children in particular always insisted that the class pray about the whales.

The time came for the voyage to Cape Town.

'Okay,' said the teacher, 'if we're going to keep praying about whales, let's get serious about it. You've seen a whale from a distance. Is that enough?'

'Oh, no,' responded the children. They had been reading up on whales and learned how shy they were, diving underwater when people were around. They had also been intrigued by the anatomy, the spout in particular. Together with their teacher, they decided on three specific items they wanted to pray for: 1) that everyone of them, including stragglers, would get a look, 2) it would be not just a glimpse but a long look and 3) they would get to see the spout.

During the voyage the class moved out of their class-room, not because the sea was rough but because the cleaning team made use of voyages to clean the carpet and on this voyage the school rooms were having their turn. Amy's class moved out into an area by the information desk, near double doors leading out onto deck on either side of the ship. Each morning the class prayed faithfully about the three points on their whale agenda.

Late one morning as the class was concentrating on school work with all thought of whales pushed from their minds, the public address system boomed out, 'Whales sighted on the port side.'

The children scrambled out of their seats, rushed through the doors to the outside deck and leaned over the railing. There were the whales! Two of them, a mother and her little calf! The whales had surfaced directly in front of the ship so that the ship's course had to be altered to avoid hitting them. That meant the ship passed right alongside the whales, so close that the whales could not get away but remained in view for a long good look, so close that the children could look almost straight down on the whales where the spouts on their back were clearly visible.

As the children were praying about whales, God answered someone else's prayer in another way. Coming into Walvis Bay, Captain Isaacson had gone out to stand the four-to-eight watch with his first officer who was new to the ship and unfamiliar with the area. Visibility was down to practically zero. Maps of the waters showed a long spit of land sticking out into the ocean. In a three-quarter-mile stretch there were two or three old wrecks and a buoy.

On the spit of land was supposedly a lighthouse, but Captain Isaacson couldn't see any sign of it either with the naked eye or on the ship's radar. In that situation the captain did what he had done on many other occasions. He prayed. Naturally, he continued his watch duties, straining to see the course markers but inwardly his heart was pouring out a prayer to God. As he prayed, a hole cleared in the heavy fog. There in full view was the lighthouse tower and off to one side was the buoy. The ship was exactly on course.

They sailed on in and a little later picked up the pilot to help navigate the harbour.

'I'm surprised you came in,' remarked the pilot.

'Why shouldn't we come in?' asked the captain.

'Well, usually at this time of morning it's quite foggy so we didn't expect you.'

And now from the sublime to the ridiculous, or at least to something more earthy. In Cape Town, South Africa, dry-dock time came round again. Everyone moved ashore except about seventy men who remained to do the necessary work. Dry-dock often presented inconveniences to the crew aboard, not only in the dirt and noise and general mess but also at times in a restriction in facilities. Electrical power was often limited. The air-conditioning was usually turned off. And, worst and most common of all, washing and toilet facilities would be shut down. Everyone had to go ashore, sometimes a considerable distance, to use the ones provided there.

Two days before the staff moved ashore for dry-dock in Cape Town, all the ship's company had been instructed to flush the toilets very thoroughly, holding down the flush lever for at least three minutes. The pipes needed to be thoroughly cleared of solids so that repairs to the system could be undertaken when the ship went into dry-dock.

During dry-dock itself the instructions to the crew remaining on board were very clear. No one under any circumstances was to use the toilets!

Someone did.

232 The plumber, working beneath a disconnected pipe, got a nasty shock as the pipe discharged its contents directly on to his head. With an exclamation of anger, he stormed out and roared, 'Who did this?' He raced around the ship, seething with indignation, He even stuck his head into the galley to ask. The workers there didn't have to see or hear him to be aware of his presence; they could smell it!

'Hey, don't look at me. I'm just cooking,' protested one of them.

The culprit was never found. He was probably too embarrassed to own up.

Those who have never felt its effects often tend to dismiss seasickness blithely as a state of mind. But to those who have staggered under its curse, it is extremely, nauseatingly real. Rudi Schmitt, a German who served as the ship's baker, was one of those who knew. Voyages became an event for him to dread.

> As long as I was the baker, I had to work. I had no choice. I would be three minutes in the bakery and five minutes out feeding the fish. It was terrible!
>
> For the first time I thought, *Maybe this is the wrong place for me. I must have got it wrong about the Lord's will for my life.*
>
> People drove me mad. I looked bad enough already, but they would say, 'Rudi how are you?' Ugh! I could have

gone straight through the roof. It was terrible! The best thing was just to lie down and relax.

I remember we sailed from Cape Town to Port Elizabeth. I was already fed up with everything. I didn't want to work any more. I was lying up on the book exhibition deck where I had slept outside at night in the fresh air in my sleeping bag. My friend next to me was going downstairs so I said, 'Would you mind passing by the galley and telling Myles Toews [the chief steward] that I just cannot work.'

I fell asleep. Suddenly I felt a hand on my face. I opened my eyes and Myles exclaimed brightly, 'He's healed! He's healed!'

I was so mad I could have thrown him overboard!

He said, 'Well, Rudi, I brought the nurse along and she's going to put a plaster behind your ear. In twenty minutes you're going to be down in the galley.'

I got up and went down to the bakery. I thought I would at least do the necessary things so there would be some bread. I stood in the bakery making bread and then spent a couple of hours cleaning up everything. Finally I took the bread out of the oven.

I felt so bad I couldn't even get down to my room. I just went outside the bakery onto the deck and lay down on one of the big wooden chests that held life jackets.

Myles came past. 'By the way, Rudi,' he remarked, 'you're not done yet.'

'I've baked the bread.'

'We need twelve trays of pizza and then refreshments for tonight.'

*Oh, no*, I groaned. *Lord, that's it! I don't know anymore if this is really the place you have called me to.*

I went up to the personnel manager and told him, 'I'm not going to sail anymore. I'm going to go home next port.'

'Well, Rudi,' he responded, 'we have three things we can try.'

'There's only one thing I'm going to try. That's to get a flight in the next port going home.'

'Well, Rudi, we can go and talk to the doctor to see what he can do with you or maybe you can change to a departments where you don't have to work as much during the voyages (but I was the only baker, so there was no chance of that) or you get healed from seasickness.'

I went back and finished my job. Then before the next voyage the doctor put a plaster behind my ear, a very strong drug, I'd heard.

It worked. For the next year and a half Rudi was not seasick. At least not until one of the voyages just before he was due to leave the ship anyway. As a grand finale, he was served up a roaring typhoon, a violent twister of a storm. And Rudi was back to 'feeding the fish'.

Kongkin Atmodjo from Indonesia worked in the galley under the chief cook. One day spaghetti was on the menu. To make it, Kongkin had to empty a huge can of tomato paste. Cleaning the last of it from the can transferred more than a little bit to Kongkin's arm. As he looked down at it, a mischievous gleam came into his eye.

The clinic was nearby, opening onto the outside deck just as the galley did. Kongkin hurried out, peeked through the clinic porthole to make sure the nurse was there and banged wildly on the door.

'Where's the doctor? Where's the doctor?' he cried wildly.

'Oh . . . !' The nurse drew her breath in horror and became panicky.

Kongkin couldn't hold in the laughter any longer; it escaped and overwhelmed him.

That confused the nurse. Was he hysterical? 'Why are you laughing?' she asked in concern.

'Because it's just tomato paste!'

The nurse couldn't decide whether to laugh or give him a hefty whack.

It was just moments before coffee-break time when people would drift into the dining room for their mid morning perk-up. That was too good an opportunity for Kongkin to pass up. Repeating his routine, he stumbled into the dining room crying out, 'Where's the doctor? Where's the doctor?'

Several people looked up in alarm.

'Ah. . . .' spoke up one cynical lad, totally unmoved, 'it's probably just ketchup.'

*What a spoilsport!* concluded Kongkin.

In Port Elizabeth, as in many other ports, believers showed their generosity. A farmer donated two tons of fresh vegetables to the ship. An eye doctor provided free eye-tests for crew and staff, and made at least a dozen pairs of new glasses for them. Someone else donated a used pick-up truck in excellent condition. The *Doulos* company realized how wonderful it was to be part of the family of God.

Wonderful most of the time, that is. There were times when they wondered.

In Durban Kongkin was again in the galley preparing lunch along with a couple of assistants. It was still an hour and a half to lunch time, but preparing a meal for over three hundred people takes considerable time. Into the busy scene walked Myles, the chief steward.

'Hey, guys!' he announced breezily. 'A truckload of flour has just arrived and needs to be carried into the bakery storage room.'

'But I have to prepare lunch,' protested Kongkin.

'It shouldn't take long.'

'Okay, twenty minutes. That's all I can possibly spare.'

All three galleymen went down to the quayside and joined Myles and another man in moving the flour. Two tons of it! Each fifty-pound bag had to be lifted onto their backs, carried up the gangway and into the storage area. It was hard work.

Twenty minutes moved far more quickly than the flour did. Kongkin began to get anxious about his cooking.

'The flour's got to be carried in first,' insisted Myles.

Finally all the flour was safely ensconced in the bakery storage room. At this point the baker entered, observed the flour and raised a vehement protest.

'That's the worst-looking flour I've ever seen,' he exclaimed. 'It's dirty! It's wet! If you keep that, you're going to have a real mess in a few weeks time. Worms and everything!'

Myles considered the matter. Obviously the baker knew what he was talking about.

'Okay, guys,' Myles conceded reluctantly, 'back to the truck with the flour.'

Kongkin exploded. They argued. Kongkin fumed but he carried the flour back to the truck.

Lunch was late.

'Blame it on Myles,' muttered Kongkin.

[Years later Kongkin asked Myles if he remembered the time Kongkin was really mad at him. 'When was that?' asked Myles. He couldn't remember. But Kongkin remembered it as the only time he got really angry at the ship's leadership. Looking back, he remarked how the Lord used even that to teach him something. It was all part of the process of building character.]

Part of the line-up team's job was to get programmes printed for the ship's visit. In Tanzania a local Christian did a beautiful job of printing these in two colours. Unfortunately one tiny mistake slipped through the proof-reading. The translator, putting the material into Swahili, had written an *f* instead of a *t* down in one corner.

David Short, the line-up man, unaware of the error, carried the freshly printed programmes back to the family with whom he was staying. When he showed a copy to the family, a young Tanzanian woman living with them began rolling about the couch shrieking with laughter.

'This is terrific!' she managed to say between bouts of laughter. 'Do you know what it says?'

David looked nonplussed.

She enlightened him, holding up the paper and translating the contents, 'Do you want to welcome to your church a team of four dead men who are going to be singing and preaching the gospel there?'

In giving orientation about Tanzania to the ship's company, David related the incident and added, 'We wondered if we should just leave the mistake on the programme and flood the port with thousands of visitors wanting to see these dead people singing and praising the Lord. But we felt we ought to alter it to *four members of the team* instead of *four dead people.*'

And finally, one last incident. While the ship was in Africa, a letter was passed on from Lawrence Tong who was making a survey trip in Central and South America to help plan an itinerary for Logos. Here is an excerpt from the letter he wrote from Panama:

> The *Doulos* ministry had a tremendous impact on the lives of many people. I was talking to one of the pastors, who introduced many ideas he had picked up from the ship ministry and his church grew from six hundred to nine hundred members. The books he bought on Doulos are now manuals for his elders and leaders in discipleship and evangelism programmes. It is exciting to listen to someone whose ministry took a leap as a result of the 1982 visit!

# AND ON TO ASIA . . . 1987–1993

| 1987 | 1988 | 1989 |
|------|------|------|
| India | India | Papua New Guinea |
| Malaysia | Sri Lanka | New Zealand |
| Singapore | Singapore | Australia |
| Thailand | Indonesia | Vanuatu |
| | Philippines | Fiji |
| | Taiwan | Tonga |
| | Hong Kong | |
| | Papua New Guinea | |

| 1990 | 1991 | 1992 |
|------|------|------|
| Solomon Islands | Malaysia | Solomon Islands |
| Papua New Guinea | Philippines | Papua New Guinea |
| Philippines | Taiwan | Palau |
| Indonesia | Hong Kong | Taiwan |
| Malaysia | Singapore | Hong Kong |
| Thailand | Australia | South Korea |
| Singapore | | Russia |
| | | Japan |
| | | Thailand |
| | | Singapore |
| | | India |

**1993**
India
Sri Lanka
Seychelles
Kenya
South Africa

# 14

# A Whole New World

In 1987 *Doulos* left Africa and moved on to Asia, where she would spend the next few years. The first Asian port of call was Bombay. The *Doulos* workers got their first glimpse of India . . . and were shocked! Utterly shocked! They couldn't believe what they were seeing. The dirt, the poverty, the wretched existence in tiny makeshift hovels around the seaport. The slums of Bombay made Africa seem like something approaching Paradise. Many ship people couldn't cope with what they saw and hung back from going ashore.

Not Prisca Ahn, a young single Korean woman from a Buddhist background. As a student in her early twenties she had had a deep experience of God and as a result wanted to give her life as a missionary to India reaching out to Muslims. She struck up a friendship with one of the Indian volunteers working on the ship and within a day or two was venturing out into the city with her friend, eager to drink in the sights and sounds of India, drawn with compassion for the people teeming through the streets. When it was time to return to the ship late one morning, the two women manoeuvred their way into a local bus which, as usual, was packed to its limits with people but somehow always able to add another. As the bus neared the port gate, the women worked their way back toward the exit.

'This is our stop,' called out the volunteer to Prisca 'Let's get off.'

Indian buses didn't linger at stops. Local people knew this and climbed out as fast as they could. The volunteer stepped out on the ground and turned around for Prisca. The bus was already starting to move off, but Prisca had just reached the steps at the exit.

'Don't do it,' warned some Indians in the bus, realizing the foreigner was going to jump off. 'The bus is going too fast.'

But Prisca was already in motion. She landed on the ground with both feet, but the momentum of the moving bus flung her backward and she fell, hitting her head. She lay there, obviously seriously injured, and was immediately taken to the local hospital.

The accident happened shortly before noon. In the early afternoon Geoffrey Morris, the ship's doctor, went to visit Prisca at the hospital. He reported that she had a concussion and severe bruising, but was in good care. By that evening, however, the condition had seriously worsened. The doctors realized there was internal bleeding in the cranium. Dr. Geoff wanted more X-rays.

That's when he plunged headlong into the frustrations of working through a new country's unfamiliar medical system. He had first to find a hospital that could do the X-rays and then he had to transport Prisca there. When the X-rays were developed, they revealed much greater damage than had been suspected.

242

By late evening Prisca was in a coma. Geoff spent much of the early morning hours with her in an ambulance trying to find a hospital with a brain surgeon available. Phoning ahead was impossible; they had to go physically to the hospitals. Finally they found a private clinic founded by the Zoroastrians. It was a big old house, but a proper hospital.

Completely swathed in bandages after brain surgery, Prisca was put on a life-support system. *Doulos* Koreans kept a twenty-four hour watch at the hospital. Prayer vigils were held throughout the ship.

In one of the prayer groups were Mike Hack and four other men whom he described as 'older and wiser' than he. They talked about Prisca's situation and one of the men pointed out a Bible passage, saying, 'I believe God will heal this young woman.' Together they prayed earnestly for her healing.

But a few hours later she passed from this life into the presence of her loving Master.

Local churches, which had been alerted to pray for Prisca, were now given word of her death. Two days later a funeral was held. In the cathedral were ship crew and staff, OM India personnel and some local people. Mike Stachura preached the sermon.

Before the funeral service Mike Hack and his four prayer friends again got together to fast and pray. 'Lord, we don't really know what we're doing,' they prayed, 'but somehow we don't think this incident is over. We think there's something more you want to do here.'

The more they prayed, the more fervent their prayers became. Finally one of them prayed, 'Lord, raise her from the dead.'

*Why not?* mused Mike Hack, recalling his experience with the African pastor who had testified to seeing a dead woman raised in response to prayer. *All India would hear of it. What a testimony to God's power!*

One of the men remarked, 'I don't know that I have faith to believe something like that, but I still want to support this prayer meeting.'

On and on they prayed and faith grew to expectation. At the funeral Mike sat close to Prisca's coffin and could see her body at rest. He kept looking, hoping at any time to see her open her eyes. She never did.

'I still don't know what to make of that,' admitted Mike reflecting over the event much later.

Edu Leite was another *Doulos* person who struggled with accepting Prisca's death. He had taken over as manager of the bookshop and she had worked with him on his team. 'One of the best people I had in the department,' he said of her.

And that was his problem. Why her? Why not him? He admitted to himself what a poor excuse he was for a Christian. Why didn't God take away him instead of one of his best?

Mulling over the question and trying to deal with his shock and grief, he travelled with other *Doulos* people to a funeral that somehow didn't seem real to him. As he passed through the city, he looked out at the throngs of people, the filth, the misery. *How come all these people are suffering?*

he asked himself. *Why is all this happening? I've seen poverty before, but this is too much. I can't take it. The first chance I get I'm giving up everything and going home.* In his confusion he alternated between telling himself God couldn't exist and lashing out at God for what was happening.

244     Edu found himself becoming annoyed by the funeral service. Very angry himself, he couldn't stand watching other people acting so positively and looking so calm and confident. Mechanically he stood when the others stood to pray and sat when they sat. But inside he was seething with suppressed anger.

Prisca's cabinmate went up to the front to lead the congregation in a song which had been Prisca's favourite. It had been Edu's favourite too . . . before this happened. The cabinmate started singing and the audience joined in:

> *Ascribe greatness to our God, the rock'; His work is perfect and all His ways are just. A God of faithfulness and without injustice; good and upright is He.*

Edu started to sing and then stopped himself. No, he cried out inside his mind, *this is not what I believe now. God is not fair. He doesn't exist. This is not God!*

At that moment Edu felt God asking him, 'Are you going to believe what you feel right now or are you going to believe what this says?'

The congregation continued to sing the short chorus again and again, lifting up their hearts in worship as Prisca herself had done many times. Like it or not, Edu could not prevent the words of the song from going through his mind. What happened then Edu himself tells:

Suddenly God gave me a clear picture of what our life is. If we have given our lives totally to him, if we have already given up all material and financial things, why then if we die, we're not losing anything. We're gaining!

That was the first time I had ever realized that death was the best thing that could happen for a Christian. In an instant my anger went away, my crying stopped and I felt a great happiness. People must have wondered about the big smile on my face, but I couldn't explain it to them.

Once again I rededicated myself to God, saying, 'Here I am. If you want to take me, take me.'

For the Koreans on the ship, dealing with Prisca's death was especially difficult. They had never experienced a funeral except a Korean one with its own culture and customs, its own language. Yet here they were caught in the confusing middle ground between an international mixture of cultures and their own. It was up to them to take the leading role in oversight of Prisca, the vigil at the hospital, the dressing of the body in her beautiful, colourful national dress. The pall-bearers were Korean. In the funeral service itself the ship's leaders tried to follow as much as they could of the Korean ceremony for a Christian burial.

The decision to cremate Prisca's body was made after consultation with her parents in Korea. They wanted the ashes taken back to Korea for proper burial. Two Koreans on *Doulos* volunteered to accompany the ashes, along with Allan Adams, OM's East Asia and Pacific director and assistant director of *Doulos*.

They carried her remains on a scheduled airline flight. Allan gave this account:

246

It seemed very strange to be carrying one of our dearest co-workers home in this way. When we came to her home town, we first went to the church, where her pastor together with one of Prisca's brothers officially welcomed us and then led us in procession through the small town to the house of Prisca's parents. On arrival in the house, loud wailing broke out as the gathered relatives expressed their grief. The ashes were placed on an altar in front of a picture of Prisca with a black ribbon draped across the corner. I sat on the floor in a corner of the room and broke into tears myself. The loss of her life and all that meant to her parents overcame me.

I participated in the funeral service the next day and also preached in her home church on Sunday. Prisca's father was suspicious and angry. Through translation he questioned me about the circumstances of her death. He let me know the extent of his grief and anger at what had happened. But by the final meal on Sunday afternoon he was more at peace. It was a work of God in his heart that he could begin to come to terms with such an awful loss. God was bringing healing already to this family.

Before he left for Korea, Allan Adams preached a powerful sermon about death to ship members. In our mortal bodies, he said, we groan for that time when we will really know Christ in his fulness. In Prisca's death there was the sense of loss by her friends but there was also a sense of her being set free.

A lot of tears were shed. A lot of concern was expressed.

A beautiful expression of concern was the way the ship rallied around Dr. Geoff. A young doctor, skilled and wholly committed as a brother in Christ, he had personally taken responsibility for Prisca, trying to do everything he could to save her life. Many, many people went to him to reassure him, pray with him or give him little notes to say they were praying for him.

'It really affected the ship,' commented Mike Stachura. 'We realized that a lot of missionaries had done this before us. They too had come to India and had lost people from the outset.

'I think it was also very sobering to come from Africa where everything seemed so alive spiritually and to arrive in India where the first thing we encountered was death. It was a powerful message that we have to count the cost when we serve Christ.' Philippians 3:10 became very important: 'I want to know Christ in the power of his resurrection and the fellowship of sharing in his sufferings, even unto death.'

In the future *Doulos* people were to learn even more what service might cost. But that was a few years down the road.

The second country on the *Doulos* Asian itinerary tour was Malaysia. Because it was a Muslim country, ship leaders anticipated a rather sensitive situation. One of the most senior line-up men was sent to obtain the permits: a British gentleman who had served for twenty-one years in the British merchant navy before he joined *Logos* in 1974 as chief electrician later he had been involved in the purchase and refitting of *Doulos* and finally moved into line-up. A short balding man, he was the epitome of a proper Eng-lishman. With his gift of diplomacy and charm, he had been

248

responsible for talking officials into waiving many fees for the ships.

Stan spent a couple of weeks in Kuala Lumpur, the capital of Malaysia, visiting government offices and submitting the necessary letters. All permits were finally in hand from the Finance Ministry, Customs and the Special Branch of the Police. Censors had checked the book list. All permits had been issued — except for one which had to come from the minister of Home Affairs.

Unfortunately, Stan could never get through to the Ministry of Home Affairs. He would always be put off in some way until he began to have a horrible suspicion that they were just playing for time. From experience he knew that was the strategy in some countries; they wouldn't say no but would just keep him waiting until the time for the event had come and permission would still be lacking.

Stan kept phoning and phoning, but couldn't seem to get anywhere. The time of the ship's scheduled arrival in Penang grew steadily nearer. Complicating the situation was the fact that it was Ramadan, the Muslim month of fasting.

The final week of preparations came. Wednesday was the last day of Ramadan. Thursday would begin a weekend of holidays celebrated with feasting and partying. And on Monday the ship was due to arrive.

Finally, on the Wednesday of this last week Stan got an answer on the phone and was able to get in touch with the man dealing with the necessary permit. Stan was informed that the permit was sitting on the minister's desk awaiting his signature. If the minister signed it, the official told Stan, he would phone and let Stan know.

The rest of the day Stan waited, praying all the while. All evening he waited. He was sure God was going to answer his prayers. Nothing happened. At midnight he gave up and went to bed.

On Thursday he awoke depressed. Holidays had commenced and the permit had not been received. He spent all morning trying to phone the ministry, hoping against hope that someone would be in despite the holiday. At about one o'clock someone actually picked up the receiver but only to say that everyone was on holiday.

Stan felt as if he was teetering at the edge of a cliff, drained of all emotional strength. The ship was arriving in Malaysia in three days and the permit hadn't come through. In his heart he cried out to the Lord.

At about three o'clock he received a phone call from the address where his mail was being sent, a different location from where he was staying.

'There's a letter here for you,' said the voice of a Chinese Christian lady there.

'Oh, well, don't worry about it. I'll pick it up in a day or two,' replied Stan. He was waiting for the phone call and didn't want to be away if it came through.

'Do you think the letter might be important?' the lady asked tentatively.

Stan brushed aside the idea, 'Oh I don't think so. I'm not expecting any important letters.'

'It's from the Ministry of Home Affairs,' she persisted.

Stan's heart skipped a beat. 'Really!' he exclaimed. 'How in the world did you get the letter?'

'I came home and found it wedged in the metal frame of the door.'

*How strange,* thought Stan. *How did it get there?* Out loud he said, 'But it's a holiday. There's no post today, is there?'

'Oh, no, there's no postal delivery today. Besides, the letter has no postage stamp on it.'

'Oh my goodness!' exclaimed Stan. 'Well, please open it.' He waited breathlessly.

'Hmm. . . . It's in Malay.'

'Oh dear me. Can you read Malay?'

'Yes.'

'Oh, please read it to me.'

It was the permit for the ship's visit.

*How amazing!* reflected Stan. *How did that letter come to be wedged in the door frame when there was a mailbox at the gate of the driveway? If it had been put into the mailbox, we would never have dreamed of looking there till after the holiday. The ship would have arrived by then and had no permit.*

The programme for Malaysia was ambitious, with seven ports filling three months. The island of Penang was chosen for the first port because it was assumed to be the easiest. But when the ship arrived, her people realized there were certain beneath-the-surface rumblings. Before coming in, ship's leaders had had to sign a statement that no one on the ship would undertake any evangelism with Malays or with anyone else of the Muslim faith. That meant an announcement must be made at each conference to make sure no Muslims were unwittingly present.

When the ship arrived in Penang, police and domestic security people swarmed onto the ship, saying no Muslims could come aboard at all, although the only prohibition in the written permits was that Muslims could not attend conferences. By Saturday afternoon police at the port gate were stopping all Muslims from coming in.

Mike Stachura had gone into town that morning. As he was returning to the ship he saw what was happening at the gate. In dismay he stood and watched a school bus that had travelled from the far end of the island to see the ship. The children were told that all who were Indian could go on through the gate to see the ship, but all who were wearing the distinctively Muslim headgear — scarves for girls and hats, called Songkoks, for boys — could not. Half the busload had to wait outside the gate. Mike watched also as the guards tried to separate a husband and wife and saw the incredible indignation of her husband.

It was a tense weekend.

Stan approached Mike, saying, 'Mike we have to go and talk with the minister of the Interior. Maybe even the prime minister.'

The two of them flew to Kuala Lumpur and spent much time in consultation with Christian leaders, much time praying. The ship was to sail on Tuesday morning from Penang to Port Klang, the entry port for the capital. Their fear was that during the voyage all permits might be revoked for the other six ports, leaving a gap of three months in the ship's schedule.

Stan's and Mike's attempt to get in to talk with the minister of Home Affairs was not successful at first, but on the second day they were granted a hearing. There Stan met the Muslim official who had processed his application a few days earlier.

'You know,' the official commented, 'it was very difficult to find that house where you were staying.'

'What do you mean "find the house"?' asked Stan in
surprise.

'Well, when I delivered that letter with the permits to
252    you, I had great difficulty finding the house.'

'What!' exclaimed Stan in astonishment. 'You mean to
say you delivered it personally?' To himself he said, *My
goodness! The man was on holiday and he took the time to find
my house!*

'Oh, yes,' answered the man and continued, 'I put it in
the mailbox, but as I was driving away, I noticed that the
door on the mailbox was faulty. I thought that if the wind
blew the door open and the letter fell out and got blown
away, you wouldn't receive the permit. So I turned my car
around and came back, took it out of the mailbox and
wedged it in the front of the house door.'

Stan could only gasp in amazement.

When he and Mike went in for their audience with
the minister of Home Affairs they found several other
officials present. One of them would address a question
to Mike and Stan in English and the answer would be
discussed among the officials in Malay. That part, of
course, went completely over Stan's head. But not Mike's.
He had lived in Indonesia where the language was very
similar to Malay. While he couldn't understand every
word, he could get the drift of the discussion. If the
government took a hard stand against the ship, they would
face opposition from a number of political parties and
individuals. If they took a strong stance for the ship, they

would get flack from the fanatical religious parties. They didn't know what to do. The affair was threatening to go into a parliamentary vote and that was one thing they didn't want to happen. They kept debating back and forth but realized certain members of parliament would be sure to call the question on them and bring it to the floor. They had to have a response ready.

That's what they were really after. They wanted to find out all they could about the ship and what assurances could be given.

Mike and Stan gave all the assurance they could. 'We will announce at every meeting that it is for non-Muslims only. As we have done in Penang, we will continue to fence off all the area that is Christian on the book exhibition and mark it clearly.'

The ship arrived in Port Klang and featured daily in newspaper headlines as the issue was debated in Parliament. Back and forth went the arguments. One of the older members of the founding party of the nation, a mature Muslim of great standing and experience, stated something to this effect, 'I am a Muslim. This is Malaysia. This is my country and no ship that is open to the public is going to stop me from going on board.'

His announcement that he was going down to visit the ship made headlines. All the newspapers picked up the issue and began taking sides on it. A retired former prime minister said, 'We are a Muslim nation, but we are also a multi-cultural, multi-ethnic nation. We have nothing to fear from a ship like this. It's not going to destroy our heritage or be a threat to us.'

Finally the government decided that the ship must display a sign declaring that the ship was open to the public, but the government was advising that Muslims should not go on board.

The ship followed these instruction. In big letters the sign at the foot of the gangway read, *DOULOS BOOK FAIR IS NOW OPEN TO EVERYONE.* Under that in smaller lettering was the government warning. Photos of the sign appeared in all the newspapers.

That Sunday the queues of visitors to the ship stretched for three miles. Traffic in the port was completely immobilized. People walked a mile into the port just to reach the back of the queue. During the ship's twenty-one-day stay 87,267 visitors came to the ship.

The interest continued on unabated for the next three months. The ship was also news in Singapore and in every port in East Malaysia. The publicity had gone ahead of the ship so that line-up people didn't have to worry about that aspect. Everybody knew about *Doulos.*

The programme turned out to be a very good one, concentrating on the Chinese. There was a great deal of prayer for the ship and for the nation. Book sales were more than double what had been anticipated, even the sale of Christian books. Bibles were sold not only by the armful but by the box load. More than a thousand tapes of messages recorded on board were sold at a minimal price, multiplying the conference ministry many times over.

After the last port in Malaysia came Thailand. The ship was given an excellent berth in the centre of Bangkok.

Christian leaders were excited, seeing this as an opportunity to give exposure to the Christian community in Bangkok.

On board for a few months was a Thai woman who had been with *Doulos* in her early days. Boonsian Chaiyasakorn was delighted to sail with the ship into her own country. She had high hopes for the visit. One of these hopes was that the ship might make contact with the royal family. To that end she began to pray. She also contacted a friend who was friends with Princess Maha Chakri Sirindhorn. The friend came to the ship, became excited about what she saw and on her next visit with the princess planted the suggestion of what an outstanding public relations event a royal visit to the ship would be.

*Doulos* had been in Thailand for a week when word came that the princess wanted to visit the ship. There followed a crash course in protocol for all *Doulos* crew and staff who would be involved in the visit. The programme director and an assistant drilled the ship's company on the proper means of addressing the princess as well as in the "informal" Thai protocol which would be appropriate on such an occasion. No eye-contact with the princess was permissible nor could anyone's head be above the eye-level of the princess, who was somewhere around five feet four inches tall — an interesting challenge for the tall Dutch and Germans on board. As director, Mike Stachura would be welcoming the princess and serving as host, so he spent considerable time practising the correct pronunciation of her name.

The palace informed the ship that they would line the outside of the ship with potted plants and provide a red carpet for the princess to walk on the quayside up to the ship. She would then be escorted up to the information desk and promenade area. A reception line of *Doulos* workers in their national costumes would be there to welcome her on board.

256     As *Doulos* leaders were planning all this with Boonsian and trying to envisage it happening, an unhappy thought struck one of them. Ship members would undoubtedly congregate on the book exhibition deck to watch the princess arrive and take photos of her. That would place them considerably higher than her in blatant violation of protocol. The media would certainly be there to pick it all up. The *Doulos* company must be warned.

The big day came. Most of the five hundred chairs were cleared out of the main lounge, leaving only about twenty-five or thirty for the princess and her entourage. When the time drew near, all visitors were cleared from the ship and it was closed to the public. Word quickly spread through the port, 'The princess is coming! The princess is coming!'

Sirens screamed, announcing her arrival. Those on board *Doulos* had no idea what kind of conveyance to expect. She came in an air-conditioned Dodge mini-van with tinted windows. When she emerged, she was greeted and presented with flowers that were handed up from a position of obeisance close to the ground.

Mike Stachura continues the story:

> We walked up the gangway. It was very difficult to lead her and at the same time not stand above her on the

stairway. She came inside and the atmosphere for us was tense for a while. However, she soon put us at ease, coming across as a normal, pleasant person with a sense of humour.

We had a reception for her where we sat and talked, telling her a little about the ship. After a cup of tea, she wanted to see the book exhibition. Up there it was very hot. We were all perspiring. We thought we would do just a quick walk around, but she wanted to see everything. She went to every section, looking at the books, pulling some off and deciding which were going to be for the royal library. When she went to pay, I told her, 'I'm sorry. Your money may be very good in Thailand, but it's not good enough here on the ship. There's just no way you can pay for these. They are a gift from us to your country.'

After the book exhibition tour, they went downstairs again into the foyer by the information desk. There the Thai volunteers, most of them young women, had gathered to see her. As she came into sight, they genuflected so low their knees almost touched the deck. And in that position they remained frozen.

'Come on. Stand up and talk,' said the princess as she approached them, 'Where do you come from? What do you do?'

For about five minutes she stood and talked with them while they giggled self-consciously. Then she turned back to Mike and the other ship's leaders. In the course of the conversation she mentioned that she was an instructor at the military college. Somehow that led on to talk about the school on board for *Doulos* children.

'Oh, that sounds interesting! I'd like to see it,' she exclaimed.

*Doulos* staff had not prepared for that eventuality. Someone was quickly dispatched to see that the school-rooms were in order. As it was Saturday, there was no school in session. However, one of the teachers was there, along with several children. They were trilled to welcome the princess.

The princess was intrigued by the thought of families living on board and schools operating for the children. She remarked on the fact that *Doulos* didn't just bring books to others, but her people used them on board as well.

And so the visit ended. The ship company had been expecting a short public relations call. Instead the princess stayed for an hour or an hour and a half.

Kendra Schneider, who had just joined the ship, watched from the dining room as the princess left. She was struck by the reaction of the Thai people:

> We stayed in the dining room and watched through the window. All those Thai girls on the quayside — I was amazed at how they reacted. They were thrilled. They had found out she was coming and it was a big event. They bowed down to her. That was a real eye-opening experience for me because, being from America, I had no concept of how people treated royalty, especially in an Asian context. It was such a shock. But they weren't embarrassed at all. They seemed thrilled that they could be so close to her.

No one was prepared for what happened after the princess left. Up to this point the numbers visiting the ship had been relatively small. But this was a Saturday afternoon and the crowd had been building up since the ship had closed at one o'clock. It was now four.

As soon as the royal party disappeared, thousands of people rushed toward the ship. They rushed the gangway leading up to the book exhibition. And there, to the amazement of ship workers, they formed neat orderly queues, waiting their turns to go aboard.

From that point on *Doulos* was on television, on the radio, in newspapers. The crowds more than doubled every day, tripling at weekends.

India, Malaysia, Thailand. *Doulos* had reached Asia and it was a whole new world for her company.

For Don Hamman, a regular visitor to *Doulos* to give pastoral counselling, a port in Taiwan stands out in a special way in his memory:

> My wife and I were standing on deck as we sailed into the port. All I could see were a few warehouses and shipping facilities with a huge empty concrete parking area. Behind that, all we could see was trees.
>
> 'Where's the city of Taichung?' I asked some people.
>
> 'About an hour's drive away,' they said.
>
> My heart sank as I thought, *An hour's distance away? Who's going to be able to make it out here in the middle of nowhere?*
>
> I believe the opening ceremony was on Saturday. On Sunday at noon my wife and I were enjoying dinner as

guests of Captain Isaacson and his wife Marion. We were sitting at his table on the starboard side of the dining room beside the window. As we were in the middle of the meal, people started getting up and coming over to our side of the dining room to peer out the windows. So naturally we looked out too. I'll never forget the sensation I had when I saw that on the vast open parking lot of several acres, a mass of humanity was running pell-mell right toward the ship. It looked like a Chinese horde invading. It was almost enough to strike us with panic because the ship was not prepared for people to come yet. Visiting hours for the book exhibition were still almost one hour away, so there was nobody out to meet the people. And here was an avalanche of humanity coming full speed toward the ship.

Immediately an announcement called for every possible available warm body to go out to the quayside and be involved in a human chain while ropes were set up to try if at all possible to steer people into zigzag-type lines. Well, it was almost a hopeless situation, but little by little they did gain some order.

We discovered that so many people had come from the city that the pressure had built up on guards at the guard-house and the gate, which probably was about a quarter of a mile away on the other side of the empty parking lot. Even though the guards knew it was not yet time for the book exhibition to open, they couldn't hold the crowd of people back any more for fear of a riot or danger of some sort. So they opened the gates, and it was like a dam suddenly bursting. Thousands of people began pouring towards the ship.

It was a very hot afternoon and people got thirsty immediately. We set up some stands to sell Coca-Cola, but in about an hour we had totally sold out of all the coke we had — about $1500 worth, I think. Someone called the coke company in the city to rush out a truck with another load, which they did, trying to provide some kind of liquid refreshment for people standing hours in the sun during the afternoon.

My wife and I managed a little later in the afternoon to make our way through the crowd back to the gate, where people were still pouring in. We looked down the main road which came from the city. As far as our eyes could see there was still a traffic jam. They said cars were backed up for a mile or more.

The people kept coming all afternoon. Between one thirty or two in the afternoon until nine o'clock at night the official count of those who had actually come aboard and gone through the book exhibition was over eighteen thousand. We were told that probably about the same number had been turned away or simply left when they saw the crowd.

During the afternoon *Doulos* people tried to provide a little interest to occupy those waiting in line. I remember the visitors were especially intrigued by two of our very tall Dutchmen who had dressed up in their Dutch costumes with little caps and huge clodhopper wooden shoes. The short little Chinese almost needed binoculars to look up into the faces of these tall Dutch fellows. They were overawed with the height of these guys and their unique Dutch costumes and wooden shoes. Then our evangelism team set up a sketchboard and had some music. Evangelistic services were held in the middle of the crowd as the people were slowly wending their way, taking a few hours, to reach the gangway and go on board the ship.

The next weekend over nineteen thousand came. They bought literature in incredible quantity. They would go off with their arms loaded with books.

Yes, this was Asia, but some experiences were not entirely new.

262

## 15

## *More Line-up Challenges*

When the ship's leaders planned to bring *Doulos* into Australia in 1989, they realized it would be a complex operation. Line-up men were sent to Sydney more than a year before the ship was due. Stan Thomson, who had lined up the visit to Malaysia, was given responsibility for arranging the technical aspects of the Australian visit. The port in Sydney was known as a 'red' waterfront because the two major trade unions were communist-dominated. Stan wanted permission for the ship to be able to use her own crew to load and unload her vans and various stores. He also wanted to obtain a waiver of the requirement for watchmen (a statutory requirement of the unions), because it would be extremely expensive to employ them. Stan watched with amazement as the Lord worked out all these problems.

The biggest technical problem Stan had to solve involved sewage disposal. Anti-pollution laws were very strictly enforced. As *Doulos* had no sewage treatment plant on board, arrangements needed to be worked out to connect up by hose to a sewage pipeline on shore. As Stan went down to survey the berth that had been allocated to the ship, he discovered to his horror that there was no sewer pipe there, no sewage system connection.

By this time Stan had developed a good relationship with the New South Wales (NSW) Port Authority. To his astonishment they bent over backwards to help the ship. They sent their engineers to find the nearest sewer connection. They got their men to fit new pipes underneath the quay and across to a sewer pipe on the other side of the quay. And they never charged a penny for the work.

With that, Stan thought all his sewage problems were solved. But he was wrong. He learned that before the ship could discharge any sewage into the city main, clearance had to be obtained from the NSW Water Board. He did not even know where to start tackling that problem.

As he was visiting a pastor on the outskirts of town, he casually remarked, 'I don't suppose you know any of the officials in the NSW Water Board.'

'Why?' asked the pastor.

'Well, I need to meet someone in the management who could put us in touch with the right person to give us permission to discharge our sewage.'

'Hmm . . .' the pastor said thoughtfully, 'I wonder if so-and-so who's in my congregation could help you. He's retired from the Water Board.'

The pastor gave Stan the man's phone number. One thing led to another until five engineers were phoning around trying to locate the right person. Eventually he was found and permission was granted.

Meanwhile Richard Beaumont had left his job as bookshop manager on *Doulos*, and was now down in Melbourne working with the line-up team. He had spent fourteen months of hard effort trying to work out the customs procedures to get permission for bookselling. He was told that it was not possible to sell anything from a foreign vessel. Australian authorities had turned down a request from the British navy for permission to sell caps and tee-shirts on their ships. Even the tall ships in harbour to celebrate the Australian Bicentennial Year in 1988 had had to set up little booths on the quayside to sell souvenir items. No, Richard was told, it was completely impossible for *Doulos* to sell books on board.

Richard managed to talk to the second highest man in Customs on the phone but soon realized he had come to a dead end. In a fit of inspiration he said to the man, 'Look, I'll be in Canberra next Tuesday. Can I come and see you?'

'Yes,' he agreed. 'Come at eleven o'clock.'

Quickly Richard rang Stan and told him, 'You must meet me in Canberra on Tuesday. I've got an appointment to see the customs man. It would be good if we went together.'

That weekend Richard spoke at a home for senior citizens in Melbourne and asked them to pray because the ship was already sailing, yet the visit to Australia depended on permission to sell books.

'Right,' the ladies had responded. 'We'll pray for you at ten o'clock Tuesday morning.'

*Ten o'clock? That's interesting,* thought Richard. *Why not at eleven when we have the appointment? Oh well. . . .* He shrugged off the thought.

Richard and Stan prayed and fasted for twenty-four hours prior to their appointment. On Tuesday they arrived at the customs office at ten forty-five just to make sure they were on time. They need not have rushed. They had to wait until eleven thirty before they finally saw the door open and a couple of people depart. Stan and Richard were ushered into the office where they introduced themselves to two men who stood to greet them.

266    On the desk lay a thick file about *Doulos* containing all the material Richard had sent the man plus some other background information as well. There was even material about the *Logos* visit ten years previously. Relaxed and casual, the official started telling Richard and Stan about *Doulos* — the history of the ship, what it was all about, why it was coming to Australia, what was behind the visit.

'Actually,' he said, bringing his recital to a close, 'I just wanted to let you know that the decision has already been made. We started our meeting at ten o'clock with the two men you just saw leaving. We discussed the whole matter again.' (Richard couldn't help but think of the ladies praying at ten o'clock.) 'And we've agreed to let you sell from on board the ship. I'll give this to you in writing, but you must understand that it is not in any way to set a precedent.'

That appeared to be his main worry — that the decision might set a precedent.

Richard thought back to his own prayer time with Stan. One of the things they had asked God was that they wouldn't have to beg for permission, but that the Lord would provide. That's exactly what happened. Not one word did Richard and Stan need to offer in their defence. The work had already been done. God had done it.

And God gave the ship a fruitful time in Sydney.

Sydney, however, was not the first port of call in Australia. That was Davenport. Richard Beaumont was chatting with Captain George Booth in one of the small conference rooms where Immigration officials were busy processing the passports of ship-members. Richard, who was in the process of emigrating from New Zealand to Australia, was telling George about the experience, mentioning the probing he had received about any criminal record and so forth.

As if on cue, one of the officials looked up from his work and asked, 'Captain, is there anyone on board who has a criminal record?'

George gave him a puzzled look and quipped, 'Do we still need that to come to Australia?'

The official looked at George sharply. Suddenly he realized that George was pulling his leg, referring to Australia's history as a penal colony. His serious expression dissolved into a laugh.

Richard let out a sigh of relief. He had had visions of all his careful line-up work going down the drain.

In Newcastle, sewage disposal was again a problem. Stan visited the port, talked to port engineers, the port director, the harbour-master. After several visits and a lot of negotiation, the final answer was, 'Sorry, we can't help you. There's nowhere you can hook up to a local sewage line.'

Just outside the harbour-master's office was a long berth. As Stan came out of the office, he looked at the berth and turned to the harbour-master, asking, 'Is this berth deep enough for the *Doulos*?'

Reluctantly the harbour-master consulted his charts and grumbled that it was.

'Well, you have running sanitation in your office. You have sewage. Isn't there a sewage line here that we could connect on to?'

268 Very reluctantly the man responded, 'Well, there might be, but you'd have to find out from the city engineers.'

Stan sought out the chief water engineer of the city who checked all their plans and gave a very firm refusal. Absolutely no. Just opposite the harbour-master's office was a huge nightclub with hundreds of patrons. It was heavily overloading the old sewer. The engineer threw up his hands and insisted, 'We can't take one drop more into that sewer.'

The captain and chief engineer of *Doulos* came to Newcastle and checked out the berth that was offered. A very long run of piping would be needed, they concluded. It was totally out of the question from a practical point of view. The visit would have to be cancelled.

Stan described his reaction, 'I can't explain this faith that I have, that I hang in even though everyone has said no. Even though the ship's leaders had decided that we would need to cancel the visit to Newcastle and were looking at alternatives, even in the last twelve hours I prayed, *God, it looks impossible but something has got to happen.*'

Something did. Overnight the nightclub closed down; it had changed owners and the new proprietors wanted to refurbish it. Stan phoned the chief water engineer and his people made the connection to the city sewer.

The way was free for *Doulos* to go into Newcastle. Well, almost free. As she was ready to sail into the port area, another obstacle presented itself — high swells, perhaps two metres high. People on the ship, anchored in the harbour, were getting seasick. The line-up team watched helplessly from shore as *Doulos*, and other ships as well, waited for the swells to subside and for the pilots to end a strike that was currently in progress.

For two days *Doulos* rode out the rough seas before the calm came, the pilots resumed their duties and the ship could sail in. She was given priority over all the other ships.

Because the ship arrived late, some of her programme had to be cancelled. Among the items cut out was the official opening. The Lord Mayor, who had been invited as guest of honour for the opening reception, was reinvited, this time as guest of honour at International Night.

The wife of the mayor, a dedicated Christian, had been praying that her husband too would commit himself to Christ. At International Night he heard the gospel clearly presented. He also met Captain Richard Prendergast. The two men immediately hit it off and Richard invited the mayor to his cabin for breakfast the next morning. That morning the two men prayed together and the mayor met Jesus Christ.

Several years later an Australian told one of the men who had worked with line-up in Newcastle, 'The OM prayer meeting that started in the mayor's home is still meeting and the group is still praying for you.'

In Kuching, East Malaysia, in 1990 the three-member line-up team was just pulling on their jogging suits for an evening run when the phone call came. It was Lloyd Nicholas, an Australian responsible for the ship's itinerary and line-up preparations.

'There's been a change of plans,' he informed them. 'The federal government has said the ship can't go to Sabah just now because it's election time there. So *Doulos* will be coming directly to Kuching instead. It will arrive in six days. Can you be ready for it?'

'Well . . . uh . . .' Edward David, a Malaysian leading the team, quickly thought over the situation, 'I guess we can be ready but I don't know if the churches can be.'

A sudden change of schedule was always a line-up team's nightmare. Unfortunately, it occasionally happened. Often the problem was that the ship got delayed for some reason. No matter how diligently the schedule was worked out, the unforeseen had a way of cropping up and upsetting carefully laid plans.

Edward's team was engulfed in panic, but that was short-lived. They collected their scattered thoughts, spent time in prayer and started working.

They were in a better situation than line-up teams often are when the dreaded phone call comes. They had been sent fourteen weeks ahead of time to Kuching. With seven weeks of the time gone, everything was in place except the printing of programmes and permission from the state government.

The printing was completed in two days, as much of the preparation had already been done. It took another day to get the programmes distributed to the churches.

The state permits came instantly after a phone call. The team simply had to go and pick them up.

The team also went to see the port manager, who gave them a berth free of charge. A free berth in a Muslim state! Sometimes everything did go smoothly.

Kendra Schneider, an American, gained her first line-up experience in the Philippines in 1991. She gives a glimpse of the everyday life of a line-up team:

> Usually the first couple of weeks are spent getting settled, finding an office and a place to sleep, getting to know various Christian leaders, meeting the agent and different people like that. It's just contacting people. After we know some people and find out a little bit about how things actually work in that city, in that country, in that culture, then we can start our work.

The ship was due in Iloilo in the Philippines on 31 January, so the team had to get started before Christmas. The team leader had gone on ahead a week beforehand and made some of the basic arrangements, but the team still had to be taken around to meet people and be given a tour of the city to help them learn their way around. Then they had to sit down together as a team and discuss what the assignments were to be. As Kendra didn't speak the local language and was new to line-up, she was given administrative office tasks like filing.

One of the challenges was adapting to a lifestyle very different from that on the ship. On *Doulos* they could go to the dining-room and pick up food that had already been prepared. When they had finished, they could leave their dishes for someone else to wash. Dirty clothes were taken to the laundry and reappeared clean and neatly folded. On a line-up team, however, all these things had to be organized. Rent for the apartment in Iloilo had been unexpectedly high, so the team tried to save in other ways to compensate. They did most of their own cooking, which, of course, involved locating and purchasing the food. At first they were also doing all their own laundry, washing clothes by hand on their one day off a week. However, they learned it was very cheap to send them out to a washer woman and it was not too long before the team decided they could afford that luxury.

Trying to agree on what food to prepare became a major problem. Eventually three agreed on European food and the fourth cooked his own. Then there was the washing up to do afterwards and when two different meals were cooked, a lot of pans were used. That was all frustrating at times. There was always so much to do. Even after dinner there was still work to be done.

At the office there were so many phone calls and so many people coming and going that it was hard to get an hour to sit down and type out something, so most of the typing was done in the evening at home. The team was constantly living, breathing, working and eating line-up.

The team leader had set up a local committee to help with the preparations for the visit. The chairman, a local pastor, was influential in getting together people from different denominations to serve on the committee. He also offered space in his church for the team to use as an office.

In many ways he was very helpful to the team and they grew quite close to him and his family. Kendra even stayed in their home over the New Year holidays.

Then on 8 January the pastor was murdered, stabbed to death in the house of one of his parishioners.

Line-up work went on hold. Kendra went out and spent some time with the widow the next day. It was a heavy emotional time and difficult for the team to think clearly or be productive.

Mourning was a nine-day process, very different from what most of the team was used to. Then the day after the funeral, one of the team came down with pneumonia and could not work for the last two weeks before the ship's arrival. Team responsibilities had to be shifted around. The team was constantly in prayer for God's help.

The pastor's heart's desire had been for Christians in Iloilo to be united and that had been adopted as one of the main aims of the *Doulos* visit. His death resulted in drawing the committee members and the churches closer together. His funeral was the first time in that city that so many Christians from so many different churches had gathered together in one place.

In 1990 Andrew Sinclair, an Englishman, was asked to go on line-up to Vietnam. With two *Doulos* men and another two men who had been working in Vietnam, he flew into the country. For a week they surveyed the situation, talked with people and generally got preparations under way. Then the other men left and Andrew carried on with one colleague.

The situation in Vietnam was very sensitive and the pair had to feel their way carefully. In the process, they got caught in the infighting between the local town people's committee and the national town organization. Contact with churches had been avoided because that was deemed too sensitive. Nevertheless, when the team returned to the ship for a week, they were confident that line-up preparations were looking positive.

Three days after they arrived back on the ship in Bangkok, Thailand, they received word that there was no berth available for the ship. The team knew very well that there had been a berth available, so there must be some other reason why the ship could not go to Vietnam.

The team prayed a lot. The whole ship's company prayed. Christians around the world prayed. People on the ship were confident that things would work out and the ship would go to Vietnam. As time went on, though, they began to wonder.

One afternoon Andrew was in the line-up office trying to work out his expenses for Vietnam when his boss, Lloyd Nicholas, came to call him into the director's office. Two or three others of the ship's leaders were there.

'We want you to go to Sattahip here in Thailand,' Lloyd told Andrew.

'What?' Andrew repeated in surprise.

'We want you to go to Sattahip,' repeated Lloyd.

'When?'

'Now.'

'How?'

'I think there's a bus or something you can get.'

'Why?'

'It looks as if we're not going to be able to go to Vietnam and we need to find out if there's a berth available in Sattahip. We want you and Craig Orr to go now so that we can know by our planning meeting tomorrow afternoon.'

'Okay.' agreed Andrew.

Neither of the two men really wanted to go, though. They wanted to go back to Vietnam. But they agreed.

They talked with the Bangkok line-up team who knew someone who might be able to lend them a car. A call was put through to the contact and he agreed. Someone went to pick up the vehicle.

Meanwhile Andrew and Craig hastily packed a few things. When the car arrived, they set out. They had only a rough tourist map to guide them. They knew that Sattahip was down in the south-eastern part of Thailand, but that's about all they knew. They started off, having no idea where they were going to stay. They just simply drove off.

They travelled for about four hours. After they had passed a big holiday resort, the road began to get narrower and narrower but eventually they ended up in Sattahip. They knew they had arrived when they reached the beach!

The main thing in Sattahip was a big military base. Andrew and Craig drove to one of the gates. That was a dead end for them, so they drove around another way and saw what appeared to be a hotel. When they reached it, they found it swarming with military people. It was indeed a hotel, they learned, but only for the military.

They went up to the receptionist and asked, 'Is there anywhere we could stay tonight?'

The receptionist looked at them uncomprehendingly. She spoke no English. The team tried to get across the idea with sign language. It was hard going.

A man who had been sitting in the foyer rose and approached them, saying in clear English, 'Can I help you?'

Turning to him, they replied eagerly, 'Yes, you can. We're looking for somewhere to stay tonight.'

The man asked what they were doing. They explained that they were working with a ship and had come to find out if there was a berth available.

'Well,' he told them, 'there's a hotel called the White Swan. It's a bit rundown, but it's on this side of town quite close to the port.'

The *Doulos* men found the hotel easily. It was half empty, probably a relic of the American-Vietnam War. But it was definitely open.

The next morning, after a good night's sleep, they made their way to the port. Using sign language, they managed to find the port director and were able to make arrangements for the ship to come for the desired dates.

Greatly relieved, they turned and started back to the ship. En route they stopped at another military hotel for lunch, which proved to be a memorable experience. They were given a menu which they were happy to see was in English as well as Thai. One entry was called *Wild Boar, Wild Curry*.

'That's it,' they decided. 'We've got to have that.' They had not the faintest idea what it would be like, but it sounded intriguing.

The waitress came over.

'Two *Wild Boar, Wild Curry* please,' they told her.

The waitress looked surprised.

'Yes,' Andrew repeated, 'Two *Wild Boar, Wild Curry*.'

The first thing the waitress did was to go to the table just behind them where generals and other military brass were sitting.

'They want *Wild Boar, Wild Curry*,' she whispered.

The military brass exclaimed in astonishment, 'What?' and turned to stare at the foreigners.

Andrew and Craig began to get a bit worried as they watched the news ripple around among the other guests. Andrew looked at Craig and joked, 'Maybe it's two whole boars.'

'No, no, it couldn't be that.'

Eventually the food came. Soup. Spicy hot soup. *Very* hot soup. *Painfully* hot.

The other guests stared in amazement as Andrew and Craig bravely downed most of it. Afterwards they bought some ice cream to tone down the effects.

The next thing on the agenda was to ring the ship and let them know there was a berth available. They managed to find a phone and take care of that item of business. Then they decided to visit churches in the area.

That brought the next problem. How could they find the churches? Go to the police station, they decided.

They found the police station easily and went in and looked around. A lady who was sitting there got up and said, 'Hello. Can I help you?'

She spoke very good English. They tried to explain what they were doing.

'Oh yes,' she responded. 'I understand. Let me take you around.'

She was involved in business and had come down from Bangkok for the day. She also knew about *Doulos*.

278

She took the men first to the Catholic Church. No one there seemed interested, so the team simply noted the location and went on to the Seventh Day Adventist Church. No one was there. They went on to a little Assembly of God church which had just been built the year before. When Andrew and Craig arrived, three people were there. By the time they left, the group had grown to eight or nine, exclaiming enthusiastically, '*Doulos* is coming!'

They told Andrew and Craig that they had been praying about going up to Bangkok to visit the ship, but decided it was too far away. 'And now look, our prayers have been answered. *Doulos* is coming to Sattahip.'

They were very excited.

## 16

## *Introducing the Master*

The purpose of being on *Doulos* was to serve God and to share with people his message of hope. Many *Doulos* workers found it much easier to talk about Jesus in a formal meeting than to initiate a conversation about him with an individual person, particularly with a stranger. That was something they had never done before and they felt insecure, ill-at-ease, unsure how to go about doing it.

Kendra Schneider tells of her first experience in this area. It took place in Sri Lanka.

> I hadn't had much experience in evangelism before joining OM, so I was really excited to be in the two-week evangelism training programme but also a little bit nervous. The first week we spent learning different evangelism techniques in the morning and practising them in the afternoons. The thing I was most scared of was personal evangelism — just approaching someone and starting to talk with them about Jesus. I didn't mind giving my testimony in front of a crowd because I had some distance, but one-to-one conversations scared me.
>
> Sure enough, one afternoon we were sent out to do personal evangelism for the whole afternoon. I was put on a team of three. None of us wanted to do it because we were all scared. But we knew that this was the time to do it. We needed to obey and step out.

So we prayed together and went out. Nothing was organized. The leaders had just told us to walk into town and approach anybody and talk to him or her about the Lord. It was easiest to go into a few shops. At least, you could look around and try to meet some people. We had a good conversation in a jewellery shop. I think we ended up having four good conversations.

One lady came to know the Lord and wanted us to pray with her. Then a young fellow, probably still a teenager, came to Christ. Wow! We couldn't believe it! Two people had prayed to receive the Lord when we hadn't even wanted to go out.

The next incredible thing was that teenager brought a friend to the ship so we could tell him about Jesus. He too prayed to receive the Lord. And then they brought back another friend. Three young people!

Kendra was in a special training programme, but much of the evangelism took place spontaneously as *Doulos* crew and staff found themselves in situations where individuals were in need or simply wanted to talk. It was a matter of being alert to opportunities.

Mike Hack recognized such an opportunity in the Philippines when his wife's passport was about to expire and the two of them had to travel to Manila to get it renewed. While there they stayed at a guest house.

One day as they were waiting for the passport to be processed, Mike decided to go outside and sit in a small shelter with a thatched roof where he could write some letters on a little table there. Out of nowhere, seemingly, a young man materialized and sat down at the table across from him.

*Oh, no*, thought Mike impatiently, *Why did he have to come and sit here? I want to be alone so I can get these letters done.*

Hardly had the man seated himself than a squall blew up. Rain pounded down. Winds swept through the open shelter. Mike and the stranger were alone, cut off from the outside world. The man introduced himself as Eddie and they started to talk. As they did, Mike noticed some men a couple of hundred yards away, standing against a wall, waving and gesticulating wildly.

'Know who those people are?' asked Eddie. It was obviously a rhetorical question for he went on to explain, 'They're my bodyguards.'

'What have you got bodyguards for?' asked Mike curiously.

Eddie pulled out a revolver and stared at it pensively.

'There are people trying to kill me,' he explained in a frightened voice and shifted his gaze to Mike's face. 'In a fight in my village recently I accidentally killed a man I grew up with. I had to buy this gun and hire these bodyguards to protect me.' He moaned, 'They're trying to kill me! They're trying to kill me!' Clearly he was very scared.

Mike and Eddie talked for about twenty-five minutes while the bodyguards couldn't get to them because of the storm.

'You know, "He who lives by the sword is going to die by the sword." ' Mike told him. 'You can't trust in guns. You've got to trust in Jesus. You can't trust in those bodyguards.'

'Yeah,' Eddie admitted, 'my bodyguards . . . all they're worried about is whether they get paid.'

'When it comes to the crunch, they're not going to lay down their lives to protect you. They'll look out for themselves. They're just in this for what they can get from you.'

Mike told him about the kind of security Jesus offers, a security based on something even more important than human life. Eddie listened intently. Yes, he decided, that was what he wanted. He would commit his life into God's hands.

After they had prayed together, Mike advised him, 'Get rid of your gun. Sell it. Get rid of it. Get rid of your bodyguards. Trust in Jesus. Now I know this is easy for me to say. There are people out to get you. But trust in the Lord.'

They talked further and arranged a few things for him to do.

At that point the rain stopped. Eddie went off with his bodyguards. Mike never saw or heard from him again.

Occasionally an opportunity to talk about Jesus didn't have to be sought; it came rushing out to meet the *Doulos* person. Rose Mundhenk, an American, experienced that in the Philippines in 1988. In her case, a team effort had been planned. They would try to hold an open air meeting in an inland village not far from the place where the team was staying.

'Oh, you'll never be allowed to do one in that village' the team was told.

'Let's give it a try anyway,' suggested one of the team members and the others agreed.

They planned who would do what. A couple of them dressed up as clowns to help gather a crowd and hold their attention by doing a short mime with a message. When the team was ready, the twelve of them set off in a motorcycle-propelled cart.

On the way they passed by a school.

'Oh, wouldn't that be a great place to have a meeting!' exclaimed one of the team.

'Yes, it would,' agreed someone else perfunctorily, dismissing the thought as unrealistic.

Inside the school building some of the children had spotted the clowns in the cart as it passed by and they jumped out of their seats and rushed to the windows, chattering excitedly.

Meanwhile, the team proceeded on to the end of the block and found themselves at a dead end. They would have to turn around and retrace their path. That was all the encouragement the schoolchildren needed. With a cry of anticipation they emptied the classrooms, running pell-mell to see the clowns.

The teachers decided to make the most of the situation. They could hardly stand in empty classrooms and teach. Nor did they see much hope in corralling the wildly enthusiastic children. So they did the next best thing. They invited the *Doulos* team into the school to do a programme for them.

Then came personal conversations. Not with children but with some of the teachers who wanted to know more about this life Jesus offers. Three of them ended up turning to Jesus and offering him their lives and loyalty.

While some of the *Doulos* company had to be taught how to communicate effectively about Jesus or be alerted to the opportunities surrounding them, Mike Mullins, an Irishman who was the radio officer on *Doulos*, was one to whom talking about Jesus came as naturally as eating and sleeping; it was in his blood. Nothing could fire him up to greater heights of enthusiasm than telling people what he himself had experienced. As a teenager at a camp he had committed his life to Jesus Christ, but later had slipped away and lost interest. Not long before he came to *Doulos* he had again encountered Jesus and his life had been turned upside down. It was the best thing that had ever happened to him, he claimed, and eagerly took every opportunity that presented itself to let other people know how they could have a similar experience.

On Sundays in South Korea the ship had what they called 'Gospel Flow' programmes. An announcement was made in the book exhibition inviting visitors to a special thirty-minute programme of music and preaching in the ship's lounge.

Each week two *Doulos* teams would be responsible for the programme. On this particular Sunday Mike's team was due to take over from the other team. As Mike listened to the tail end of the message being preached, his attention was drawn to the young Korean woman standing beside the preacher. *Now that's what I call a good translator!* he thought. *Fiery, enthusiastic. It's going to be great to have a translator like that!*

Unfortunately that was the young woman's last meeting for the day. She had to leave, so another translator came in to take her place.

Mike made his way to the *Doulos* man in charge and asked, 'Can't we have that last translator? She was good, really good!'

'Sorry. She had to go. This one will have to do.'

'Well, okay. God has brought her, so we'll just have to trust him.'

The meeting started with some singing. Then a *Doulos* man went forward to tell of his experience with Christ. He started off by introducing himself and saying, 'I came from a Christian family. . . .'

The translator looked flustered. 'Please . . . uh . . . repeat.' she asked politely.

*Oh, no!* groaned Mike. He turned to the team member sitting beside him and whispered, 'We've just got to pray. We've got to pray.' And they did.

Then came the time for Mike to preach. Usually he was never at a loss for words, but in this situation he had no idea what to say. Stalling for time to think, he walked up to the front where a blank sketchboard was standing. On it he drew a huge red cross.

'God loves you,' he said, turning to the audience. Suddenly the words came. He talked about why Jesus died. 'He cried from the cross, "Father, forgive." Even on the cross Christ was saying, "I love you." '

As he said those words, Mike glanced at his translator. He saw tears coming into her eyes.

Hastily he looked away and carried on preaching, getting

more and more enthusiastic about what he was saying. It dawned on him that the translator was now translating fluently. The more fired up he got, the faster he spoke. She spoke right along with him, in spite of the fact that tears were spilling down her face.

286     After the meeting Mike found out that the translator was not even a Christian. She had just been standing around when someone asked her if she would translate. She had tried to refuse, protesting that she didn't think she could do it; she wouldn't know what to say. But she had finally yielded to insistent persuasion. And God used her. Several in the audience cried along with her and a number of people met the Lord that day — including the stand-in translator.

A Greek-registered ship was berthed in Pohang, South Korea when *Doulos* sailed in and tied up just ahead of it. Costas, radio officer on the Greek ship, walked along the quayside, intrigued by the newly-arrived ship. With a Greek name like *Doulos*, that was no wonder.

He strolled over to the gangway and asked to meet the radio officer. Mike was called down. He greeted the Greek warmly and took him aboard, giving him a tour and showing him the radio room and, finally, bringing him into the dining room to have a cup of coffee and chat.

Costas couldn't get over the fact that everyone on board was a committed Christian and was working for no salary. In the following days Mike had many conversations with him, always managing to bring the talk around to Christ. He told his own story of how he had met Christ, how God had spoken to him, how God had changed him. The Greek had difficulty understanding that. He had never heard about a relationship with Christ and was amazed that a person could be excited about it.

Every day he came to the ship. On a Thursday evening Mike took him to the ship's prayer night. Mike explained that the people on the ship were going to pray and how they were going to do it. The man was very interested. He sat there looking around at all the people praying. Afterwards he told Mike that this was one of the most incredible nights of his whole life; he had never experienced anything like it before. 'God is here,' he said with awe.

Mike invited the Greek to International Night. In the programme Mike sang with some other officers. After the message the group sang again and the preacher gave a challenge, 'If there's anyone here tonight who would like to trust in Christ, stand up.'

Mike had already spotted Costas in the crowd, far to the right, seated between two officers from his ship. As soon as the invitation was given, Costas stood to his feet. Mike was so elated he could hardly restrain himself from running down and giving the man a big embrace.

After the programme was ended, Costas went back with Mike in the bus provided for *Doulos* people. Several of them came up to him to talk and comment on his decision. Costas was excited.

'Michael, Michael,' he said and continued in his broken English with words to this effect, 'I think it happened last night. After we talked I went back to my cabin on the ship.'

I sat down on my bed and I wanted to open my Bible and read it. Before I did, though, I closed my eyes and confessed to God all my sins. I started crying. I cried for an hour and a half. I could see all the things I had done and I was saying, "God, forgive me. God forgive me."

288 'After I cried, I opened my eyes. I felt like a piece of paper. Everything was clean and new for me.'

During the last few days of the *Doulos* visit, his speech, his whole manner was different. Saying goodbye to Costas was one of the hardest things some of the *Doulos* crew had to do, because they had grown close to him. He ran up and down the quayside, filming everyone. He ran up onto the bow of his own ship to the closest spot to *Doulos* and waved his hand, shouting, 'I love you. God bless you.'

A few months later Mike received a letter from Costas. In it he wrote in his broken English, 'Michael, during our common time in Pohang, I had said to you that a new life borned in my soul. I felt the really bright spot of God. For me this change was enough to make me insert a new target. My principal target in my life now is to be continuous close to Jesus Christ. By keeping myself close to God and his rules my life has a different colour!'

In Japan the parents of one of Mike's co-workers came to visit their son on the ship. One evening they invited Mike to go with the family to a McDonald restaurant. *Doulos* workers received a little pocket money to spend in each port, but Japan's cost of living was so astronomical that their little bit of pocket money would hardly stretch to treats at McDonald's. It was with great joy therefore that Mike accepted the invitation.

When they had collected their food, carried it to a table and settled down to eat, the family asked Mike to pray. He was glad to do so. He thanked God for the food and added, 'I pray that you will give us an opportunity to share the gospel here tonight and that we may even see someone saved.'

They began eating their food and talking with each other. A lady from the next table turned around and asked, 'Are you from *Doulos*?'

'Yes, we're from *Doulos*. I'm Michael and these are . . .' and he introduced the others. He then invited the Japanese family — husband, wife and child — to join them at their table.

The family had just visited the *Doulos*.

'Oh, are you Christians?' asked Mike.

'Oh, no,' they hastened to assure him, 'We're not Christians; we're Buddhists.'

The conversation turned to God and religion. They mentioned how they revered their ancestors and how they respected their bodies and looked after them.

Wanting to share the good news of Jesus Christ with them, Mike looked around for something he could use to illustrate his point. His eyes fell on the carton that had contained his hamburger. He picked it up and compared it with the human body.

'What do you eat, the carton or what's inside?' he asked. 'What's more important? The contents, of course. The carton itself is thrown away. Your soul is what matters and that must be right with God.'

Mike explained the Christian message to them. 'All you have to do is believe in the Lord Jesus. Believe that he died for your sins and that he rose from the dead to give you new life. When we go to heaven, we're going to get a new carton, a new body. . . . All you have to do is say "Yes".'

'Yes,' said the Japanese woman and looked inquiringly at her husband.

'Yes,' he agreed.

The child too wanted to do this. Right there at a McDonalds table they all joined hands and prayed together.

In Madras, India, a student radio officer about nineteen or twenty years old visited *Doulos* and asked if he could meet the radio officer. Mike was summoned. He took the young man to the radio room, showed him around and, in the process, also shared his testimony.

'Do you anticipate any problems with your exams?' asked Mike casually.

'Well, I do have a few questions.'

Mike gave him some personal tutoring, taking him around the equipment and explaining how each part worked.

*And that may have been a mistake*, thought Mike a few days later as he was inundated with student radio officers coming to the ship and asking to see him. Sixty or seventy must have come at some time or other. Mike felt completely drained.

Then he received from a principal an invitation to visit a radio officer training school. A student came to the ship to pick him up and take him there.

'Lord,' Mike prayed, 'give me an opportunity to talk to the students about Christ.'

Mike was taken to the principal, a Hindu. As they talked, Mike told him what *Doulos* was all about and shared his own testimony. From the way the conversation was going, Mike began to fear he was not going to be let in to talk to the students.

Finally the principal said, 'Thank you very much for coming,' and rose to his feet.

Mike searched around in his mind for some way to delay what appeared to be his imminent departure. He came up with an idea.

'I remember when I was in my college we used such and such transmitters. . . .' Mike went on to mention the kinds of transmitters at his college. 'Do you think maybe for just one minute I could see the transmitters that you are using here?'

'Yes, yes. Come and I'll show you quickly the equipment we have in here.'

The principal took Mike into a room where some of the students were working with the equipment.

'Ah, you radio officer?' asked some of the students as he looked at the transmitters and made comments.

'Yes, I'm from *Doulos*.'

'From *Doulos*! Ah!'

Eighty or ninety students crowded around Mike excitedly, all of them wanting to meet him.

What could the principal do?

'Please . . . um . . . all students . . . um . . . you come into this classroom here.' Turning to Mike he said, 'They say you are a teacher. Maybe you can teach them something.'

292

They went into the classroom where the students sat down and began to shower Mike with questions.

'Just a minute,' Mike said. 'Let me tell you about *Doulos* first.'

He had a poster with him which he held up as he told them various things about the ship and about the radio room and its equipment.

'Okay, now you can ask questions.'

They had many questions about radio things. One of them came up with the question, 'Mr. Michael, have you ever experienced a distress in your life?'

That was too good an opening for Mike to pass up. 'Have I ever experienced a distress? Let me tell you. About two and a half years ago . . .' and he went on to tell about how he came to meet Christ. It had nothing to do with radio distress calls, but the students listened intently.

Mike followed up with a rope trick for them, likening the rope to a radio aerial for communication.

'What happens when it is cut?' he asked.

'Ah, broken.'

'Even if you tie a knot?'

'Ah, it doesn't work.'

The principal was quite pleased because he saw the students were interested. They were actually *enjoying* learning about radio, and that was welcome in any shape or form.

At the end, the students wanted Mike's address so they could write to him.

'Well, let's see,' he said. 'Is there a Morse key here? I'll test out your Morse.'

He sent the OM address via Morse code. When they were able to receive it correctly, they all laughed and burst into applause.

More students came to the ship. Other schools invited Mike, but he was unable to go to them. A number of young men indicated a desire to know Christ. Mike kept in touch with many of them by letter.

The ship offered a unique opportunity to tell people the good news about Jesus Christ, not just a religious creed but a way of life that *Doulos* people had personally experienced. That's what made their message so powerful. It rang true.

# 17

## *More Snapshots of Ship Life*

On the six-day voyage from India to Malaysia, the crisp voice of the captain came over the public address system, 'Will Gunnar Stokke please come and take the fish off his line.'

Everyone on board knew about the Norwegian boatswain's elaborate fishing contraption trailing behind the ship. Consequently, half the ship's company rushed up to the book exhibition deck at the stern. They leaned on the rails and cheered Gunnar and two or three other men pulling on the line. The catch flopped up and down on the surface of the water, while the crowd cheered and made pertinent — and impertinent — remarks. After a great final heave, the object came flying up to land on deck.

The baker doubled up with laughter as he saw the big empty cloth flour bag he'd just thrown overboard.

The next day the fishing line was gone.

That was just one of many snapshots of life on *Doulos* in Asia. Here are some others.

One of the duties of pantry workers was to set tables, serve and clear away afterwards when receptions were held on board. Kendra Schneider had just been made a shift leader when a reception was held in Indonesia, an unusually elaborate reception requiring large dinner plates to be brought up to the reception area from the dining-room a deck lower.

It was a busy and pressure-laden time for Kendra who was new to the job, but all went well. As the team was clearing up afterwards, washing dishes in the decidedly limited kitchen facilities of the reception area, Kendra realized how awkward it would be to handle the big dinner plates in the tiny sink.

'Wash up the small dishes that belong here,' Kendra instructed her co-worker, 'but leave the big dinner plates. We'll carry those downstairs afterwards so they can be put in the dishwasher.'

'Yes,' nodded the young helper . . . and proceeded to start washing the big dinner plates.

'No, no!' exclaimed Kendra. 'Leave those, I said. You can wash these smaller things.' She indicated the stacks of cups and saucers sitting on the counter.

The young woman nodded again and went back to washing dinner plates.

Kendra, tired and on edge, exploded. 'I said to leave those,' she yelled.

The words were hardly out of her mouth when she realized that the young Indonesian woman was doing her best to please but probably couldn't understand Kendra's American English. Oh, no! thought Kendra, cringing inwardly, *What have I done? An Asian girl, new on the ship and here I am making her lose face! How could I have done it?*

There was too much work to stop and sort out the situation at that moment, but postponing it simply prolonged the discomfort because Kendra knew what she would have to do. For the moment she thrust the matter away and quietly showed the Indonesian woman what was to be done.

When the work was finished except for the dinner plates, Kendra released all the workers but the Indonesian. As soon as the others were gone, Kendra turned to the young woman.

'I'm sorry for what I did.' The words came tumbling out as Kendra tried to apologize and ask for forgiveness.

'Oh, no, it was my fault too,' protested the Indonesian. 'I said yes when I didn't understand.'

Suddenly the tension dissolved. The two women looked at each other and smiled. Happily they picked up the stacks of plates and carried them downstairs where they stood together companionably dealing with the dishes and singing songs of praise to the Lord.

'That was the first time I had ever got angry at someone, expressed that anger, forgiven her, apologised, and enjoyed being with her — all in the space of a few hours',' explained Kendra, looking back. 'It made me realize how right the Bible is when it says, "When you're angry, don't let the sun go down on your anger." '

Ironically, another incident Kendra remembers involved the same young woman. Kendra's cabinmate had borrowed an adaptor from the Indonesian in order to listen to some music cassettes on her tape recorder. One day Kendra had a few items of clothing to wash by hand. She took the tape recorder along with her to the bathroom so she could enjoy music while she worked. Unfortunately, she forgot one thing, small but important. The electrical current in the cabin was 110 but in the bathroom it was 220. The adaptor reacted in predictable fashion. It blew.

Kendra stared at it in consternation. The adaptor hadn't even been loaned to her but to her cabinmate. Furthermore, Kendra realized that replacing it would surely cost a couple of months' pocket money and she had no money at all to hand. She couldn't even afford to replace the adaptor right away.

Shamefaced, she went to the owner to tell her what had happened. Together they took the gadget to the audio-visual department in the hope that it could be repaired. That was not possible.

'Don't be upset,' responded the Indonesian graciously. 'Don't worry about replacing it. You are a lot more important than this little adaptor thing.'

Kendra was amazed. This was not the kind of reaction she had anticipated. It gave her another perspective to be incorporated into her own life.

Kongkin Atmodjo lived in Cabin 211, a dormitory cabin holding about eighteen bunks. With so many young men in one room, practical jokes were inevitable. One day one of the men secretly took some black shoe polish and spread it liberally around the listening end of the telephone receiver. Afterwards, he went into a nearby cabin and dialled the phone number of his own cabin. As soon as someone answered, he hung up. The person who answered, of course, ended up with black shoe polish all over his ear. The prankster then returned and basked in the enjoyment of his cabinmate's discomfiture. It was a great joke, he decided, and repeated it again and again over a period of time as long as there was a supply of victims. With people continually moving on and off the ship, there was an endless supply in a room of eighteen bunks.

298

Now it so happened that four Asian pastors came to visit *Doulos* for a few days and observe the ministry firsthand. They were put in Cabin 211.

The phone rang. By this time most of the cabin occupants were wise to the trick and ignored the ringing. They simply glanced briefly in the direction of the phone and returned to their reading or whatever else they were doing. That's why they didn't realize what was about to happen.

One of the pastors stared undecidedly at the ringing phone. Should he answer it? The phone continued to ring insistently. The pastor finally stood up and reached for the phone.

'Hello. Hello,' he said in heavily accented English.

There was no answer. The pastor looked perplexed. He shrugged, laid down the receiver and climbed back into his bunk to lie down on the clean white pillow on his clean white sheet.

The *Doulos* men, becoming aware of what was happening too late to prevent it, stared at one another in dismay. *What should we do now?* they wondered and looked around, waiting for someone to get inspiration. Kongkin, himself an Asian from Indonesia, finally climbed reluctantly out of his bunk and walked over to the pastor. He felt embarrassed for himself and for the pastor. What else could he do but apologize and point out the washroom down the alleyway.

He didn't dare wonder what the pastor must have thought of *Doulos* after that.

When the perpetrator heard what had happened, he exclaimed sheepishly, 'Oh, I never thought one of the visitors would answer the phone!'

But that didn't end the pranks, though it may have instilled a little more caution. One evening he put shaving cream in a big manila envelope and took it up to the engineers' accommodation area where he stuck it partially under one of the doors, with the open end of the envelope protruding into the cabin. He then took a heavy book and dropped it on the part of the envelope still outside in the alleyway.

Instantly the cabin door flew open, revealing a bespattered young man in a far from amiable frame of mind. Behind him, the cabin appeared a disaster area with white blobs scattered everywhere. The prankster, standing in a clean alleyway stared in mock surprise and then broke down laughing.

'Where in the world did you get all these tricks?' Kongkin once asked him.

'Oh,' he replied blithely, 'I was at a Bible College in Chicago for a year.'

Kendra and her co-workers had just celebrated the opening of the newly-refurbished pantry when the time came to leave Taiwan. Before a voyage the captain always instructed the crew and staff to secure things to avoid breakage if the ship took a roll. But for over a year the ship had never taken a roll; it had been smooth sailing with no rough seas. Staff had become lax about tying things down and stowing away breakables. On this voyage the ship had no sooner left the breakwater than she encountered high waves which continued to get higher and higher. This was a new experience for many of the pantry workers and they crowded around the dining room windows to enjoy the spectacle.

Suddenly there was a loud crash and the sound of shattering glass. They rushed back into the pantry.

Everything that had been on the table was on the floor. The entire contents of one refrigerator had spilled out, splattering condiments, sauces, jams and butter all over the deck. The butter as well as the jam had been in glass jars so there was broken glass everywhere as well. It was a huge mess.

Myles Toews, the chief steward, arrived quickly on the scene to assess the damage and help in cleaning it up. He showed the young workers how to wet tablecloths for the tables so that plates wouldn't slip so much. After that, it became a joke for the pantry women to talk about watering the tables instead of watering the plants on the window sills. But they learned to take the captain's orders seriously!

It was as well they did because a few weeks later in Manila, the ship was ordered out to anchor to ride out a typhoon heading straight for Manila. Kendra tells what happened when it hit:

> We were having lunch and I was sitting at one of the tables now used for a buffet. These big tables, which used to seat eight people, were not bolted to the deck. Instead, they

had foldable legs so they could be moved or stowed away. Well, I was sitting at one of these when a wave came at us the wrong way and the ship rolled sharply. One person in the dining room fell out of his chair. Someone else went flying across the room. Those on the port side had it much worse because that was the way we rolled. Kids were screaming. All of a sudden my table started coming up in my face.

*Oh my goodness!* I thought. As I jumped up to push the table down, my plate slid down through my legs.

The officers and the captain who weren't on the deck at the time went tearing up the stairs to help get the ship on a better course that would hit the waves the right way. We didn't have any more problems, but that was one of the few times I have been scared on the ship.

On the next voyage Captain Tom Dyer left Manila promptly in order to avoid another typhoon heading in. The typhoon, however, didn't do what it was supposed to do. Instead, it veered and headed straight for *Doulos*. Islands offered some protection from the violence of the seas but not from the high winds. The storm made for a motion-packed night but *Doulos* came through safe and sound. A ferry didn't fare so well; it sank with about three hundred people on board.

Three typhoons in less than two months after a year of calm sailing. Captain Dyer, who had came to the ship just in time for the first one, was jokingly accused of bringing them with him. From that time on he was known as Typhoon Tom.

302

The autumn of 1989 was an exhausting, emotionally-draining time for people on *Doulos*. Several rough voyages took their toll. The ship's director and assistant director had both just left and been replaced by others. The new leaders needed time to get a feel for the ship and their responsibilities, while the ship's company had to adjust to them and their styles of leadership. Dry-dock brought its own demands, compounded by a long delay in getting into the dry-dock.

Tensions began to rise, especially in the deck department. Some of the men felt misused as they saw *Doulos* staff leaving the ship and apparently going off to enjoy themselves while the crew had to stay aboard and work hard. Negative feelings were expressed and began to snowball. Other people were drawn in, particularly ones who already felt a bit negative towards leaders or ship life in general. At times deck officers would give orders and their men would refuse to co-operate.

It was swelteringly hot and people were very tired. There was a lot of complaining. Leaders began to realize that things were happening on the ship that shouldn't be happening, things that were clearly sin.

Captain Dallas Parker, who had come to fill in temporarily as captain, felt deeply burdened for the ship's company. He instigated a regular early morning prayer time in his cabin for all who were interested. Most days a small group gathered there to join him in prayer for revival on the ship as well as for other concerns.

About halfway through the voyage from Papua New Guinea to New Zealand, Markus Chacko, an Indian worker, was leading the weekly prayer evening on a Friday. One of the *Doulos* men was under discipline for having violated ship policy. He was counselled by ship leaders that, as he had wronged the ship community, he ought to stand before them and make an apology. He agreed. Having made arrangements with Markus Chacko, he went forward during the prayer night and turned to face the lounge full of *Doulos* co-workers. Humbly he said what he had done and also asked forgiveness.

Then he returned to his seat.

Shortly afterwards, another *Doulos* man stepped up to the microphone and said, 'I want to make a confession too.' He told what he had done and asked forgiveness.

A few seconds after he sat down, someone else came up to the microphone and confessed. Then another person. And another. People began running up to the microphone, even grabbing the microphone from someone else's hand as soon as he or she finished. Confession after confession poured forth, with humble pleas for forgiveness. The Holy Spirit was clearly putting pressure on people to get their lives straightened out.

The prayer night was finally brought to a close around two o'clock in the morning. But on the next evening the same thing started up again. People got up and confessed sins like being rebellious or having bitterness toward leaders, stealing money, taking forbidden food from the galley, having problems in personal relationships or with lust.

The atmosphere on the ship changed completely. People felt forgiven. They embraced with breaking voices and tears. A heavy load seemed to have been lifted. God had brought the community close together again.

Dale Rhoton, who had left *Doulos* in 1981 to join the leadership team in Germany flew out with his wife to visit the ship in Papua New Guinea. They flew on the first tiny aircraft allowed into Kieta after a recent outbreak of fighting in Bougainville. Looking around in bewilderment, they tried to puzzle out the strange-looking airport: various buildings without roofs and paved areas without walls. *What is this?* they wondered. *And where do we go to pick up our luggage?*

The airport, they learned, had been destroyed by rebel forces. The luggage problem was solved by watching as it was being unloaded from the plane onto a baggage wagon and making their way to the wagon when it came to a stop.

Getting into town was another problem. Town was on the far side of the island, a thirty-minute drive. Apparently *Doulos* hadn't received word of their expected arrival time or else had been unable to off-load their vans, they concluded. Public transport appeared non-existent. They were able to hitch a ride, however, with several Australian journalists who had flown in to cover the fighting.

They reached the ship with no difficulty but had to wait to talk with the current director, Bernd Gülker. He was a at a church meeting as it was Sunday morning. When he returned to the ship he told them what had happened.

The ship was not in any danger as foreigners were not targets. The fighting was concentrated inland, anyway, up in the hill country where the rich copper mines were located. Actually, it was the mines that had sparked off the rebellion, *Doulos* workers had been informed. The fighters were seeking independence from the rest of Papua New Guinea and hoping to conserve their rich resources for their own use.

But that was up in the hills and the ship was down on the coast. The church that Bernd's team was scheduled to visit, however, was up in the hills. That had posed a problem which was neatly resolved. Both rebels and government troops had agreed to a one-day truce so *Doulos* teams could speak in various churches on the island that Sunday. For one day all was peaceful and quiet. On Monday the fighting resumed.

During an eight-month period in 1989-90 five very special people joined *Doulos*: babies born to families working on the ship. All five newcomers were boys.

When news of the fifth arrival was given during the customary meal-time announcements on board, six-year-old Daphne, whose second brother had been born a day earlier, exclaimed plaintively, 'Has God forgotten how to make girls?!'

In 1991 the ship went into dry-dock in Hong Kong. Technical and practical crew stayed aboard to work while others went ashore, many of them on teams for outreach. One team of eight stayed in a high-rise apartment with a pastor and his family, which included a grandfather and an uncle as well as the parents and two children. That meant close fellowship. Very close fellowship.

One day Debbie, one of the team members, decided she needed some personal space; she needed to be alone for awhile. There was only one nearby place she knew to go for that empty space: the flat roof of the twelve-storeyed building where she was staying. So that afternoon she made her way to the top.

A neighbour spotted her up there . . . and panicked. She quickly consulted her family and they called the police.

'Please come here right away!' the agitated voice of the spokesperson came over the police phone line. 'There's a woman sitting on the roof. We think she's going to jump!'

The police took the call seriously, sending ten plain-clothes men to the apartment building, where they hurried up to the top and hid behind air-conditioning vents. Presumably they didn't want to startle the woman and send her over the edge. One of the men called out to her to engage her attention and keep her calm. But Debbie had earphones in her ears, listening to her tape recorder. Intent on her own thoughts, she was oblivious to the men behind her.

Dusk was setting in and with it came dinnertime. Marlies, another team member, ran upstairs to tell Debbie it was time to eat. Coming out onto the roof, she was shocked to find it full of men crouching behind vents. *What are they doing here?* she asked herself in horror. *They must be going after Debbie! What are they going to do to her?*

Turning abruptly, she rushed downstairs for help. One of the men saw her and immediately separated himself from the others to run after her. Marlies, undoubtedly setting a personal record for speed, reached the apartment seconds before her pursuer and was let in. That didn't stop him. He pushed on the buzzer, identified himself and tried to explain his strange action.

'There's a crazy woman up on the roof. She trying to kill herself.'

At these words, Sharon, another team member, jumped up, *Debbie's up on that roof!* she thought, suddenly frightened for Debbie. *A crazy woman up there too? Maybe she'll try to push Debbie off!* In a panic Sharon turned to go to Debbie's rescue.

'No, no!' The policeman shouted, trying to restrain her. 'Don't go up there. The lady is crazy!'

'But my friend is up there. I've got to help her.'

On the team was yet another young woman who had just joined *Doulos* and didn't yet know anyone well. The situation was well beyond her. She sat there crying, crying, crying. She had misunderstood, thinking Debbie had jumped off the roof and was killed. The Chinese maid in the home was standing by the young woman trying to comfort her, saying, 'No, no, no. Debbie would never do that. She has no reason to commit suicide.'

Sharon managed to shake off the plain-clothes policeman and run upstairs. Meanwhile Debbie suddenly realized it must be about suppertime. Putting up a hand to remove her earphones, she turned around and caught sight of the men. She watched in alarm as they slowly walked toward her.

'Don't do it! Don't jump!' said one of the men in a pacifying voice.

'Jump? What are you talking about? I'm not going to jump.'

'You're not?'

'No, I was just listening to a cassette.'

'Oh. . . .'

308

Relieved and probably rather embarrassed, the group made its way to the apartment, where explanations were duly made.

*Doulos* needs a continual supply of seawater to operate toilets, cool engines and generators and provide for fire hydrants. Probably a million gallons of seawater circulate around the ship in the course of a day. As the seawater comes into the ship, it passes through filters, but many sea creatures are so small they slip right through the filters. These crustaceans collect and harden around the valves, making them difficult or even impossible to close if the necessity arises. So the valves have to be periodically taken apart, ground out, wire-brushed, cleaned and sometimes even turned on a lathe. Then they are ready to be reassembled with new packings. The grand finale comes only when water flows through at great pressure.

Since the engine room is below water level, anything that comes in from the outer hull has tremendous pressure to it. No valves can be taken apart to be overhauled unless the water is shut off. But, of course, water is needed for the daily operation of the ship. Only in dry-dock when the engines, generators and pumps are shut off and the ship is lifted out of the water can such work be done.

David Salisbury, a middle-aged Australian, gives a

glimpse of what happens when life is restored to the ship:

I remember the day we finished dry-dock. It was decided to start the generators and the fire pumps that circulated the seawater around the ship. This was very interesting to me because it was my first time to see such big machinery set alive again. I was in the entrance to the alternator room, looking down on the compressors that keep the ship cool in the air-conditioning. As the pumps started up, the room clouded into a haze of water everywhere. Water was coming out of all sorts of valves and out of a filter chest.

All of a sudden people were running everywhere. The first engineer yelled out to tighten some of the valves which he hadn't wanted to overtighten before. Some of the rubber packings we put in weren't quite so good as they could have been, but we found that by tightening them or replacing them while the water was running was the best way to fix them. I looked up and saw two fellows sitting with their legs straddling a fifteen-inch pipe, a huge valve between them on which they were working like fury, tightening huge nuts. They were both being hit about chest level with a heavy spray of water. The more they got the valve tightened down, the more enthusiastic they became because the water was getting less and less. When they finally got the job done, they cheered and yelled out, 'Hallelujah! Praise the Lord!' Everyone else joined in. One of the men lifted both of his big long boots into the air to let the water run out of them. There was probably about half a pint in each.

That wasn't the finish, of course. Over in the corner was a big chest which was a filter for the seawater to come in. I saw water gushing out at such a rate that we had to shut off one of the sea valves and take the lid off to reseal it. We got that tightened. As I looked around behind me to see what else was going on, I saw Steve from Malawi down a hole in the steel plates in the deck. The water was coming up both sides of his face. He and a second man were working like fury to see if they could shut the water off from another valve that wasn't sealing properly.

After about half an hour things came back to normal again. There was a dead silence, or at least, it seemed so after all the banging and crashing that had been going on for the last thirty minutes. People were standing, sitting, lying there with grins all over their faces and saying, 'We're floating again.' Later they sat up on deck and laughed and joked about it.

The majority of workers joining *Doulos* went first to a general OM conference in early autumn. Afterwards, they would fly as a group of perhaps fifty or sixty to the ship. And then the culture shock hit them. Not only in relation to the particular country the ship was visiting at the time, but to life on the ship itself. A time of orientation to ship life was badly needed. Accordingly, a two-week pre-ship training programme was initiated after the newcomers had arrived on *Doulos* and had had an opportunity to see it for themselves.

In Thailand in 1993 this orientation programme took place at a Christian academy on shore. Along with explanations about various aspects of ship life, the group was also given training in ministry skills and some opportunity for outreach.

Mercy Koh, a Singaporean ship leader involved in the training, recorded one ministry outreach in her diary:

> Water Buffalo Race at Chonburi. Big event. Hundreds of buffaloes were assembled. The usual fanfare goes with such an event.
>
> Four churches in Chonburi united for the first time in their history for a major tracting blitz. Seventy-three of our pre-shippers and their trainers were also involved.
>
> It was an immensely hot day. At the end of our tracting, many of us were very sunburned, but seventy thousand tracts were distributed.
>
> In the history of my tracting experience, Chonburi is the only place where I have had to humble myself and pick up 'rubbish' from the ground. The fine for littering in Thailand was five hundred bahts, so the missionaries instructed us to pick up all tracts that were thrown away lest the churches whose addresses were stamped on the tracts be charged for littering. We did just that — picking up tracts that had been thrown away by those who did not want them. Torn tracts, crumpled tracts, dirty tracts, wet tracts, unread tracts — as far as we could, we picked them all up. This very act, I think, was a testimony to the Thais who must have wondered why we foreigners were stooping so low as to pick up 'rubbish'.
>
> After we were finished, it rained cats and dogs.

As they took stock of the event they estimated that twenty thousand tracts must have been thrown away. A discouraging beginning for *Doulos* newcomers in their first attempt at ministry. But it was a beginning that reflected the realities of life: many who hear God's word will spurn it.

There was, of course, another perspective to the event. On one day fifty thousand people did *not* throw away the tracts; they carried off with them a message that could bring hope to their lives.

312

In another country most of the *Doulos* crew and staff had gone to their cabins for the night when a roll-on-roll-off ferry of a thousand tons sailed into port. The ship called in regularly, bringing food, machinery, and passengers and carrying away fish and other products.

Chief Officer Graeme Bird and his second officer were still up and around on *Doulos*. Drawn by the irresistible appeal of observing another ship manoeuvre itself into a berth, they stood and watched as the ferry backed up to the quayside and let down a loading ramp at its stern. With the bow pointed out to sea, the stern ramp was the only part of the ship against the wharf. Two anchors were let down to help hold the ship steady. The *Doulos* officers noticed that the end of the thick ramp lacked the usual tapering-off fitting which provides a smooth transition for vehicles driving off the ramp onto land. That posed no problem for the inventive crew. An old mooring rope lying discarded on the wharf was pulled over and carefully laid out against the end of the ramp. The thick rope cushioned to some extent the abrupt descent of the vehicle from the surface of the ramp to the pavement several inches lower.

'Aha, so that's the way it is done!' laughed one of the *Doulos* officers.

Meanwhile, passengers had already started to disembark, taking their lives in their hands in darting among the vehicles zooming around. An operator trying to manoeuvre his forklift out of the ship, across the ramp and onto shore ran into problems and had to submit to the humiliation of being towed by a much larger shore-based forklift. Behind him, another forklift operator, determined to avoid such ignominy, rushed out of the ship and down the sloping ramp at breakneck speed. Suddenly he lost control and the forklift went into a spin on the narrow ramp. Disaster was narrowly averted as the machine caught in the hoist chain of the ramp, teetered at the edge and came to rest on board.

All that was needed was a short length of good strong rope to haul the forklift to safety. The *Doulos* men watched in disbelief as a rope was brought onto the scene, a rope that had already been mended in various ways in at least four places. The rescue attempt ended in failure after causing the driver to flee the scene when the forklift nearly toppled over into the water. Again the shore-based forklift had to be brought to the rescue.

With amusement the *Doulos* onlookers watched the next item of business — unloading cargo. The standard practice, based on simple logic, is to stow at the back what will be discharged last and to reserve the front space for cargo that will be unloaded first. The ferry crew had never come into contact with the logical approach, the *Doulos* men concluded.

Finally calling it a day, Graeme and his second officer went down to their cabins and climbed into bed.

About 1:30 am Graeme was aroused by the gangway watchman.

'The ship in front of us has sunk!' he announced in a tone that suggested he still could not believe what he had seen. 'It just rolled over and sank.'

Apparently, instead of shifting cargo temporarily on shore to get at what was stored behind, the crew had decided to save time and effort by simply shifting it around inside the ship. That might have worked if port holes had not been opened to alleviate the discomfort of an unbearably hot tropical night. Shifting the cargo had created a strong list and water had began to pour in through the port holes.

Deadly serious now, Graeme immediately pulled on his clothes and called together some of his men. Within minutes a lifeboat was lowered and a search-and-rescue operation commenced. A couple of the *Doulos* mates spent the next few hours climbing over the upturned hull, systematically tapping the steel and pausing to listen for replies from any survivors who might have been trapped inside. Other *Doulos* crew endeavoured to stop all fuel leaks to prevent pollution of the beautiful tropical island and destruction of the fish life which was the mainstay of the inhabitants.

Later it was learned that everyone on board at the time had managed to get out in those few minutes when the ship was in the process of capsizing.

Graeme wondered afterwards what would have happened if, instead of laughing, he and his second officer had pointed out to the crew what they were doing wrong. Would they have listened and heeded? Probably most wouldn't have done so, concluded Graeme, but one or two might have.

'How this reminds me of God,' Graeme wrote later. 'He saw man's sin and sent a messenger, his own son Jesus Christ, to tell them how to do it right. Some wanted him to go away. Others listened, believed and did things right. I, for one, am glad that God didn't just laugh.'

# 18

## To Russia with Love (packs)

'Vladivostok! We're going to be so close to Vladivostok next year. Can't we take the ship there?'

'Out of the question. Vladivostok is a closed port. No foreign ship has called there for decades. You realize, don't you, that Vladivostok is the home port for Russia's Pacific Fleet?'

The year was 1991. The communist regime in the Soviet Union had fallen a few months previously and the ship's leaders couldn't resist the exciting thought of bringing the ship into a country that had been completely closed to Christian activity for so long.

'Vladivostok is the major city on the east coast. There must be some way to get us in there,' they insisted as they discussed the situation with Ronnie Lappin, OM ships' most knowledgeable man about Russia.

Ronnie was doubtful but agreed to make a survey trip to the nearest accessible city, Nakhodka, a city far smaller than Vladivostok. As he was preparing for the trip, the news broke that Yeltsin was going to open the port of Vladivostok as of 1 January.

Ronnie's trip, however, was in November. He went as planned to Nakhodka, investigated the possibility of bringing the ship into that small port city and encountered no hindrance. But his heart wasn't in the survey. *Vladivostok is the place for the ship to visit, he told himself. I just know it is. How can I get the information I need about Vladivostok?*

'Well, Lord,' he finally prayed one day, 'if you want this ship to go to Vladivostok, surely you will open up some way for me to visit the port.'

To visit any city in Russia required a visa, but Vladivostok, being a restricted area, required special permission, which was more difficult to obtain. Ronnie had no visa or special permission. He kept asking the shipping agent if there was any way he could get to visit Vladivostok. The agent had contacted immigration officials, but they were very slow moving.

Then the shipping agent discovered that he himself needed to travel up to Vladivostok on business. He agreed to take Ronnie with him in his car and see what happened.

The trip was memorable. The speedometer needle hovered around 90 mph as the Suzuki jeep sped over bumpy roads, not too icy but peppered with pot-holes. Along the way Ronnie could see radar stations sticking up into the sky on the tops of many hills. Destroyers and cruisers seemed to lurk in every second bay they passed. Sprawling out along the way was military installation after military installation.

Only as the Suzuki entered the outer environs of Vladivostok did the other passengers in the vehicle become aware of the fact that Ronnie possessed no visa. They were horrified.

'Just keep quiet — absolutely quiet — if the military police stop the car and search it,' they warned him in panic.

318

*Yes, I get the message*, thought Ronnie. *Just act deaf and dumb.*

Fortunately they were not checked.

Ronnie remained in the city for a total of six hours. The only person he was able to meet was the shipping agent, and that for only half an hour. He quickly tried to explain about the ship ministry. The shipping agent said he would contact the mayor's office about it and then get back to Ronnie.

That was all. Ronnie wondered pessimistically if anything would come of it.

Surprisingly enough, Ronnie did receive a response from the shipping agent saying he had contacted the mayor's office and they were very happy with the prospect of *Doulos* visiting Vladivostok.

Another problem soon arose to put the Vladivostok visit into jeopardy. Ronnie was not free to pursue the line-up much further, yet the situation was too complex for anyone except an experienced line-up person to handle. None was available.

It was Dale Rhoton who came up with the solution as he was visiting the ship early in 1992. 'How about George Barathan going?' he suggested.

George, the Sri Lankan who had tried in vain to arrange a ship visit to Trinidad in the early days, was no longer involved in line-up; he was part of the main leadership team on *Doulos* and was just moving into a new responsibility for pastoral care on the ship. He had many years of experience in line-up, but he knew virtually nothing about Russia. He felt very inadequate.

In April Ronnie took him into Russia to introduce him to various officials and church leaders whom Ronnie had already met. They arrived in the evening and were picked up by a Christian man. As they drove along, George looked out at the city. Still in winter's grasp, it looked bleak and forbidding. The people appeared depressed. Their features looked western, but that was all that looked western to George.

Buildings seemed at least two or three decades behind the times. There was not a single modern high-rise to be seen. Most people apparently lived in apartment buildings. Houses were rare. The buildings had not been maintained and presented a shabby, run-down appearance.

Several times they passed long queues of people waiting patiently to buy food, usually bread. In the days to come George would also stand in such queues and experience first-hand what the people went through. Shops lined the major streets, but there was little on the shelves inside. A filled shelf, he found out later, would often consist of a generous supply of only one product.

On George's second trip to Russia he went with a couple of other *Doulos* men instead of Ronnie. He was amazed at how openly he could talk to customs and immigration officials about a Christian ship coming to carry out a Christian programme. None of the officials reacted negatively, but none of them smiled either. They steadfastly insisted in following rulebook procedure to the letter, which led the team to much frustration working through all the red tape. Still, there was nothing to block the visit.

Usually one of the first things a line-up person does in getting the programme planning under way is to form a committee of local Christian leaders from as wide a spectrum as possible. Vladivostok contained six or seven churches for its five hundred thousand inhabitants, but there were deep-rooted divisions among them arising from problems dating back to the 1960s and 1970s when some of the churches went underground, refusing to be registered with the government and conform to its demands.

For example, the government had said that children were not allowed to attend church services. The unregistered church refused to accept that regulation. Other churches, however, decided it was better to go along with the government and accept its restrictions in order to be able to keep the church open for worship. Now there was no longer government regulation, but the suspicions, sense of betrayal and recriminations remained. It was not something that could be resolved overnight.

George eventually had to give up the idea of forming a committee with these churches. The team would have to work on an individual basis with each church. Surprisingly enough, all did support the ship to some degree.

The needs of the Russian people were not only spiritual but also physical. The media had not exaggerated when they made much of the scarcity of common commodities and poverty in the face of escalating costs. The *Doulos* company wanted to respond in some way to these needs as well as to the spiritual needs. They especially wanted to help Christians in a practical way because they saw Christians as brothers and sisters in the family of God.

George wrote a report about how to help the church. One of his suggestions was to provide food items, medicines and a few other things. When he returned to the ship, he discussed his report with ship leaders. Several of them began brainstorming. One person suggested, 'What about making up little food packets with things like milk powder, coffee, tea, sugar, and so forth and giving these to individual Christians?'

More discussion followed until an idea began to take shape. 'Love-packs' containing food items and clothing were to be made up and given to individual Christians, one per person. Not only that; extra packs were to be given to needy people outside the church, but distributed through individuals within the church.

*Doulos* was at this time in South Korea, where it remained for two and a half months prior to the Vladivostok visit. The idea of love-packs was presented to the *Doulos* local committee in each port and to the churches as teams visited them. Korean Christians embraced the project with enthusiasm. Special bags were sold very cheaply. In the bottom, the Korean would put his name and address and perhaps even a photo so that the Russian who received the pack would know who had sent it. Next came foodstuffs and clothing. Not shabby cast-offs, but new good-quality clothing: tee-shirts, warm nylon jackets, a variety of things. Toiletries too, like soap. Perhaps a toy or two. Enough to make up a bag weighing about twenty or twenty-five pounds.

A goal of ten thousand love-packs was set. As the ship's visit to Korea progressed, Christians would bring the packs to the quayside and ship workers would carry them aboard to stow them. That's when ship-members began to get an idea of the magnitude of the project. Bag after bag was carried aboard and ship people learned how heavy twenty pounds can feel. When the pile of bags on the shore grew large, chain gangs were formed to pass them up the gangway and back down into the bowels of the ship. Boards were placed on stairways so the bags could slide down.

322

The ship's holds filled up. Every available nook and cranny was filled up. Over six thousand love-packs had come aboard and the flow had not yet stopped.

At the other end, in Russia too, storage space had to be found.

'All taken care of,' reported the line-up team. 'We've got the use of the basement of the main Baptist church.'

'Do you have any idea how much space ten thousand love-packs will occupy?' they were asked. *Doulos* officers had estimated it to be the space of at least five or six huge ship containers. The line-up team reacted with shock. However, their storage space proved adequate.

When the ship arrived in Vladivostok, she was given the passenger terminal, which was the best possible berth. This was next to the railway station frequented by thousands and thousands of people daily and right in the centre of the city, next to Lenin Square with its large statue of Lenin looking out toward Japan and gloating over dreams of conquest of that country for communism.

The line-up team was told the ship could stay at the berth for only a limited time. For at least three days near the end of the visit *Doulos* would have to move either to anchor or to a cargo berth. That would restrict the ship greatly in its operations.

Those on board prayed about the matter before and throughout the visit. Not once during their week and a half in Vladivostok did anyone come to the ship to mention even the possibility that the ship might have to move.

As usual, the official opening was the first event scheduled for the ship. Russians had already begun assembling for the book exhibition but were not allowed on the ship until after the opening ceremony. They stood patiently in line and waited.

Those on board had not yet been cleared by Immigration to go ashore. Some of them stood on deck, looking down at the line forming on the quayside. Mike Mullins, the radio officer, was one of them. Dressed in his smart white uniform, he had been greeting guests for the reception and was now waiting for it to finish. As he leaned on the railing, he spotted two young Hare Krishna men with rucksacks on their backs. The two men surveyed the situation, observed a dozen eight- or ten-year-olds amusing themselves on the quayside, laughing, talking, playing. The Hare Krishnas glanced over at the adults crowding around the barrier near the foot of the gangway. Then they looked back at the children and walked over toward them. The children appeared fascinated with the men in their startling attire. The men began talking to them and giving them literature.

*Oh, no!* groaned Mike in frustration. *Of all times to be confined to the ship!*

He called one of the deck cadets standing nearby. 'Look at those Hare Krishna guys,' he said. 'We've got to do something. Let's pray about this.'

They began praying, 'Lord, do something. Don't let those children be deceived.'

324 They prayed with their eyes open, watching all the while what was going on. As the did, they saw a large strong-looking older woman with the typical Russian scarf on her head and a Bible in her hand turn in the line and glance toward the children. She nudged the woman next to her and gestured toward the children. Three of the women broke out of line and began hurrying toward the children. When they reached them, they brusquely shouldered the Hare Krishnas out of the way, almost knocking one of them to the ground.

Whatever the women said to the young men, it was effective. They started running away, with the women chasing after them.

The women returned to the children, took the leaflets from them, pointed to the pages and began talking earnestly. The leaflets were ripped up and Gospel tracts given in their stead. One of the women opened her Bible and pointed out something to the children. Then the women patted the children on the back and returned to the line.

Mike, up on deck, couldn't contain his elation. 'Hallelujah!' he shouted.

The women looked up surprised. Then they caught sight of Mike waving to them. 'Hallelujah!' they shouted in return. That seemed to encourage the women. They began singing. The crowd gathered around to listen. The women passed out tracts and talked to the people. They were having their own open-air meeting.

Eventually the ship's crew and staff were cleared by Immigration. Andy Isles, who could hardly wait to go ashore, hurried down the gangway and began giving out some of the three hundred thousand tracts which would be distributed during the ten days in Vladivostok. 'But,' he wrote afterwards, 'my excitement slowly waned as I saw what Russia was like. The best way I can describe the streets of Vladivostok would be to say it was like taking a time walk back into the 1950s. The trams were old; the buildings were old; the streets were old. It seemed that only people were young. And it was the people who got my heart excited again. Never before had I seen people so hungry for the word of God! People could be seen sitting on the side of the street, reading the tracts we had just given them.'

Unfortunately *Doulos* people were not the only ones doing evangelism. The cults, as demonstrated by the Hare Krishna men on the quayside, were there as well. A short time later Andy was travelling with a ministry team on a commuter train to the suburbs where they would be working for the next six days. Seated opposite Andy was a man holding a Hare Krishna book. With his limited Russian, Andy tried to tell the man that the book was bad and he should throw it out the window. The man didn't take the advice. Andy pulled out a copy of the New Testament, pointed to it and said it was the true word of God. At this point, the team's translator came up and helped in the conversation, explaining the good news of salvation. Andy tried to give the man the New Testament, but he refused.

Nor would he accept any Christian tracts. His stop came and he got off the train.

'This was the first of many spiritually confused people I would meet in Russia,' wrote Andy.

A week later this same man showed up at the ship's youth festival and was spotted by a *Doulos* person who had been on the train with him. The man seemed interested in talking further, so arrangements were made for him to come to the ship the next day when there would be more opportunity to talk. The director of the training programme on board was asked to talk with him.

The two men talked for an hour on the following day, contrasting what the Hare Krishna believe with what Christians believe. This was near the end of the ship visit and the supply of Russian Bibles had been sold or given away, but the training director happened to have one on hand — probably the last one remaining on the ship — and offered it to the man. This time the young man accepted it and took it home with him.

The next day, shortly before the ship sailed, the man appeared on the ship again. He just wanted to report that he had made a decision for Christ after he had gone home that night.

Deanna Ricketts was on another ministry team. Hers went inland. Here are some impressions she jotted down:

> I am sitting at a camp for children in Russia, and my team is about to put on a programme. It is day five and I am feeling overwhelmed. People may tell you and tell you

what it is like to do ministry here, but until you are actually here, it is difficult to understand.

People are so confused. They have been told what to do and what to believe for seven decades. Now suddenly they are on their own and they don't know what to believe. Christians are not the only ones coming here to tell them what to believe; many cults are here too.

They are searching for more than just a glib answer. I do not think I have or could possibly begin to touch the tip of the iceberg, but I see that they are occupied with deep issues of life. They do not care so much about outward things like looks and material things. They want to fill the hole inside. Some are very angry. It used to be that everybody was guaranteed a job and food. Now they have no such thing. Prices have gone up to five or six times what they were.

Yet people give us all they have. We are staying in people's homes and they give all they can. They have so little, but they give it to us. Sometimes I find it hard, almost embarrassing. What do you do when you know that you have had plenty to eat and don't need more of the food they have waited in line for and spent time in preparing, food they probably rarely eat themselves? Yet they are so proud to be able to put it in front of you. You want to refuse it but you cannot; it would be like rejecting them. You can see on their faces how happy they are to put it in front of you.

We have meetings all day. One meeting was at a hospital with many older people. They were very interested in us. Even the staff listened to most of our programme. Afterwards one lady stood to thank us for coming. She began telling us that some of the people there were Christians, but they had no Bibles. Many of them, even non-Christians, wanted Bibles but they were just not available.

She did not realize that we had brought some New Testaments and Bibles with us. Eric and I stood at the back of the van selling the Bibles as fast as we could until we suddenly realized they were almost all gone. How sad to have to tell the other people we had no more!

However, we were able to come back the next day and provide more Bibles, as well as have another programme for them. After the programme they kept us for over an hour with intense questions.

The ship was given much publicity in the media. Even national television picked up the event and gave it considerable coverage, all positive. This served a much greater purpose than just bringing crowds to visit the ship. It gave credibility to Christians in Russia. As one local person remarked, 'Before the ship came, Christians were seen as scum.'

Some of the love-packs were picked up directly from the ship, but most of them were transported to a church which served as distribution centre. Two days had been allotted for a small *Doulos* team to accomplish the mammoth task of transporting them from the inner depths of the ship to the storage place, but other personnel pitched in to help in their spare time and local believers volunteered their aid as well. As a result, the two-day job was cut down to one. The goal of ten thousand love-packs had not been reached, but seven thousand seven hundred proved to be enough of a job to transport.

When the team delivered some to one of the churches, they presented a short programme and offered teaching on how to study the Bible. Afterwards church members crowded around the team, introducing themselves and talking eagerly. One older woman told them that in 1957 she had had a vision of a white ship with foreigners coming to Russia to preach the Gospel freely in the streets. [Apparently this vision was widely known in Russia, as *Logos II* had heard of it in 1990 when she visited Leningrad, now St. Petersburg, seven times zones from Vladivostok.]

In one of the staunchly conservative churches, members had been suspicious of *Doulos* at first. Pastor Alexander himself had led them in praying that *Doulos* would not bring bad influences into the church. When love-packs were distributed, many church members held back, not wanting to be tainted by accepting gifts from questionable sources.

As the ship visit progressed, however, attitudes began to change. At the end the pastor remarked to *Doulos* leaders that his church members had been won over by the lives and testimonies of the *Doulos* crew and staff. Two things that particularly impressed him were the times of prayer and the central focus on Jesus Christ in all the meetings. (And in the end, his congregation couldn't get enough of the love-packs!)

These were not the only ones to change attitudes as they saw *Doulos* in action and became involved with it.

Ronnie, on his second visit to Vladivostok when George was with him, had met with the few pastors and Christian leaders they had been able to locate up to that time. One of them was Pastor Dula, who had been pastor of an unregistered, or underground, church. He had undergone much persecution and suffering during the reign of communism. Many of his bones had been broken during interrogation sessions with the KGB. Yet Pastor Dula was quick to point out that not only had he and members of his church suffered but also members of the registered church as well.

At the first meeting to discuss a ship visit, Ronnie and George had sat and drunk coffee with the pastor. (Coffee that Ronnie had brought with him — a real treat for Russians. And not only coffee, but coffee with sugar!) This might suggest a friendly, relaxed social occasion. It wasn't.

Ronnie and George had been subjected to a thorough grilling about the ship, polite but unmistakable. The pastor posed all kinds of difficult questions. Questions concerning drinking, smoking. Questions about the position of women and about headwear. Questions about co-operation with other denominations. The likelihood of this pastor agreeing to work with the ship seemed remote. His line and the policy of his denomination was not to work with other denominational or interdenominational groups. They held to a very traditional fundamentalist position.

All through the discussion Ronnie noticed that the pastor seemed unable to keep his eyes away from George. Ronnie surmised that he had never seen a Sri Lankan before. He seemed fascinated. As time passed, he appeared to warm to George's presence. Learning that George was planning to make another visit to Vladivostok, the pastor invited George to visit him and also come and visit his church.

Of all the pastors Ronnie and George visited, Pastor Dula

was the most reserved and suspicious in regard to the ship visit: both its aims and the actual content of its message.

And then the ship came.

'It would be difficult to describe the transformation in this pastor during the course of the ship visit,' Ronnie reported. 'And the transformation that took place in his church as well. I have rarely seen such taking place. He must have become the warmest — even the hottest — person towards the ship ministry by the end of the visit.

'I was at one of the last services in his church before the ship left Vladivostok. He stood up and confessed to his church that he had been narrow-minded and blinkered and had learned so much from these young people who came from many nations around the world, who had come to teach them and to help them in their own church situation. They had given a great deal to his church. He said he realized now that his church was seventy years behind where the rest of Christianity and the church were nowadays. That was quite some admission to come from a Russian pastor. And to say this in front of his own church!'

When the ship was preparing to leave, many of the crew and staff were out on deck singing and clapping their hands. Getting caught up in the emotion of the moment some of them began dancing around exuberantly. Ronnie, standing on the quayside, saw Pastor Dula lean toward his wife and heard him remark, 'Even David danced before the Lord.'

Ronnie always became nervous when he saw *Doulos* people doing something which might appear extreme to some of the very traditional members of the church in Russia. He had been quite wary about the thought of including folk-dancing in the International Night, which was held on shore. Ronnie was amazed and relieved to hear Pastor Dula explaining to his church that these were nothing more than traditional dances and therefore permissible for Christians. Ronnie found it quite impressive to see a pastor standing up before his church defending the actions of a foreign group. Wholeheartedly defending them because he believed these things were right in their context and they as a church had much to learn from this group.

Nevertheless, at a final meeting with pastors and Christian leaders, George Barathan, speaking for the ship, in his gentle, unassuming voice asked the Russian believers to forgive ship people if they had offended them in any way.

A final comment by Ronnie:

> I cannot think when I have been so touched or seen pastors so touched by a visit of the ship.
>
> In Russia it is customary for believers to kiss members of the same sex on the mouth, so the pastors were all going around kissing each other on the mouth — which, of course, to us westerners was not quite the done thing. But I do recall that at the farewell breakfast on *Doulos* for the pastors and Christian leaders, quite a few of us were so caught up in the emotion of the moment and the sense that God had done a great work there in Vladivostok that there were kisses all around.

George had not been able to get pastors to come and work together in a committee to plan the ship visit. Yet when the ship was leaving, they not only came together, they were kissing one another. Amazing what God can do when he is the one at work!

# 19

## Terrorist Attack

The time in Vladivostok came to an end just before the first anniversary of what had undoubtedly been the most traumatic event in the history of *Doulos*, an event that occurred on 10 August, 1991 in Zamboanga in the Philippines.

Following normal procedure, a line-up team had gone to Zamboanga weeks ahead of *Doulos* to prepare the way. The team had set up a committee of local Christian leaders to advise and help plan the programme. This too was customary practice, but it was particularly important in Zamboanga because there was a lot of tension in that part of the Philippines, with many Muslims wanting to make the island of Mindanao, where Zamboanga was located, an independent state. The team relied heavily on the advice of the committee for safety procedures as well as for planning a programme.

The big fear of the committee was kidnapping. A number of people — particularly westerners, who were assumed to be rich — had been kidnapped and held for ransom. Kendra Schneider, the only woman on the line-up team, rarely went anywhere alone. If it was absolutely necessary, she went in the middle of the day and took a 'tricycle', the popular three-wheeled taxi of the Philippines.

334

As long as sensible precautions were taken, local Christians saw no danger for *Doulos* crew and staff, but the ship took extra safety precautions nevertheless. The 'two by two' rule of going ashore in groups of at least two people was strictly enforced; at night the group had to be larger. Watchkeeping procedures were also made more stringent. Nothing was to be left in public rooms or alleyways; items found there should be assumed to be dangerous. Visitors coming on board should be searched for firearms or explosives. The list went on.

As the visit progressed with no signs of trouble, however, vigilance was difficult to maintain and some ship-members — though not the crew on duty — became relaxed about observing safety rules.

Zamboanga was a busy port for *Doulos*. There were many church meetings and a wide-open opportunity for evangelistic outreach. Teams were able to hold open-air meetings throughout the city and visit universities and colleges to share the gospel.

Many of the ship's company had had little or no experience of working in a country with a high proportion of Muslims. What little experience they had was in countries where it was illegal to talk with a Muslim about Christ and consequently there had been little interaction with Muslims. The ship's leaders were quite concerned about giving proper orientation for the situation in the Philippines. A local pastor with sixty years of experience among Muslims was invited to live on board and give the *Doulos* community teaching about Islamic beliefs and culture. He gave guidelines and advice in relating to

Muslims, cautioning *Doulos* people to show sensitivity in what they said and did. The bottom line of his message was this: show love and don't be confrontational or say negative things about another person's beliefs, his prophet or his holy book.

On Saturday, after *Doulos* had been several days in port, George Barathan, who was programme manager at the time, approached the guest pastor after dinner to make sure everything was going well for him and his wife and that they were being made to feel at home on board. As the pastor had some free time, he and George went for a stroll on the deck to talk and pray together.

In the course of the conversation the pastor mentioned his disappointment with a *Doulos* meeting in a local high school. His granddaughter, who attended the school, had reported that one of the team members in the course of his testimony had made a derogatory remark about Islam. While most of the students showed no emotional reaction, a few had clearly been offended. The pastor himself was quite upset about the remark and George promised to make sure such a situation was not repeated.

On Monday morning George plunged into a day filled with appointments and paper work. When tea break came at ten thirty, he was glad to dash down to his cabin to make himself a cup of tea. He was in the middle of preparing it when the phone rang. Three Muslim students on board wanted to talk with a ship's leader. George went up to meet them.

The students were very keen to set up a debate at the university on the subject of Christianity versus Islam.

George tried to refuse in a diplomatic way, saying 'I'm sorry. We already have a very busy weekend planned. Besides, we don't like to get involved in debates about religions. We'd be glad to send a team, though, to share about the ship if you would like that.'

336    No, they wouldn't like that. They wanted a direct confrontation. A debate.

'I have an appointment now so I can't talk any more now,' George finally had to tell them, 'but I'll check about your idea for a debate and get back to you on Wednesday morning at ten thirty, if that's all right with you.'

Promptly at ten thirty on Wednesday morning George was informed that three men were at the information desk asking for him. Feeling he needed someone with maturity and experience to help him handle the situation, George sought out the Filipino pastor on board and gave him a quick overview of what had happened as they went to the visitors' lounge where the students were waiting. Two of the students had been to the ship on Monday; the third was new to George.

George introduced the pastor, who began talking with the visitors in their own language and getting acquainted with them. After a few minutes, one of the students turned to George and asked in English, 'What about the debate?'

'Well, we've thought through your request,' George told him, 'but for several reasons we believe we cannot have the meeting.' He went on to give his reasons. The coming weekend was a busy one with International Night on the Saturday and many church meetings on the Sunday. People were simply not available for another meeting on Saturday.

Furthermore the ship was not into debates and dialogues about Christianity and Islam. Her purpose was to share the love of Christ wherever her people went but not to condemn any religion.

The Filipino pastor nodded his head, expressing agreement.

One of the students turned to him and with mounting anger began rattling off something in the local language. George rightly conjectured he was telling the pastor about what had happened at the school meeting. After a few minutes, the pastor broke off the conversation and turned to George to give him the gist of what had been said. He informed George that the tallest student, the one who was doing the talking, was president of the Islamic Student Body at the university. The student admitted that he had not been at the high school meeting himself, adding that if he had been present when the negative remark was made, he would have stoned the speaker.

George turned to the students and said in a gentle voice, 'Please forgive us for saying anything like that. We as a ship are not here to condemn Islam. If such a statement was made by a person from the ship, it expressed only his own opinion and did not represent the view of the ship.'

As the conversation continued, the students seemed to cool down and appeared more friendly, even accepting gracefully the refusal of a public debate. They talked further about the ship, wanting to know what those on board normally did when they went to a port. George explained the usual programme and emphasized the fact that they always worked with local churches.

Before the students left, they thrust two booklets into George's hands and strongly urged him to pass them on to the person who had made the remark and make sure he read them. George agreed in a pleasant tone. Then turning to the pastor, he asked in a low voice if it would be appropriate to give the students a New Testament in return. The pastor thought that would be fine. George excused himself for a moment and returned with three New Testaments.

'I have something to give you too,' he told them. 'It's a New Testament. If you'd like to have it, you're welcome to it.'

Without any hesitation they each reached happily for a New Testament. Goodbyes were said, hands were shaken and they left the ship, apparently satisfied with the visit.

Some of the people involved in the International Night scheduled for Saturday evening began to express misgivings. Without any tangible reason they were becoming fearful. Suzy Bus, co-ordinator for the programme, suggested cancelling it. She got together with the line-up team leader and several ship leaders to discuss the matter and pray about it. They came to no conclusion but agreed to get the advice of the Filipino pastor who was on board and also to discuss the matter with the local committee members.

The pastor felt the event should not be cancelled. The committee members agreed, arguing that this was the first time the mayor and his staff had publicly provided support for the Protestant church. (He had offered help in building the stage for the event and in blocking off the street in front of the city hall. He was also planning to provide fifty security personnel.) With such support from the mayor's office, it would be inappropriate to cancel the event now. Besides, a cancellation would reflect adversely upon the evangelical community. And they were the ones who would be left behind when *Doulos* departed.

Bowing to the opinion and counsel of local Christians, the ship's leaders decided to go ahead with the event.

The *Doulos* company prayed for a nice day for International Night, especially important since the programme was to be held outdoors. Saturday dawned and with it came the heaviest rain of the entire stay in Zamboanga. A nearby island was completely blotted from sight by the downpour and a strong wind was blowing in as well.

The technical crew usually started immediately after breakfast to set up for the programme, but on this day they had to delay preparations because they didn't know where to make them. Would the rain pass over so that International Night could be held in the city square? Or would the venue have to be changed? They could only wait and see.

After lunch the rain was still coming down. The ship's leaders met with the advisory pastor and other local Christian leaders to discuss alternate venues. It was suggested that they hold the programme in the nearby ferry terminal. Local believers saw no problem with security for an event within the port area. The decision was made. City authorities were informed and the message went out to the public via radio and television announcements.

The ferry terminal had a number of advantages, chief of which was its corrugated roof to provide shelter from the rain. It was really a sort of shed with a concrete floor and breeze-block walls about four feet high. At one end were two or three offices and at the other, a few shops. In between was open space with benches set around for waiting passengers.

By five o'clock the rain had tapered off into a light drizzle. It was a muggy, oppressive afternoon as about fifty *Doulos* cast members filed down the gangway and walked five or ten minutes along the quayside to reach the terminal building. The ship's carpenters were already there hastily constructing a makeshift stage and a technical crew was arranging lighting and sound.

Rehearsals had been held on the ship to allow the technical preparation to proceed unhindered, so all that the cast needed to do at the site itself was to run through the main items quickly. After that was done, the group gathered backstage for prayer. One of the participants wrote about this time of prayer: 'I had been to the International Night in almost every port since I joined, but never had we had such a powerful and moving prayer-time before the show. We sang praises to the Lord together and particularly asked God for protection as we shared his message with the Filipino audience. Suzy Bus, the show co-ordinator, requested that we have a prayer chain during the whole performance so that at all times prayer would be going on.'

The port area was busy as usual when the International Night got under way shortly after six o'clock. Ferries were coming and going, discharging passengers and picking up new ones. Enterprising merchants were hawking their wares. Even the crowd visiting the *Doulos* bookshop was almost as big as usual. All that in addition to about fifteen hundred Filipinos assembled in the ferry terminal to watch the *Doulos* performance.

Inside the building a two-foot-high stage had been erected in front of the offices. One of the offices was being used as a dressing room, with a heavy blanket hung over the large plate glass window to provide privacy. To make a backdrop for the stage, a number of big flags had been draped along the back. Most of the cast sat huddled on the floor in a small space of about eight by fifteen feet between the back of the stage and the dressing room/office. A bench had been set to one side of the stage; the captain and four other people sat on it. High barriers placed perpendicular to the stage on each side screened the backstage area from the audience.

The performance began with a colourful parade as representatives from different countries marched on stage in their national dress. Participating for the first time was Sofia Sigfridsson. A friend noted in her diary about Sofia, 'Thank the Lord. She has finally found the courage to stand black and beautiful to represent her blond-hair-and-blue-eyed-dominated country of Sweden . . . .'

Sofia had been adopted from Ethiopia as a baby and taken to Sweden to grow up. Finding her own identity had been no easy process. Yet that afternoon after rehearsal when a *Doulos* friend had put an arm around Sofia, giving her a friendly squeeze and teasing, 'Everyone will know you're from Sweden because of your blond hair and blue eyes,'

Sofia had laughed along with the woman. A genuine laugh, knowing she was accepted for who she was.

Another item in the International Night programme was the Papua New Guinean *Paravetta* dance. Sometimes when there were not enough *Doulos* performers from a particular country, other nationalities would be recruited to fill in. Fawzia Abd Elnour had been pressed into service this evening to fill out the numbers for the *Paravetta* dance. Fawzia, who had grown up in an orphanage in Sudan, was one of those who had felt uneasy about International Night, not just because she was participating but because of something else. Something undefinable. She had hoped the programme might be cancelled. During rehearsals on the ship she had seemed to hear an inner voice saying, 'Prepare a small bag for the hospital.'

*Now what does that mean?* she had wondered. *Is it a warning or simply a bad thought come to trouble her?* She had prayed that God would take away any evil thoughts, but she did take along an extra blouse just in case it should be needed.

It was her first time performing the dance and she was rather nervous. Her eyes searched out Suzy Bus, directing from the front row of the audience. Bouncing and swaying in rhythm on her seat, Suzy was doing all she could to encourage the performers. Fawzia fixed her eyes on Suzy, smiled at her and danced, forgetting everything else.

A new item on the International Night programme was the Scottish Country Dance. Because this was the first presentation, its dancers were understandably both apprehensive and excited. They'd had lots of fun practising together, praying together and even partying together after their final practice the night before. They too had recruited a 'foreigner', Karen Goldsworthy from New Zealand. Just before the show as one of the cast members helped her with her hair and make-up, Karen had commented, 'If only Mum and Dad could see me now! I look so *feminine!*' She did indeed look lovely in her red and white dress.

The dance had become special to Karen because in preparation for it she and another participant had gone shopping for black shoes. The two had used the expedition as an opportunity to clear up some tension that had developed between them. The result was a much greater closeness and appreciation of each other.

All the time the programme was going on, people were praying behind stage. Kendra Schneider recalls that as she came off stage dressed as a southern belle from the United States, she felt hot and very thirsty. 'I got frustrated because there was a group of people praying and one of them was sitting on the water jug. I couldn't get a drink. I had just come back from my performance and I was thirsty, but I also respected the fact that they were praying and I didn't want to interrupt. *It's great that they're praying*, I thought, *but why couldn't they be considerate and realize somebody might want a drink?*'

Much of the International Night programme was pure entertainment, but some items had a serious thought embedded within. The mime-dramas fell into this category. The chicken drama could always be counted on to raise a lot of laughs as various *Doulos* people flapped around on the stage like chickens. The point of the drama was that acting like a chicken doesn't make one a chicken; just so, acting like a Christian doesn't make one a Christian. The second and last drama portrayed a twentieth-century traveller trying all sorts of things in an effort to find meaning in life; at the end he realized it could only be found in Christ.

344

Finally Chacko Thomas, an Indian who was assistant director on *Doulos*, came on stage with a short but very direct message about the five wounds of Christ: in his hands, head, back, feet, and side. He pointed out how we sin against God with these parts of our bodies. Christ, the sinless one took all our punishment.

As all this was going on, the building was packed and people were standing outside peering over the low wall. Behind them, others were milling around or walking past. On one side of the terminal a number of jeepneys, the Filipino taxi-buses, were parked and spectators had climbed on top of them to see better over the heads of the crowd. A Filipino *Doulos* volunteer standing at the back noticed a tall dark man with wavy shoulder-length hair milling around, throwing an occasional glance toward the stage. Several times he commented in the local language to no one in particular, 'You *Doulos* people see what will happen to you now!' Intent on the programme, people near him may have given him a curious glance, but no one paid him much attention.

Nate Fawcett, an American who had performed in the last mime, was sitting behind stage with the rest of the cast. He takes up the narrative at this point:

After our drama, Chacko Thomas, took the microphone to give the closing challenge. Meanwhile, backstage something seemed to compel the rest of the participants to pray. I have never seen a group of people so united in prayer. I'm not trying to spiritualize things, but that's the way it was. God was there!

As I stood there dressed all in white, praying that God would save and call people to himself that night, I heard a loud, flat explosion followed immediately by the sound of shattering glass. A round, black object came sailing backstage from outside. It hit a bench and skittered along the floor until it came to a stop about two metres in front of me. I stared at it, thinking it was a rock. Suddenly, everything moved into slow motion as I realized it was not a rock but a grenade! I couldn't move. I just stood there dumbly staring. Joe Parker, the book exhibition manager and my boss, jumped in front of me and threw himself at me, hurling both of us back into the doorway of the dressing room. As we staggered back, one thought flashed through my mind: *What is it like to die from a grenade blast?* And then it exploded.

Immediately there was complete and utter silence. Then everyone in the audience began screaming, shouting, and yelling hysterically, madly pressing toward the exits. When I raised myself up, my foot fell in a puddle of warm liquid. Blood! I stepped out of the dressing room, and my first thought was, *I must find Cynthia* (a special friend of mine)!

My mind in a fog, I limped around backstage desperately looking. One of the first people I saw was Sofia. She was lying on the floor, her eyes wide open, staring at nothing. She had been dressed in white, but all I could see now was red. I took her hand and began praying for her, but I soon realized that she was beyond prayer. God had already claimed her for himself.

I stood and once again began searching for Cynthia. I remember being irritated because blood kept flooding into my eyes from a cut on my head, but it didn't register in my mind yet that I needed help myself. At this point, God clearly said to me, 'Nate, Cynthia is in my hands. You need to help others.' I turned and looked around. There was blood everywhere, covering everything. I saw Elmar from Germany trying to carry Darek from Poland who was delirious and bleeding profusely. I limped over and took Darek's legs, helping to carry him to the waiting vans and ambulances. As I stumbled along, I knew I needed to start singing. It was as if Jesus was forcing my vocal chords to work.

> *Praise the name of Jesus*
> *Praise the name of Jesus*
> *He's my rock*
> *He's my fortress*
> *He's my deliverer*
> *In him will I trust*
> *Praise the name of Jesus!*

© Word Music UK 1975
used with permission.

When we arrived at a van, we put Darek inside. Just then I felt someone tap me on the shoulder. I turned around and there was Cynthia! I hugged her and held her, thanking the Lord that she was safe. She said she was okay but, looking at me, she was shocked. Evidently I looked a lot worse than I thought I did. By this time my foot was just a bloody pulp with blood streaming out of it. I was covered in blood, my white clothes accentuating the effect. As we stood there, I was grabbed by a man in an army uniform who shoved me toward the van. I tore my arm away and tried to convince him that there were people who needed to get to the hospital much faster than I did. He wouldn't listen, as much as I protested. He yelled at me. 'You're bleeding all over and you can't walk! Now get inside!!!' At that point, because he was stronger than I was, he half lifted, half pushed me into the van.

Then the pain hit! Up to this point, my foot, back, thigh, and head had been mercifully numb, but as soon as I lay down in the van, waves of pain began spurting through my body. I didn't realize that I was capable of hurting so much.

The ride to the hospital was very short and on the way God gave me the strength once again to sing. The van was literally crammed with wounded and helpers, all together about fourteen people. On the way, we decided who were the most critically wounded, so that they could get inside the hospital first.

As soon as we arrived, Trudy Stearns, the American who was driving the van — and rivalling any Grand Prix champion — jumped out of the driver's seat, ran around to the side door, single-handedly hefted Darek up and hurried toward the emergency room yelling, 'I bet you've never been carried by a woman before, have you, Darek?' On her way, a motorcycle blocked her path. With Darek still in her arms, she calmly kicked it out of the way. Although the humour of the whole thing didn't fully strike me until later, it still served to lighten the atmosphere a bit.

I hopped, hobbled and was finally dragged into the hospital. The doctors, nurses and staff were in a panic.

348

Imagine a peaceful Saturday evening suddenly shattered by dozens of people being carried in, absolutely drenched with blood, and not having decent facilities to handle them. Add the fact that it was impossible to tell who was injured and who was just helping, because *everyone* was bloody. At this point I don't remember exactly what happened, but I know I was left lying on the floor in the foyer of the hospital in intense pain for quite a while. Eventually, as the hospital staff saw more and more people coming in, they realized that there was no way they could cope. They arranged for eight of us guys to be transferred to another hospital. We were put in an open-backed van belonging to a local Christian and were driven — or flown, it seemed — to Zamboanga Doctors' Hospital, where we were taken immediately to the emergency room.

Trudy Stearns, the driver of Nate's van, tells something of her reactions:

More than any other International Night that I've been involved in, almost everyone spent the whole time in prayer instead of socializing and preparing for what would be next on the programme. So while we were loading people into the van, my mind kept yelling at God, 'We were praying. Why did you let this happen?' As I slid behind the wheel, I made another mental comment to God, 'I hope you don't expect me to pray at a time like this. I have nothing to say.' That's when the injured in the van started singing. Never have I felt the overwhelming presence of God so strongly. I was immediately calmed and just repeated over and over for hours, 'Father, Father, Father.'

Kelly Inae, from Papua New Guinea, had been seated behind stage on the floor writing a letter when the compére Joe Parker, came looking for somewhere to sit down. Kelly had picked up the towel lying beside him and offered it to Joe to sit on so he wouldn't dirty his suit. Five or six minutes later a grenade had landed on the cement and slid in front of them.

349

'A bomb!' exclaimed Joe.

Kelly had never seen a bomb or a grenade before. Into his mind flashed pictures from war comics he had read at home. The object on the floor looked like what he had seen in the comic books. He scrambled up and tried to get away, but it exploded and caught him on his left leg from the foot up his side to his arm. Some bits caught him on the right leg as well. He fell face down on the concrete floor. Some of the shrapnel had gone into his stomach. The pain was awful. *This is it*, he thought. *This is the end of my life!* He cried out to God, 'Lord, forgive whatever wrong I have done today. Restore my life.'

In his mind a voice seemed to say, 'My purpose has not been fulfilled in your life.'

From that moment fear of death left him. He tried to stand but found it difficult because his left foot was numb. Although he didn't know it, the shrapnel had entered below the knee and severed a nerve. He clutched his stomach and hobbled along until two Filipino friends he had made in port came and helped him out to the vans.

Lynn McKane remembers:

> I was listening to Chacko speak on the wounds of Christ and praying when I heard the metallic bounce on the floor.

I caught a glance from two girls who saw the grenade and I knew what it was. Perhaps my Northern Ireland background had heightened my awareness of danger. I started to run. My reaction was to get away. I expected the whole place to erupt into violence. I shouted, 'No, no, no . . . !' but had taken only a couple of steps when I felt a searing and paralysing pain in my hip and hand. I thought my hand had been blown off and my relief at seeing it still there lessened the shock of finding it covered in blood from my injured forearm. I ran on some more steps into an office. A man stood there counting money. I yelled at him to help but he looked stunned. Then I fell on the floor and the pain in my hip prevented me from getting up again. Cynthia came in. She ripped off the apron from my costume and tied it round my arm. I had the absurd idea that nobody would find me there so I kept shouting to Jesus and anybody else! Minutes later I was carried to a jeepney and taken to hospital.

Cynthia Smith was another one of those who saw the grenade and realized what it was. In the next few minutes she heard sirens and saw wounded people being piled into vans and *Doulos* people hugging each other. With a dazed feeling that none of this was really happening, she went all the way back to the ship without realizing she was hurt, except for one of her arms which was bleeding. She later recalled:

I wandered around for awhile looking for a Band-Aid and I remember thinking, *This is very strange. People are bleeding and no one has a Band-Aid. I should be able to find a Band-Aid right now because so many people are bleeding.* I went into the main lounge where some of the ship's nurses were helping people. When they had me lie down to clean my arm, I realized my entire back and rear end were wet with blood. It was only then that I discovered I had lots of pieces of shrapnel in me. I was taken to the hospital.

Fawzia's account went like this:

> Participants were praying behind stage. Suddenly we heard what sounded like a gunshot which broke the light backstage where all the participants were praying. This was followed by two hand grenades. One fell about a metre from me, just in front of Sofia, and exploded. When I could not stand the smoke and the strong smell, I bowed my head and prayed.
>
> I heard different voices crying, 'Everybody lie on the ground; they are coming with guns!'
>
> 'Watch out!'
>
> 'Run!'
>
> 'Blood! . . . . Blood!'
>
> I was still sitting on the seat and could not move. I looked to my left. Everybody had gone. I looked to my right. People were still there but seemed far away. I decided to join them.
>
> The moment I stood up I noticed blood flowing out of my neck. I asked one of the brothers for help. I was shocked, trembling and the brother was shocked too. He was trembling; his eyes were wide open and he tried to back away. At that moment I became unconscious.

Mark Laing, the ship's dentist, was backstage sitting with the others. He initially thought the public address system had blown out because the place became dark and fragments of glass were blown toward him. He had the impression of someone falling towards him: Then he heard screams coming from the audience as they tried to get out of the building, pushing over benches and trampling on each other in the process.

352     He ran toward them, thinking there must be gunfire. He tried to climb over the barrier fence that had been placed beside the stage. Another man joined him and together they pushed it over and ran toward the exit.

Reason finally reasserted itself and he returned backstage to see what had happened. He saw a *Doulos* man lying face up on the rear left corner of the stage, bleeding from his legs but conscious. Beside him lay Fawzia. People were standing around her. She had been injured in the neck and blood spurted from a small puncture in her neck.

A local Filipino said they must get her to the hospital. 'Put pressure on her neck,' he said to Mark, 'See if you can stop the bleeding.'

Fawzia had regained consciousness and wanted to hold Mark's hand. In the meantime, the Filipino located a blanket and with the help of a couple of other people they put Fawzia on it to carry her out to the ambulance.

They hurriedly made their way through a crowd of people, some of whom were trying to peer backstage to see what had happened. Running around the outside of the building toward the quayside, they saw a vehicle with red lights. It turned out to be a police car rather than an ambulance. To the left, though, they spotted a van and headed towards it.

As Joe Parker, the American manager of the bookshop, had come off stage from introducing a performance, he had seen Sofia sitting in his seat on the bench. She didn't look as if she was feeling very well.

'Oh, I'm in your seat,' she apologized and started to get up.

'No, no,' Joe told her, 'that's okay. Just stay there.'

He moved backstage where Kelly offered him a towel to sit on. Sitting and listening to Chacko's message, he heard what sounded like a couple of coke bottles breaking. He looked up and saw what he took to be a rock headed for the cast seated behind stage. His eyes followed it as it hit someone on the shoulder, flipped up and landed about two feet from where he was sitting.

*Oh, no!* he realized in horror. *That's not a rock; it's a hand grenade!*

In retelling his story he said,

> My first thought was to try and pick it up and then I felt God speaking to me. He said, 'No, that's stupid. You have a family. Just go.'
>
> I turned around toward the dressing room and started to run when the grenade went off. Several of us were trying to get into the room and the force of the explosion blew us right in. In some ways I felt closer to God at that time than I ever have in my life. I remember waiting to see Jesus. I figured being that close to a hand grenade I had to die and I was just waiting to stand in front of Christ. So many things go through one's mind in such a short period of time. In some ways I was disappointed when I realized I was still alive and able to move. I had been waiting to see Jesus.

354

I got up and went out into the open. Dead silence. People were lying on the floor, but there was dead silence. I remember then having such tremendous anger in my heart. I wasn't directly mad with God, but I was mad with the angels. I said, *Where were you guys? You were supposed to be here to protect us.* I remember then God's prompting and telling me to get out of there. Just leave. I knew people had been injured but I felt in my heart that God was saying, 'Go back to the ship. Go back to the ship.'

I went out and climbed into the back of a jeep. The guy wanted to take me to the hospital but I said no. I had quite a fight with this guy to get him to take me back to the ship.

It was good that Joe persisted, as events would soon show.

## 20

## *Crisis Response*

With so many people involved in International Night, the *Doulos* information area had been very quiet. The Singaporean woman on duty was coming to the end of her shift. She was deliberating whether to vacuum the area while it was empty, when suddenly the Zamboanga line-up team leader burst in, obviously agitated about something. He demanded the keys to a van, barked out an order to summon all medical personnel to the International Night venue and rushed out again, flinging out an explanation as he left. Something about a bomb.

Stunned, confused, apprehensive, the Singaporean and her Swiss co-worker immediately phoned down to the director in his cabin and to the women's leader. Seconds later they were paging for deck officers, the doctor, nurses. Emergency procedures were activated. And then blood-covered people with shocked white faces began to stumble in, many of them being helped by others. They were taken into the main lounge where chairs were pushed aside to allow them to lie down on the carpet as needed.

The women at the Information desk, however, were not the first workers on board to learn the alarming news. An Australian, Glen Doris, was leading the shift working on the book exhibition, which was well attended but not over crowded. The first indication that something was wrong came when one of Glen's workers suddenly shouted loudly to the visitors, 'The ship is being evacuated. Will you please put down your books on any table and go to the exit.'

Glen was taken by surprise. As shift leader, he knew that any emergency procedures like evacuation needed to go through him. He hurriedly made his way toward the man who had made the announcement.

'What's the trouble?' he asked.

'I don't know, but Joe's come back to the ship all covered with blood. Something has happened at International Night. He says to get the people off the book exhibition.'

Glen immediately went to the microphone. 'Attention, please! There has been an on-shore emergency and we are asking you to leave the ship. There is no danger to you here on the ship. I repeat. There is no danger here, but we need to evacuate the ship.'

He went on to give instructions about leaving behind the books that had not yet been purchased and proceeding toward the exit. A translator repeated his words in the local language.

The crowd left in a relatively calm and orderly way as workers watched to make sure everyone actually left the ship.

When the last visitor was gone, book exhibition workers gathered together, alarmed, concerned, confused. Some were crying as they joined hands in a circle and began to pray. They still didn't know what had happened or that anyone besides their boss had been injured, but they prayed for the people who had caused Joe to bleed.

[An interesting sidelight given later by Bernd Gülker was that in the three years he had served as director, he had never seen or experienced a full evacuation of the ship. Not until Zamboanga, that is. Emergency drills were normally carried out during times when the ship was closed to the public, so only ship crew and staff were involved. But at the beginning of the Zamboanga visit about nine hundred students had come aboard from a naval college. They happily agreed to serve as a sort of rent-a-crowd for an emergency evacuation drill. They were told what was going to happen, so the main value of the drill was the experience for *Doulos* crew and staff. As a result, when the real emergency came, *Doulos* people knew exactly what to do and the evacuation could be completed within minutes.]

Shortly before the evacuation several *Doulos* people had spotted a man coming on board carrying something metallic in his hand. Suspicious, the gangway watchman had reported it immediately to the book exhibition shift-leader, as well as to one or two other people. Just after the call, Joe Parker arrived covered with blood and the order was given to evacuate the book exhibition. Visitors began streaming to the gangway. The man with the metallic object was caught in the stream.

Unfortunately, no one knew if the man had been able to plant the device on board before he left. Once the ship was secured on the outside, a complete sweep was made of all areas which had been opened to the public. No bomb was found, but several suspect parcels were turned up. Not equipped to handle this kind of item, the ship safety team left the parcels untouched until bomb disposal teams were made available. The professionals pronounced the parcels harmless and then proceeded to give the area another search before leaving, satisfied that no bomb had been planted aboard.

358      As soon as the evacuation of the public was completed, all available crew were summoned by five rings of the alarm bells and a call for the control team to report to the gangway. One of the crew was a Malaysian deck-hand who had returned early from International Night immediately after his part in the programme. He was in his cabin bathroom when the alarm sounded. *What a strange time to be having a drill!* he thought. But he pulled on his clothes and went up on deck to investigate. As soon as he stepped out on the cardeck near the gangways, he saw people on the quayside running toward the ship from the International Night venue. Police were scrambling into their vehicles and driving off. Several of the *Doulos* crew had already assembled on deck. One of them informed the Malaysian that a grenade had been thrown. His heart started racing.

Second Mate Steve Baker shouted orders. Someone was already on one winch to lift the gangway but no one was manning the other one. The Malaysian shouted to the mate that he would take the winch. Within ten to fifteen minutes with only two officers, a cadet, two deck-hands and a few volunteers, both gangways were raised and secured. That was record time.

Volunteers were posted at several points as watchmen. Several canoes on the starboard side evoked concern, but an army helicopter came and hovered above until the canoes moved off.

Meanwhile, *Doulos'* rubbish bins and waste buckets sitting on the quayside were carried aboard via the mid-ship crew gangway. Within minutes everything was on board so the ship could be closed up at a moment's notice. A couple of deck-hands ran to fire stations on board and grabbed two axes to have at the ready to cut the mooring ropes in case of an attack on the ship.

After seeing and hearing Joe Parker, the immediate reaction of *Doulos* leaders was to get everyone back on board and accounted for. A couple of drivers were sent to the terminal building to bring back the injured who had not already been taken to the hospital. An announcement was made on the public address system that everyone on the ship should come to the main lounge for muster. Their names were then checked from an alphabetical list.

About this time, a group of local people, mainly businessmen, came aboard and offered their services, which proved invaluable. They had organized themselves into a communications network called *React* to help in disasters or other emergency situations. Carrying their own powerful radios, they based themselves on the ship and at the hospitals where *Doulos* people had been taken. With their help, *Doulos* leaders were able to account for almost everyone within an hour of the explosion.

Some of the more seriously injured who had returned to the ship were taken to the hospital. George Barathan helped to carry Joe Parker to an ambulance at the foot of the crew gangway. After lifting Joe inside, he climbed in after him. Joe's wife went along as well.

On the way to the hospital Joe kept saying, 'We shouldn't have had this event. It was a stupid thing to do.' George felt guilty because he was one of those who had made the decision. Joe's wife diverted their thoughts by starting to sing some well-loved choruses.

George takes up the narrative:

> When we arrived at Brent Hospital, we found a large crowd there already. No one seemed to be in charge to monitor the people, especially inside the wards where our patients were being treated. Joe was brought to a bed. I tried to go from bed to bed to visit, but there were too many local people, along with a few nurses, rushing here and there. It was hot and stuffy without adequate ventilation.
>
> I was relieved to find Simon Slator, a six-foot *Doulos* deck-hand, helping at the hospital. 'Sofia is gone,' he told me.
>
> I was deeply shocked! He took me to her room. Sitting with her was a Filipino brother, keeping watch and mourning. Anger mixed with sadness filled my heart. I kept asking, 'Lord, why did this happen?' After a few minutes I left the room with Simon. The Filipino brother remained.
>
> While I was going around to see the patients once more, Simon came to me again and said, 'Karen is gone too.' In one corner of a ward I saw her lying on a bed with her eyes closed. There were a few people standing around her.
>
> I felt then that I needed to get back to the ship soon and inform Bernd [the ship's director] about the two deaths.
>
> I returned to *Doulos* and as I walked through the main lounge, I saw the ship's staff praying in many parts of the

main lounge and port lounge. Bernd was at the front, with Chacko [the assistant director] standing a bit further away. I broke the news to Bernd about the deaths of Sofia and Karen. He immediately turned away and broke down in tears. I sat beside him on one of the chairs and put my arm around his shoulders to comfort him. Soon Chacko joined us and he too was deeply disturbed by the news.

Five minutes later, Bernd got up to announce the news of the deaths. As Bernd mentioned the home-going of each person, the ship staff began to cry, hugging one another for comfort. It was a very moving sight for me. After a little while, people began praying together in small groups. Chacko took much of the responsibility to lead the people in prayer. He was a great strength to Bernd during those difficult hours.

Requests were coming in from the hospital for blood donations, first for a specific type and then for other types as well. Many of the ship people volunteered to go to the hospital. One of them was Kendra Schneider.

Because Kendra had helped with the line-up and knew her way around Zamboanga, she was in constant demand for information, for communication, for talking with the media, for many things. Not until two o'clock in the morning did she finally fall into bed. But first she left her name and blood type on record at the information desk in case her blood type was needed. At two-thirty the call came. Kelly had her blood type and needed blood for an operation. Kendra got up and dressed.

At the hospital she spent forty-five minutes undergoing various tests to be sure her blood was acceptable. Four people had gone in from *Doulos*, but only two were accepted as donors. Kendra was one of them. Kelly needed 1000 cc. for the operation. The hospital would take only 500 cc. from any one donor. The first donor gave blood with no problems, but when it was Kendra's turn, her small veins collapsed. Nothing would come out. The hospital technician tried her other arm and managed to draw out only a very tiny trickle.

'Try my leg! Try anywhere else! You've got to get blood for Kelly!' begged Kendra.

'Sorry. We can't do it. You can't give blood.'

*Now what's going to happen to Kelly?* wondered Kendra. Frustrated that she couldn't force the hospital to take blood from her, she walked over to the desk where the lab was located, put her head down and broke out crying. It was the first time she had cried that evening. She cried and cried. 'Oh, God,' she pleaded, 'you can't let this happen. Don't let him die just because my blood won't come out. Please don't let this happen. Bring in blood somehow.'

After she had cried herself out, she wiped away the tears and sought out one of the hospital staff. 'Isn't there someone else who has blood?' she questioned. 'Don't you have some blood in store that could be used?'

The nurse obligingly investigated and discovered 250 cc. that belonged to someone else. The someone else had died two days earlier and obviously had no further use for the blood. It turned out to be just enough to get Kelly through the operation.

Blood was not the only thing needed by the hospital staff. It soon became apparent that they lacked many basic supplies. Quickly a supply line from the ship was organized to take medicines, bandages, syringes, blankets, toilet paper, and even food and drinking-water. The ship also provided someone to stay beside every injured *Doulos* person in the hospitals. The ship's doctor was already moving from hospital to hospital checking on *Doulos* patients.

Claudia Schroeder, an Australian, was one of six nurses on *Doulos* who attended International Night. Because she wasn't participating, she sat in front of the stage. Like the other six *Doulos* nurses, all of whom escaped injury for one reason or another, Claudia was immediately pressed into service. She accompanied one of the *Doulos* women from the ship to the hospital and remained there all night, wandering around and filling in as needed, sometimes attending to patients, sometimes talking with reporters. When it got too much for her, she would slip outside for a few minutes. That didn't get her away from people, though. Outside were crowds of people. She found herself talking to them about her faith, surprising herself with an uncharacteristic boldness.

By three in the morning most of the chaos had died down. A number of patients had been shifted to other hospitals. Claudia stayed with two patients requiring the most care. Sometime early in the morning when she was not needed, she slipped into the room where Karen and Sofia lay, accompanied by a Filipino friend of *Doulos*. No one had yet had a chance to take care of them, so Claudia cleaned the bodies. She had no idea how long she remained there. Time had lost all meaning for her.

Around six in the morning she and another nurse went into Joe Parker's room. His wife had been with him all night. The three women sat together for half an hour or so, their conversation gradually leading toward prayer. While they were praying, the sun began to rise. It was during this brief respite that Claudia finally stopped and thought over what had happened. Up until this point everything had been a big blur. There had been an emergency and she had simply been doing what had to be done. Now for the first time it sank into her consciousness that a grenade had exploded.

Her adrenaline kept her going almost non-stop throughout the next day, although she did go back to the ship and try to sleep. An hour was all she could manage. Then she was awake and restless, feeling the call to action. Back to the hospital she went.

During that Sunday she accompanied Sofia's and Karen's bodies as they were transferred to another hospital where the morgue was located. For Claudia this trip was an ordeal. Everyone seemed to be staring at them as they drove through the main street of the city. As Claudia looked out at the people, her mind was tormented with the thought, *Any one of you out there could have done this*. She remembered the night before when she had stepped outside the hospital for a few minutes and heard someone remark, 'Oh, you mean only two were killed? We were hoping there would be more.'

When Claudia had washed the bodies of the two women a few hours earlier, she had been dry-eyed and professional. At the time she had thought, *This is crazy. These are two very good friends of mine and I can't cry over them*. Now, open to public view on the streets of Zamboanga, the tears began to flow. Yet she didn't know why she was crying. Nothing seemed quite real.

Lynn McKane, the young woman from North Ireland, tells of her experiences that night in the hospital:

> After an initial examination when they had established that my life was not in danger, I was left in a room. Above me was a single strip light from which cobwebs hung in ribbons. I had no pain killers and I couldn't move much because of the pain. I couldn't believe what had happened. I lay there thinking, *I hope they don't have to tell my parents* because they were older and I didn't want to shock them. Little did I know that it would end up on international news.
>
> Lilias, a local Christian lady, looked after me in *loco parentis*, caring for me as my mother. She stayed by my bedside, despite all my protests that she ought to go home to her family. She prayed for me, held me, washed me, helped me with the bedpan (terribly difficult with my hip injury) and just sat there ready to react at any moment all night. She dozed off sometimes but if I moved she was awake and reaching out to help. I was deeply touched by her love and care.
>
> All through the night *Doulos* nursing staff carried in supplies: bandages, medicines, toilet paper. The hospital had very little. In the middle of the night the surgeon came in to say that he had run out of instruments so I would have to wait a few hours for my operation. I wasn't going anywhere anyway!
>
> At nine o'clock I went into the operating room. I was relieved that there seemed to be no cobwebs there but

thankful that I couldn't look closely! Three hours later I emerged with forty-one stitches, mostly in my hip and arm.

I awoke at around seven in the evening to see two *Doulos* people smiling over me, excited that I was awake. They read to me from the Bible, prayed with me, wept with me.

366

Nate Fawcett, the American who had sung as he was being taken to the hospital, continues his story:

One of the most precious memories I have of that night was when a Christian man came into the ward and asked me if I wanted a Bible. My voice shook as I told him that yes, I wanted a Bible. Five minutes later he returned. Tears filled my eyes as he handed me his own personal Bible and said, 'Here, this is for you. You keep it.' I immediately turned to Psalm 23 and read it out loud. Most of the others in the room quoted it from memory along with me. We then passed the Bible around the beds and each person read his favourite passage out loud. It really was a blessed time!

We were in that hospital for one day and two nights, and it was quite an experience in itself. We had cats wandering around under our beds and no air conditioning. If anyone needed a painkiller, he first had to sign for it and then the hospital would send someone down the street to the local drugstore to buy it!

'In that hospital I truly realized for the first time in my life what the body of Christ is. The whole time that we were there we had a non-stop stream of local Christians coming by. They were very sensitive and didn't stay for long, but just came to pray with us and to express their love and pain at what had happened. Some brought us small presents, even some ice-cream, but above all, the love they showed us was amazing. I watched person after person come into the ward, look at us, and have their eyes fill with tears as they helped to carry our pain. I felt so much support from these wonderful brothers and sisters. Many times since then I have begun to cry when I remember their actions.'

Later on Saturday night when things had largely settled down, Greg Hallam decided it was time to return to the venue to retrieve the expensive sound-system he had set up there. He was told that it was too dangerous for foreigners to go ashore: only Filipinos were being allowed to go back to the venue. The problem was that Greg alone knew how to dismantle the equipment and pack it away. And that was something which needed to be done soon or, despite the guards around the terminal, the equipment would undoubtedly prove irresistible to enterprising looters.

Greg organized a group of Filipino friends to help him. With high motivation, the job which normally took an hour and a half was accomplished in thirty minutes. The group also collected into bags the left-behind shoes, clothing and other belongings of *Doulos* people. Greg found it 'an eerie job to go back to the venue again. To see the place empty, to remember what started as a night of joy and celebration but ended in death and chaos. To see the many pools of blood all over the ground and to view the hole in the concrete floor where the grenade exploded. We finally hit bed emotionally and physically exhausted around four o'clock in the morning.'

*Doulos* leaders and many other ship members worked through most of the night, organizing, communicating, keeping the *Doulos* community updated on what was happening and caring for the hurting and grieving. Sunday brought more of the same.

Chief Engineer Tim Wilson took responsibility for making arrangements to send the bodies of the two fatally injured women to their respective countries. A Catholic youth group held vigil outside the funeral parlour where the bodies were taken. A vigil was customary in the Philippines and this group decided to stand in for the families who couldn't be there. One of the *Doulos* local committee had a good conversation with the group about death and assurance of salvation.

A Sunday morning service was held on board, offering an opportunity to express to God and to one another what people were feeling. No message was given, but various individuals spontaneously led the singing of hymns and choruses, prayed or simply shared thoughts.

Bernd, who had planned to lead the service, was called away a few minutes before the start. The mayor and some senior military officers wanted to talk with him. The military had already offered help in transporting the injured to Manila for better care and greater security. On Sunday morning the decision was made to airlift as many as possible. One of the military officers offered to bring a special plane from Manila. The patients would be flown out as soon as possible, preferably that same afternoon.

Arrangements proved too numerous and too complex for a Sunday afternoon departure, so Monday morning was set as the time for lift off. On Sunday night the *Doulos* chief engineer and the chief steward drew up a plan of action. Twenty patients and their aides had to be moved simultaneously from four hospitals to avoid delays once the plane had arrived in Zamboanga. Most of the patients had to be carried on stretchers, as they were still weak from the surgery they'd just undergone. For security, all of this had to take place without the benefit of radio communication to co-ordinate movements.

That was the major part of the operation. There were other smaller yet important matters to attend to as well. X-rays and medical reports for each patient needed to be collected. Their friends on the ship had to pack some extra clothing for them. Food, drink and medical supplies for the two-hour trip had to be organised. Someone had to check each hospital for personal belongings that might have been left behind. Many such behind-the-scenes details had to be foreseen and taken into the planning.

At eight o'clock on Monday morning Operation Airlift went into action. By ten o'clock the patients began arriving at the military airfield in ambulances. George Barathan went around checking on each arrival and ticking the name off his list. Some of the patients managed a weak smile as they were transferred from the sturdy comfortable ambulance stretchers onto extremely narrow, purely functional ones designed for the aircraft. By this time the sun was high in the sky and blazing hot. The only shade was offered by the big, squat, full-bellied Hercules military aircraft sitting on the runway. Patients were placed under the plane to take advantage of its shade.

A large door in the rear underside of the plane folded down to form a ramp. Military personnel lifted the stretchers one by one and carried them up the ramp into the primitive interior of a plane designed to transport troops, vehicles and supplies in time of war. The sides were lined with upright metal posts containing hooks at three different levels. The poles on one side of the stretchers were fitted into the hooks. The poles on the other side of the stretchers went into clips on straps that hung down from the ceiling. The results were three-tiered bunkbeds, repeated again and again along the sides of the aircraft and down the centre as well.

Two of the seriously injured remained behind. All the other injured were carried on board. Last to arrive was Fawzia. George noticed that she was struggling to cough out the phlegm in her chest. Her mouth looked dry. A couple of *Doulos* nurses wet some tissues and pressed water around her lips.

When everyone was inside the plane, Bernd prayed, committing them to the Lord. The noisy engines began to rev up. *Doulos* personnel who were not going to Manila moved back out of the way and the tailgate was closed, making it even hotter inside.

The take-off at eleven thirty went smoothly. There were no instructions to fasten seatbelts. George stood beside the stretchers to make sure everything was all right. The Air Force medical team had been very helpful thus far and continued to monitor the patients, particularly Fawzia and Kelly, the two in the most critical condition. Earplugs had been handed out to provide relief from the deafening noise of the aircraft.

370

Lynn McKane had been told as soon as she woke from her operation on Sunday that she would fly to Manila the next day. Her later comment was:

> I thought they were crazy I imagined trying to sit in an aircraft seat. Impossible! But as it turned out, in spite of the circumstances and discomfort the airlift was quite exciting. It certainly helped me to stop thinking of the tragedy.
>
> Some people were singing, praising God and very joyful. I wasn't. I felt numb. I didn't doubt God; I just couldn't understand the meaning of protection any more. When others sang or prayed, I felt very moved and cried. It was a very emotional time.

A gentle landing at 1:24 pm was followed by a bit of a shake-up on the bumpy runway. Stretchers bounced and intravenous feeding apparatus jiggled. George looked with concern at some of the more seriously injured patients.

The plane came to a halt. The tail door was opened. And a storm broke loose as the press swarmed in!

George was taken completely off guard. This was, after all, a military base. How did members of the press get in? And how did news leak out about the airlift here? George expressed his feelings in a diary:

> I was very tired by this time and very concerned for the patients. I had no time to meet the press. I wished they would go away! Couldn't they be a little bit sensitive for the moment? I could understand why some cameramen and journalists get punched!

He had his hands full as at least twenty-five or thirty mediamen swooped on the patients, badgering them with questions, particularly about the unfortunate remark about Islam that had been made in a school meeting. Afraid that one of the *Doulos* people might come out with an unconsidered statement that could set a spark to a potentially explosive situation, George rushed around urging them to reply, 'No comment.'

The dentist, Mark Laing, who had also accompanied the patients, had his share of frustration with newsmen as well. He noted in his diary:

> The tail door was lowered while we were still coming to a halt. Once stopped, we were immediately swarmed by over thirty photographers and a few TV cameramen. They didn't wait outside the aircraft but came right inside. . . . I allowed them in for a few minutes until one photographer jumped on top of our luggage. I pushed him off and, getting angry, started to clear them out.
>
> They stood on the tailgate, not making room for us as we brought out the luggage. I said, 'Excuse me,' to no avail. So I pushed them out of the way.

George stood in the plane and watched as one by one the patients were carried out by the stretcher party and loaded into military trucks, vans and ambulances. Then he stepped out onto the runway, hoping to blend into the anonymity of the crowd. No such luck. Word quickly spread that he was spokesman for the group and he was rushed by reporters. He gave them an interview which was cut short as the medical motorcade began its journey toward the hospital, racing with army escort and sirens blaring. Even so, some of the reporters managed to make their own way to the hospital in record time to be there and waiting for the hapless victims.

The hospital in Manila was fitted out with the latest equipment. Doctors and nurses began making their rounds, testing blood pressure, checking blood types and X-rays. Five hours passed before the last patients were finally accommodated in comfortable wards with two or three in a room with its own bathroom. They were well looked after by both hospital staff and local believers who came to visit them.

Back in Zamboanga *Doulos* people who had been less seriously injured returned to the ship. They arrived hobbling on crutches, with arms in slings, or with bandages on their bodies, but their mood was joyful, and joyfully they were welcomed 'back home'. Rohan, an Australian, came with patches covering both eyes. He laughed as his friends tried to direct him around the ship. The doctor had assured him that his eyesight would be fine, but Rohan commented to ship people that as long as what was upstairs — he tapped his forehead — was working okay and as long as he could still worship God, that was what was important to him.

When the *Doulos* contingent returned to the ship after sending off the airlift patients, Bernd learned that the captain had been warned of further threats ahead, particularly when the ship sailed through the islands to Tawau in East Malaysia. *Doulos* leaders discussed the threat and tried to decide what should be done.

The navy had requested that *Doulos* leave as soon as the current made departure possible, which would be around dusk. *Doulos* leaders decided that would be wise, even though it meant leaving a day sooner than had been planned. One problem was that a group of Filipino young people were planning to join the ship for a three-month STEP (Short Term Exposure Programme). They were due to arrive on the ferry from Manila at 7:00 pm. *Doulos* was scheduled to leave at 6:30. They would just miss each other, probably even seeing one another in passing. The decision to sail without them was a difficult but necessary one.

Amazingly, instead of arriving late, as often happens, the ferry arrived early, which almost never happens. Two hours early! In less than half an hour the STEP people were through Immigration and Customs, on board and ready to sail.

Another decision made by *Doulos* leaders was to have the hull of the ship combed for limpet mines. Again the armed forces offered their help and expertise, sending down trained divers. The ship was clean.

Shortly afterwards *Doulos* set sail into the sunset, escorted into international waters by a naval vessel. Her route was kept secret.

374

# 21

## Lingering Pain

What lay behind the attack in Zamboanga? Who had done it? Why?

Rumours flew thick and fast in Zamboanga. Steve Baker, safety officer on *Doulos*, pieced together what little was known and gave this report:

> Two grenades were thrown. One hit the captain on his shoulder. We believe this was the grenade which failed to explode…. The grenade which did not explode was investigated by the local bomb disposal experts, and this revealed that the grenades used were M 55 Fragmentation Grenades, fitted with a three-second delay fuse. This grenade is not designed to kill, but to cause maximum injury….
>
> We consulted both our own people who were at the events and the Armed Forces and bomb disposal experts to put together a full picture of the events. It seems that this hit was highly organized, the two grenades being thrown simultaneously so as to get maximum effect. We think probably up to twelve people would have been involved: the two that threw the grenade, a few people just mingling as look-outs and some to drive a vehicle so as to attain a getaway for those who threw the grenades.

A search by police at the originally-planned venue in the town square turned up five hidden grenades. If the attack had taken place there as planned, the carnage would have been far more terrible.

No one claimed responsibility for the attack at the time. Not until a couple of years later after the budding terrorist group *Abu Sayyaf* had successfully carried out several kidnappings and armed assaults against Christians, leaving a number dead or wounded, did they finally begin to boast about their part in the bombing of a missionary ship in 1991.

According to a report in the *International Herald Tribune*, of 26 May, 1995, the leader of the terrorist group, as the teenage son of a poor Muslim fisherman, had been attracted to the fiery anti-government diatribes of an Islamic scholar. Though he was young and quiet at the time, his rapt attention had been noted by the revered orator. On closer acquaintance the Islamic scholar became so impressed that he arranged a scholarship for the young man to go to Saudi Arabia and on to Syria to become grounded in Islamic teachings.

Abubakar Janjalani left the Philippines as a shy young man. He returned as a fiery fanatic calling for a *jihad*, a 'holy war,' against the government and against the Christians whom he viewed as settlers on the island of Mindanao. His message of hatred, violence and destruction became a magnet for disaffected young Muslims.

Apparently ideology alone was not enough to satisfy the group. They wanted action. Something big, decisive, shattering. Something that would capture the attention of all the Philippines. Something that would strike a devastating blow to Christians and demonstrate to the world that Abu Sayyaf was a force to be reckoned with.

And yet they remained silent after the attack on *Doulos* people, perhaps disappointed that the response to their horrific action had not lived up to their expectation, whatever that might have been. At any rate, the newspaper *Malaya*, on the Wednesday after the bombing carried this statement: 'The remarkable thing is that one of them [*Doulos* victims] said he had forgiven "the people who did this" in true Christian fashion, while Muslims of Zamboanga issued a statement of apology and disclaimer.'

And elsewhere in the paper: 'A Muslim religious leader, Ustads Abdulagani Yusop, condemned the attack in an open letter and expressed hope that the perpetrators would be brought to justice.'

And on a personal level many individuals, Christian and Muslim alike, expressed their abhorrence of what had happened and offered sympathy and support for *Doulos* people.

*Doulos* crew and staff had been dealt a heavy blow and the pain was terrible. Yet in the midst of the shock, confusion and suffering was a sense that God was in control, a confidence that he loved his people and would carry them through.

Why had two women, not yet twenty years of age, been snatched away by death? There was no answer. Nevertheless, God's hand could be seen even there. In the port before Zamboanga, Karen had gone out on a ministry team called an A-team and something significant had happened to her. She wrote out a brief account to share in the last Sunday evening service of the team:

. . . . There have been many hard times where God has been at work moulding and shaping me. Before leaving for this A-team, life was difficult for me. Everything seemed to be going wrong and I was hurting. I did a lot of crying, but I made a big mistake by not crying out to God. I tried to sort things out in my own strength. The night before we left the ship, I realized I couldn't go on as I was. I was just getting into a mess. I spent time till early in the morning talking, crying and praying with a friend. I left one prayer request with her: that while on A-team I would see God in a new way and regain my first love for him.

'We arrived here and began our programme. I was involved and doing my part, but my heart wasn't in it. I felt God was a long way away. At many of the meetings there was praise and worship, but I couldn't worship. There was an uncomfortable barrier between God and myself — my pride and stubbornness. As the first week went on, I tried to ignore the emptiness, the restlessness I was feeling in my heart, but I could see all around me Christians who had great joy and an obvious love for the Lord. I realized I needed to get right with God! I finally gave in, handed over my burdens to the Lord, and came back into his waiting arms! Then what a *joy* it was to go out on meetings! I *enjoyed* the times of praise and worship with churches. God is so loving and forgiving. The first week I had felt so alone; it was good to turn around and go running back to my father's arms!'

Karen Goldsworthy and Sofia Sigfridsson had gone into the arms of a loving father. They were beyond all pain. They were safe.

For the living the pain was only beginning.

The first evening at sea Bernd called the ship's community together to give an update. He told them of the grenade found in the port area by a lamp post. He mentioned that he had heard that another man had been apprehended moving toward the ship with a grenade. He tried to give people as complete a picture as possible, though he did keep silent about one thing: further threats to the ship. *Doulos* people had enough to handle without adding another fear.

Bernd realized that in the aftermath as people tried to put everything together, questions would surface. Why did *Doulos* go to Zamboanga in the first place? Why was International Night not cancelled? Why? Why? Why? While these were legitimate questions, they could stoke up criticism and accusations against ship leaders, against fellow-workers and even against themselves. Bernd talked frankly about this. He then told them that the leaders wanted to release them as much as possible from any pressures. If they had any needs, the leadership was available to help. The meeting ended with a fresh sense of commitment to one another.

On board were about thirty Filipinos. On Tuesday, the second night at sea, Bernd held a meeting with them. He told them he realized they too were suffering in a different way. Because this had happened in their country they might assume people were blaming them. Bernd reassured them that no one blamed them, that those on board *Doulos* had made many friends in Zamboanga. It was not just members of the ship who were wounded, but also the Christian community in Zamboanga.

The audio-visual team had taken video footage of *Doulos* patients in the hospital and as they were airlifted out of Zamboanga. The team worked throughout Monday night editing the film so that it could be shown on Tuesday evening after the Filipino meeting. Most people had not seen the bodies of the two young woman who had been killed nor had they been able to see the patients leaving. hospital because security precautions had restricted crew and staff to the ship. Seeing the video of their friends and fellow-workers brought the events of the past days into the realm of reality.

On Wednesday the ship arrived safely in port and lay at anchor. The next morning a farewell service was held for Sofia and Karen. Goodbyes must be said, so that *Doulos* people would be able to put the past behind them and move forward. Bernd gave a message based on Revelation 12, but much of the two-hour service was devoted to voluntary sharing by many of the crew and staff. Tears flowed freely.

Dale Rhoton and Peter Maiden (associate international director of OM) flew out to Manila and arrived the day after the injured were airlifted. For a couple of days they spent time with each of those who were hurting, individually and in community. To the astonishment and delight of *Doulos* patients, the international director of OM, George Verwer, phoned each one of them and talked personally for a few minutes.

Having spent time encouraging, comforting and reassuring those in Manila, Dale and Peter went on to the ship, which by that time had reached Tawau, East Malaysia. There they spoke to the ship's company, giving them a report from Manila and offering counsel and affirmation. Much time was spent with the leadership, trying to get the feel of the situation and help in planning what to do next. The rest of the time they were simply there to be available for individuals to talk with them on a personal level.

Another person who flew into Tawau to be of service to *Doulos* people was Dr. Marjory Foyle, who had worked for many years as a medical doctor in India before focusing on stress and trauma counselling. She was a highly qualified psychiatrist with much experience in counselling trauma victims in war-torn parts of the world.

One of the first things she did when she came aboard was to speak to the entire ship community to help them understand what happens when people are grieving, why they felt as they did and reacted in ways that might have seemed out of character.

In counselling leaders, Dr. Foyle advised them to watch the sleeping patterns of people, as many were having trouble in this area. Food, fluid and sleep were extremely important at this time. If people couldn't sleep, the doctor should provide medication to help them sleep.

Those who had been at International Night were divided into four groups, each with a ship's leader. Dr. Foyle told them that in any such situation, there is loss and there is gain. She asked them to discuss what the loss was and what the gain was. This helped people to realize that there was gain as well as loss.

For the rest of the week Dr. Foyle was available for people to make appointments to talk privately with her, particularly those who had been most severely affected.

Recognizing symptoms of grief and trauma didn't eliminate them, but it helped in working through them. Some of the *Doulos* people did that quickly and relatively easily. For others it was a long and painful process.

382 Several comments a couple of months later give an idea of some of the struggles the *Doulos* people were going through. Suzy Bus wrote:

> Lots of us have had sleep difficulties. For me that has been the greatest strain — bad dreams and lack of sleep so much so that my stomach and arms hurt. The good days are now getting better and the bad days are less often.
>
> I am seeing God's word in a new light. Some of its promises have taken on new meaning and new delight. Worship is more precious because my Saviour is more real to me. There has been a deep hurt and longing inside me to go back home and 'be safe' but slowly the Lord has been showing me the essential importance of finishing my job here, facing all the issues here and now and not leaving them till later.

Markus Zaugg of Switzerland commented:

> That I had not one thought of hatred or revenge really showed me God in us makes the difference. Before I always wondered, *Is it possible really to forgive such a terrible thing out of our heart or do we make it up in our mind because we have to?*
>
> When we came together in the hospital room, we sensed the presence of God like never before. We had such pain we couldn't sleep that night, so we started singing praise songs, prayed and read Bible passages. It was nearly unbelievable.

And Cynthia Smith, from the USA:

> Physically I am fine now, though I lost twenty pounds due to stress and a lot of sickness in the weeks after it happened. In Singapore I had an operation on my hand, and they were able to remove three pieces of shrapnel. That has healed, so I can play my flute and guitar again.
>
> But emotionally I still feel very strange. This sort of traumatic situation affects many areas. One of the hardest to deal with is my concentration span. I can't read or write for a long period of time. Also, I have flashbacks where suddenly the entire event replays like a movie and I can't turn it off. And I miss Karen so much!

The first time Claudia Schroeder, one of the nurses, returned to the ship for a short relief from hospital demands was on Sunday morning. Not knowing if her best friend on the ship had been injured, she made her way to the woman's cabin, knocked and opened the door. The cabin was pitch dark. Claudia let out a scream and ran as fast as she could upstairs again to be with people.

On another brief visit to the ship, Claudia had gone to her cabin to gather a few things to take back to the hospital. Her cabinmate walked in behind her and touched her on the shoulder. Claudia screamed. She explained later, 'I didn't realize how much on edge I was, because I felt very calm inside, very controlled.'

Later as she had watched the air-lift plane take off, it had felt as though part of her was gone. She had spent most of the past thirty-six hours nursing the patients and now they were gone.

Returning to the ship she needed to sleep but was restless.

She didn't know what she wanted to do. For the first few days there seemed to be people crying everywhere. Claudia herself felt completely frozen. She didn't know how to react or what to do. She just sat there day after day trying to comfort those who were crying. The ship was very quiet. If she went to the dining room to sit, she would find people whispering quietly there. Occasionally something would bang or someone would unexpectedly brush against another person and that person would jump in panic.

When the time came to sail, three hundred people gathered on the quayside to see the ship off from Zamboanga. As they waited, they began to sing, *Onward Christian Soldiers*. Claudia was very touched. The sun began to set. Everything was still, very still. Suddenly the atmosphere seemed like that at International Night just before the attack. Tension was in the air. One of the ship's officers came out on deck and told *Doulos* people lining the railings, 'Everyone go inside. They've found a grenade near the bow of the ship on the quayside.'

*This is it*, thought Claudia. *It's all over.*

She went into the dining room. People sat there silently, no one saying a word.

Claudia sat down and closed her eyes, thinking, *Lord, it's all over. They're going to throw it. We're all going to die now.* She was scared.

A verse came to mind, 'For his sake we face death all day long.' *Am I willing to die?* she asked herself. She couldn't answer the question.

She joined a couple of friends. As they held hands and prayed, her fear gave way to a sense of peace.

She continues her story:

When they announced in the main lounge that Karen and Sofia were dead, a lot of people started crying and spent the next few weeks working through their feelings. But I was busy, doing what had to be done. If I broke down and started crying in the hospital, I knew I would be useless. I had to keep going.

Finally when everything died down, I thought with relief, *Now I can cry.* But I couldn't. My emotions were completely frozen. I had got to know Sofia really well just a few months earlier. The night before the attack I had been sitting on the stairs with her and another girl, talking and laughing and having a great time. The next day she was lying dead. I remember telling myself, *Cry, Claudia, cry! Cry! Come on. This was your friend!* But I couldn't cry. Then I felt guilty.

I started getting frustrated with myself, thinking, *What's wrong with me? Am I such a hard person?* I'd think and think and think about what had happened to try to make myself cry, but I couldn't.

For a long time it all seemed like a big dream and not reality at all. There was so much confusion. I couldn't make sense of anything. I couldn't explain to people when they asked how I was feeling. I didn't know how I was feeling. I didn't know how I was doing.

The first time I felt there was a breakthrough really deep into my emotions was when we were in Taiwan seven months after the attack. I was walking along the street with another woman. We were talking and laughing when suddenly there was a huge explosion next to the building we were walking past. It sounded exactly like the explosion in Zamboanga. I jumped and then kept on walking. All of a sudden my whole body went completely numb. I came back to the ship and I must have cried for four hours straight. I couldn't stop crying.

I went up to the bow. I didn't want anybody around me; I just wanted to cry. People kept coming and putting their arms around me to comfort me and I thought, *I don't want comfort. I just want to cry. I need to get this out.* After I'd cried it out, I felt, *Now I am human. I've been able to cry. I'm not so hard.* I felt that the ice had melted away. There was pain and yet release.

# CONTINUING ON 1994–1995

| 1994 | 1995 |
|------|------|
| South Africa | |
| Tanzania | Cyprus |
| Sri Lanka | Djibouti |
| India | India |
| United Arab Emirates | United Arab Emirates |
| Bahrain | Qatar |
| Oman | Kuwait |
| Jordan | Seychelles |
| Turkey | Kenya |
| Ukraine | Tanzania |
| Romania | Mozambique |
| Italy | South Africa |
| Malta | |
| France | |

# 22

# Business as Usual

Malaysia provided a safe haven for the ship. During the week in Tawau *Doulos* people were free to go ashore or remain on board, to take part in ministry or not to do so. Above all, they were encouraged to rest.

While proceeding with the scheduled two-week visit to Singapore, where several of the injured took advantage of the top quality medical help available, ship leaders hastily rearranged the future itinerary of *Doulos*, looking for ports that would release crew and staff from as much stress as possible: ports in which they would feel safe, where English — the common language of the ship — was spoken and where ministry demands would be light. Western Australia was the choice and the next three months were spent there before resuming the rest of the Asian tour.

In October a number of *Doulos* people came to the end of their term on the ship and were replaced by new recruits. A year later most of the others who had been through the Zamboanga experience, apart from leaders, had left the ship. Gradually thoughts of the horror were pushed into the background by the demands of the present and the increasing presence of people who had not been in Zamboanga.

Yet some of the injured continued to struggle with pain,

both emotional and physical. After the attack Fawzia was unable to use her left hand. That meant she couldn't cut up her food but had to ask someone else to do it for her and risk getting an off-putting response from someone who didn't understand. Fawzia found it very humbling to have to explain. Sometimes the person would then apologize and do it for her — but sometimes, not. Occasionally Fawzia threw away food even when she was still hungry simply because she couldn't cut it up.

She was told she should have another operation on her hand, but she was afraid it might only make her hand worse, bringing a lot of pain but no help. Eventually she did have the operation and found it helped considerably in bringing motion to her fingers, but she still couldn't grip well with them.

There was other pain too. Even four years later the pain in her neck sometimes made it impossible for her to get into a comfortable enough position to be able to sleep. The pain was particularly bad in the heat and *Doulos* was usually in hot places.

Then there was the pain in her foot where shrapnel had lodged between the toes. It hurt whenever she did much walking.

Most ship workers came for a two-year commitment and then left. Fawzia was one who remained for a longer period and was given the responsibility of looking after the volunteers in each port. As a long-termer, she was expected to take her turn giving lunchtime an-nouncements near the end of the meal. She found the process very awkward because she couldn't grip with her

390

injured hand. She had to pick up the paper on which the announcements were typed and carefully situate it in her injured hand before picking up the microphone with her good hand. Because she felt very self-conscious with everyone looking at her, her injured hand would begin to shake. Then the shaking would spread to the hand holding the microphone. The experience was such an ordeal that she asked to be relieved of the responsibility. The person in charge evidently didn't understand the extent of Fawzia's anguish and simply encouraged her to look upon the task as a challenge.

Someone on the ship, however, did notice her discomfort and offered to take her place. From then on, every time her turn came up on the list, the announcements were made by her stand-in, George Booth. *Captain* George Booth.

The incident in Zamboanga had left a scar, a pain that would never be completely eradicated, but it had not put an end to the mission of *Doulos*. *Douloi* continued to go and work faithfully aboard her, serving their God and reaching out to people in need.

But in 1993 as *Doulos* left Asia for Africa and points beyond, she faced another very different crisis which threatened to end her days at sea.

The grand old lady needed a 'heart transplant', as it was termed. Her direct current (d.c.) electrical system with its aged hotch-potch of wires was fast becoming obsolete. Most ships had long since switched to the more efficient alternating current (a.c.) and it was becoming increasingly difficult to find men who had experience with the old d.c. machinery. Replacing old equipment and finding spare parts had also become more difficult and expensive.

The time had come to face the issue. Was it worth the huge expenditure of money and labour to convert the system to a.c., a project estimated to cost two million dollars even when all labour was freely donated? Or had the time come to lay the old lady to rest and look for a newer ship or perhaps even a completely new one made to order?

Research gave a clear answer. *Doulos* was such a soundly built ship that she could sail well into the next century if she received the 'heart transplant'. The cost of replacing her with another ship which would require extensive renovation was astronomical.

And so began a project that was to last six months, at least the visible part of it that took place while the ship was laid up in Cape Town, South Africa. Much thought and effort went into preparations. Ten thousand hours of thinking, discussion, planning, ordering supplies and building electrical panels. Volunteers at two Swiss electrical factories constructed 170 of the latter, the most complex of which required 350 hours of work and contained 400 relays, 180 pushbuttons with lights, 5,000 terminals and over 3,000 yards of wires. More than thirty miles of cable were installed throughout the ship.

From around the world practical workers came to offer a week, two weeks or several months of their time. All *Doulos* staff not involved in the project were sent ashore, most of them on ministry teams, and the ship was turned into a giant, cluttered, grime-laden, junk-strewn workshop and construction site. Labour was intensive and working conditions Spartan, but the camaraderie was great as people worked with a will.

The financial cost of the project hung heavy over the *Doulos* leadership. The ship barely managed to keep afloat financially as it was. What would happen when the considerable income from book sales was eliminated and two million dollars of project bills added?

Dale recalled his conversation with George Miley shortly after entering the ship ministry. The ship ministry hadn't changed in the way in which it encountered one critical need after another, but God hadn't changed either. When the ship sailed from Cape Town, all but three hundred thousand dollars had come in from people in many parts of the world. The remaining amount soon came in as well. The Cape Town port authorities waived port fees for the entire six-month stay, a huge saving for the ship. In addition local people donated goods and services of many kinds: bed linens, food stocks and so on.

For a group of *Doulos* people a highlight of the time in Cape Town was an invitation to tea at the official residence of Mrs. de Klerk, wife of the then president of South Africa. In the course of the conversation she remarked, 'You on *Doulos* know what it means to be servants and to have responsibility towards one another. That's what we want to see happening in this country. South Africa is experiencing a time of freedom, but with freedom comes responsibility. We are in the process of establishing a government built on justice and righteousness, which we know comes only from God. Please pray. . . .'

When *Doulos* had sailed into South Africa in early 1993, only about five hundred South Africans were involved in world missions outside of their country. Because of apartheid South Africans of all races were barred from many of the most spiritually needy countries in the world. But in 1993 those barriers began to fall. When *Doulos* sailed away the following year, she carried with her over forty South African workers.

Their presence was a great blessing but also a potential source of problems. Because there were so many of them on board, their presence was strongly felt. Tension among them would inevitably radiate out and affect the rest of the ship's company. And with the prospect of South Africa's most crucial election coming up in late April, uncertainties, fears and distrust had fertile soil in which to grow. No black South Africans were on board at this time, but there were eight or nine 'so-called coloureds'. The other 80 per cent were whites.

Theo Dennis was one of the 'so-called coloureds'. As preparations were being made for International Night in Tanzania, Theo approached the young white woman who would be representing South Africa in the costume parade.

'What flag are you going to carry to represent South Africa?' asked Theo.

The woman looked at him in surprise. 'Why, the South African flag, of course.'

She meant the traditional one and Theo questioned the wisdom of that. The flag had become a controversial issue as it represented all the regime had stood for in the past decades. Unable to convince the white woman that there was a problem, Theo finally walked off a bit upset but willing to drop the matter rather than make an issue of it.

In India a short time later, though, Theo took his frustration to Mike Hey, an Australian currently serving as ship's director. 'Carrying the old South African flag in the countries we have been visiting is a high security risk,' Theo told him. 'It's the symbol of an oppressive regime. No sports group would dream of carrying it outside the country; they'd use the new one designed for the five-year transitional period.'

Mike looked thoughtful as Theo continued, 'Not only that, but the flag is offensive for some of us on board. It's like someone was walking around sporting a big black swastika.'

Mike nodded. 'I see what you mean. I guess if it's not representative of all the South Africans on board, we shouldn't use it.'

It was never again used on board. The new flag was ordered. It took many weeks to arrive and in the meantime, South Africa dropped out of the flag procession at International Nights.

One issue might have been dealt with, but tensions didn't ease up. By the eve of elections the strained relationships were obvious to others on *Doulos*. South African whites and coloureds would pass each other with averted eyes and no greeting. Suspicion had become a major divisive factor. *What are you really thinking? You don't know what I'm thinking and I'm not going to tell you.* Distrust grew sending ripples throughout the ship's company.

On 25–27 April elections took place, the momentous elections that swept Mandela into power at the head of a new South Africa. *Doulos* South Africans eyed each other warily.

Mike Hey finally decided something must be done. On the Sunday after the elections, he called together all the South Africans on *Doulos* and talked about the fears of South Africans. Yet Theo felt that what he addressed was basically the fears of the whites. No recognition was being given to the election as a victory for righteousness and for the kingdom of God after seventy years of apartheid and three hundred years of oppression in southern Africa.

People sat tense and silent as Mike spoke. Theo decided it was time to bring his point of view out into the open. 'It's a new day for the oppressed. We coloureds on board feel this is our day. We've been liberated from white oppression. Finally our voices can be heard and democracy can be fully implemented.'

The meeting proved to be an exercise in futility. There seemed to be no way to build a bridge of understanding between the two races. It was not that the whites did not want changes to come in their country; it was more a that they feared what might happen as the changes were attempted.

A couple of weeks after the elections, Mike called all the South Africans to come forward during the ship's Thursday evening of prayer. The rest of the ship's company prayed for them, asking God to reconcile them to one another. Later on in the prayer meeting, one of the coloured women stood up in front of everyone and explained how she felt.

Her family had been oppressed for many years, really oppressed, and now this new day of liberation had come for them.

A white South African woman stood up and, speaking in behalf of all the whites on the ship, asked for forgiveness for the oppression and apartheid. Even though she tried to speak for everyone, however, individuals were at different stages and each one had to work through things on a personal level.

'Nevertheless, since that prayer meeting,' Theo reported a couple of months later, 'relationships have improved. We, a coloured family, are now receiving white South Africans into our cabin and sitting around joking, having fun, praying together. Just this afternoon my wife was counselling one of the white South Africans. Somehow we are starting to find each other. The ship has been a wonderful platform for that because we're so close. You can't jump off and say, "Well, I've had enough now." It's a time when you have to work through relationships.'

Just how fragile these new relationships were, South Africans discovered on Christmas Eve. Each person on the ship was asked to meet in a group with the others from his country. Together the group was to decide how best to present to the ship's community their respective country's Christmas customs.

The South African group, being the largest contingent, met in the main lounge of the ship. As discussion got under way, it quickly revealed how fragmented the group was. English-speaking whites, Afrikaans-speaking whites, coloureds, Indian South Africans. Each composed a distinct entity. An argument erupted and old suspicions resurfaced. As some of the group began to cry, the South Africans realized how scarred they all were from the old system. In an attempt to lessen the tension, someone began to sing. The others joined in, hesitantly at first and then with more force.

One of the Afrikaner men got up and left. About ten minutes later he returned and, obviously upset, tried to express in words his feelings. The group, which was trying to start up a game to lighten the atmosphere, paused and listened. The Afrikaner confessed how God had healed him in his thinking and attitude in regard to the racial issue.

'I feel the Lord is leading us to have a footwashing ceremony,' he said to the others.

They did so. Black hands washed white feet. White hands washed black feet. Tears of repentance and joy flowed.

'This proved to be the breakthrough we were all waiting for,' Theo commented later. 'It was the best Christmas present we could have asked for.'

While South Africans were working through their tensions and trying to build a new identity as South Africans, *Doulos* was entering an excitingly different part of the world which brought a large measure of stress with it. For the first time she was going into the Gulf, the heart of Islam, and on up into Turkey. *Logos* had been in this part of the world, but that had been many years earlier. Much had changed since then.

Ministry, of course, had to be greatly curtailed. Those on board were given extensive, almost overwhelming, instruction about what they could or could not do and say. For most *Doulos* people this was strange and even a bit scary. It was certainly oppressive to have to consider carefully every word and deed.

For the public at large, the message of the ship was to be love. *We are here because we love God, we love one another and we love you.* Local people would know the *Doulos* was a Christian ship; for them that simple message of love would be a powerful testimony to what God can do for people. Islam has no concept of a God of love.

More explicit spiritual ministry would be directed toward local churches — and there were several of them among the large expatriate segment of the population — encouraging, challenging and, above all, supplying them with large quantities of Bibles and otherwise unavailable Christian literature.

Literature was to be the major focus of the ship. Line-up people wondered how much freedom there would be for distribution, and how much demand. Their highest hopes were exceeded as the ship was besieged with visitors and record amounts were sold. Secular books, of course, were the drawing card for the general public, yet *Doulos* people were amazed at the freedom given to sell Christian literature as well. Regulations varied from port to port. In one place, the books had to be isolated and marked with a big sign indicating they were Christian. In another port Bibles were banned but other Christian books could be sold. In still another place, all Christian books were prohibited, but after some hasty negotiations, authorities allowed *Doulos* people to take Christian books to a local church and sell them inside the church building. Local Christians were elated as they saw this setting a precedent for future Christian bookselling in churches.

Some of the Gulf ports came before the *Doulos* visit to Turkey and some afterwards. To reach Turkey, *Doulos* had to pass through the Suez Canal. As she was steaming north through the Red Sea and into the Gulf of Suez, expecting to reach the canal by morning, something occurred that had always been a remote possibility but never seriously considered.

Late in the evening the radio officer went to his office to finish some work. Hardly had he seated himself and switched on the radio, when over the static-filled waves came a Mayday call. It was not at all unusual for a radio officer to pick up distress calls, but almost always the calls would come from a great distance. This one came from only fifty nautical miles to the south of *Doulos*. The speaker reported that his ship was burning as a result of a fire in the engine room that had got out of control. End of the message. No name was given to identify the ship nor any information about the kind of ship. Just its location. The time was 11:30 pm.

As several vessels closer to the burning ship responded to the call, *Doulos* continued on her way while monitoring the radio for further developments. The first vessel to reach the area was a British container ship which had been only ten miles away. It was frustrated in its attempt to move in close to the burning ship because the waters were filled with lifeboats and inflatable rafts. However it picked up survivors from a lifeboat, including an officer who reported that the ship in distress was an Egyptian vessel carrying 588 crew and passengers.

Other vessels converged on the area. One reported hearing people screaming in the water out in the darkness. Small rig-tenders came and were able to move up under the sides of the listing ship and try to persuade people to jump into the water and be rescued. A US warship arrived on the scene and took over as co-ordinating vessel.

At 12:30 am reports of serious injuries were received on *Doulos*. A few minutes later *Doulos* contacted the warship, *US 977*, to offer medical help if needed. (*Doulos* is often in need of a medical officer in order to be able to sail, but at this time she happened to have three doctors and twelve nurses aboard, as well as five Arabic-English translators.) The *US 977* replied that medical assistance might be needed and medical supplies also. *Doulos* altered course, turning south, and increased her speed to 13.5 knots.

Fifty miles may seem a short distance, but at 13 1/2 miles an hour, several hours were required for the journey. Not until 7:30 did she reach the distress location, having stopped en route to investigate an overturned liferaft. Scores of empty lifeboats and rafts were bobbing around everywhere, but it appeared that all survivors had already been rescued. Smoke from the burning ship could be seen in the distance.

Bob Bailey had been on watch when the Mayday call came, but it was his wife Tracey who got involved in the rescue. She was a nurse. Here is her account:

400

During the night I hardly slept. We were going into the waves and I'm not a good sailor. Sometimes I get seasick in port when the ships go past and cause big waves.

At 6:00 am we had a phone call asking if I would like to go and help. I said, 'Yes . . . if I am feeling okay.' Straightaway I felt fine.

To join the US ship where the survivors had been brought, we had to climb down the pilot ladder [a rope ladder hanging down the side of the ship] and get into a small rubber boat. Going down the pilot ladder was very scary. I prayed all the way down and held the rope so tightly that my arms were sore for days afterwards.

Fortunately the US ship was very large and stable. . . .

Dr. Strachan, *Doulos* medical officer, takes up the narrative:

We were hurried downstairs to find 270 survivors crowded on to two decks of the ship. The obviously injured ones were in the well-equipped hospital area, filling all available beds, floor-space, corridors and nearby rooms. There was an eerie atmosphere of stunned silence and quiet dignity. Not a raised voice, not an angry word, no hysteria. Yet many were seriously injured, in pain, shocked, bereaved and cold.

The only doctor on board and his small nursing team were fully occupied treating a four-year-old boy with a horrific head injury. After a hurried medical conference, it was decided that one of our doctors and a nurse should join the US medical team until the boy was eventually transferred to hospital via helicopter, accompanied by one of our nurses. The two other *Doulos* doctors, along with nurses and interpreters, set about the task of seeing to the other injured. The serious cases we put into available beds, the less serious were diagnosed and treated on the floors and corridors.

The US ship had informed *Doulos* of the various medical supplies needed, including specific drugs for a heart patient. Those very items happened to be on *Doulos*. Also, in Dubai a hospital had donated to *Doulos* a number of intravenous drips which proved invaluable at this time. The US radio officer commented to us, 'Your ship and medical team have been an absolute godsend!'

402

The *Doulos* nurses and translators were kept busy not only attending to medical needs but also in trying to comfort people. One of the things they found hardest was helping survivors look for family members and having to face the realization that a husband, wife or child was not among those rescued.

At 9:30 *Al Qamar El Saudi*, the burning ship, rolled over and slid beneath the waters. Apparently, according to reports, so much water had been pumped into the engine room to try to extinguish the fire that a list was caused which eventually led to the sinking of the ship.

Of the 588 crew and passengers aboard the Egyptian ship, 269 survivors had been brought aboard the *US 977*. Another vessel had picked up about forty but refused to transfer them to the warship. Apart from these 309 people, mostly men, there appeared to be no other survivors. One of the rescued men aboard the warship had pulled out a passenger ticket and showed it to a *Doulos* nurse, saying, 'This is all I have left. I have lost my wife and daughter.'

Survivors were transported to a hospital ashore. *Doulos* medical personnel returned and *Doulos* resumed her interrupted journey north with her people in a sober frame of mind. More than ever they were aware of God's faithfulness and protection for the ship during more than a decade and a half, yet it was hard to understand why such a tragedy as they witnessed had to happen. There were no answers. They could only pray that God would in some way bring something good out of it all.

On a summer evening in 1994 *Doulos* left Istanbul and sailed up the busy but beautiful Bosporus Strait separating Europe and Asia. The European side was lined with elaborate three-storey wood houses trimmed with intricate wooden lacework, a mute testimony to the grandeur of a century past.

As the ship approached the historic city of Yalta in the Ukraine a day and a half later, her decks filled with crew and staff eager to catch a glimpse of their next port. A line-up man pointed out the dacha where Gorbachev had been detained during the critical time when it seemed his government might collapse before the attempted coup by the old hard-line communists. As the ship sailed past a palace which nestled high on the hillside among a luxuriant growth of trees, the line-up man identified Livadia Palace where Stalin, Churchill and Roosevelt once met to work out a treaty. The *Doulos* berth in Yalta was right in the heart of the small city which in better times had been a popular health resort and holiday centre for the wealthy and influential.

The first snag in Yalta was with Customs, which wanted to levy a 98 per cent tax on all book sales. Unthinkable! Fortunately, one of the ship's most experienced line-up men was on board. Hoping to bring the tax down at least to 60 per cent, Ronnie Lappin went to talk with officials while everyone on board *Doulos* prayed. Just in time for the scheduled opening ceremony, word came that the tax had been reduced to 38%, based on the cost of the books rather than on their selling price.

Bibles were easily the best sellers, going out at the rate of 500 an hour, even though sales were limited to one per person. Within twenty four hours, the supply was exhausted, but more were obtained from the Bible Society in Kiev. *Doulos* Bibles had been subsidized so they could be offered at a very low price, but they would probably have gone out at any price, ship workers discovered, as they searched bookstalls throughout town, trying in vain to locate a single Bible for sale. In all, six thousand five hundred Russian Bibles were sold, two hundred and fifty English ones and thirty-six thousand other Christian books.

At the opening reception Dale Rhoton, again visiting the ship with his wife, was introduced to Yuri, a thin, gaunt man with greying hair circling a bald spot on the top of his head. Alert eyes peered through the thick lenses of his glasses. In later meetings the Rhotons were to discover that Yuri liked to dress casually with his shirt partially unbuttoned, revealing a thick growth of frizzy salt-and-pepper hair on his chest. When he talked — and even more when he smiled — his brown-stained teeth were exposed.

Whenever Yuri walked, he shuffled, dragging one leg slightly, but that didn't seem to bother him or even slow him down. The Rhotons had constantly to hurry to keep pace with him as he led them back along the scenic coastal path after viewing the beautiful Livadia Palace and Yuri's place of work in nearby buildings that had once housed one of Russia's proud Hussar regiments. Yuri informed his guests that he frequently walked this path, taking about thirty-five minutes to get back to the city. With his guests it took him an hour!

Yuri was happy to show his new friends around town, but most of all he wanted to talk. He was a psychotherapist, married to a neural surgeon. All his life he had been a dedicated communist, completely convinced that it offered the best life in the world. He believed the line he had been fed about Americans being masses of poor workers exploited by a few unscrupulous people in power. With *perestroika* came disillusionment and disorientation. He learned of the atrocities committed by the revered Soviet leaders and of the pack of lies the populace had been fed. Belief in communism was suddenly swept away, leaving a void which Yuri was desperately trying to fill. Whereas earlier he would have arrogantly spurned any offer of a Bible, now he was eagerly trying to find out about Christianity. 'The biggest dream of my life,' he said, 'has been to get a Bible in English.' He wanted to learn about God and practise English at the same time.

'But,' he added, 'I am no longer a little child. I cannot just hear something about God and believe it. I have to have good reasons.'

At his place of work he showed where he held therapy sessions for twenty to thirty heart-patients at a time. It was a large room with a circle of comfortable green armchairs lining three walls. Behind the chairs on one wall was a huge mural of an outdoor scene. Dotting the other walls in various places were the outline drawing of a man, indicating acupuncture points, another drawing depicting a person in the yoga position with black 'blobs' showing the magnetic points in his body, the text of the Ten Commandments and another text with Jesus' words about loving God and one's neighbour as oneself.

The Rhotons spent many hours talking with Yuri, even inviting him and his wife for a meal on the ship. Dale gave him several Christian books, including a couple of apologetic ones. Yuri's gratitude was obviously genuine.

On their final Sunday in port the Rhotons were invited to Yuri's home for afternoon tea — a prospect he candidly admitted his wife found rather daunting. She had briefly visited England and Sweden and felt very self-conscious about the difference in living standards. Yuri, however, insisted that his friends should see how an ordinary person in Yalta lived. He was proud that after *perestroika* he had become the owner of his own home.

His visitors were not quite sure just how ordinary he was. Yuri himself received a pension but still worked so he brought home a double wage of about $25 a month. His wife, as a neural surgeon, must have had something comparable as well.

'Just enough to provide us with food,' commented Yuri, adding wistfully as he nodded at one of the numerous roadside book stands that had sprung up after *perestroika*. 'We couldn't get such books before. I see so many that I'd like to read, but now there's no money.'

The Rhotons had already been told that salaries were usually about $10–20 a month. And that it cost $10 to feed one person the most basic food for a month. Bread and a few vegetables. Nothing more.

How did people survive? The Rhotons never figured that out. To buy an ordinary tee-shirt cost many people a whole month's salary. At least most people had a home, either owned by themselves or provided free by the government.

The Rhotons appreciated their friendship with Yuri, who gave them a little glimpse into the daily lives, the needs, the deep yearnings of Ukrainian people at the difficult transitional time.

In some ways Yalta brought a breath of fresh air to those on board *Doulos*. After months in the Middle East where evangelistic activity was severely restricted, they suddenly found themselves able to talk freely as much as they wanted. Furthermore, Ukrainians were curious, searching, eager to learn whatever they could about what had been so long forbidden to them. Conferences were held on board. Open-air meetings — sometimes led by *Doulos* people, sometimes by a local church — were held on the quayside and always drew crowds. Several *Doulos* teams went out into more distant towns. One of these teams was sent to an ethnic Turkic-speaking people, the Tartars.

In 1944 the Tartars had been uprooted en masse by Stalin and exiled to Siberia, the Urals and Uzbekistan. Packed into cattle-trucks for more than two weeks, nearly half of them died en route or soon after. Those who survived faced the daunting prospect of starting a new life in a strange place with nothing. In time they built homes, planted gardens and accumulated cars and other trappings of society, but as soon as communism fell and the way was opened for them to return to their homeland, they sold everything and moved.

408     Calamity struck in the form of spiralling inflation. By the time they arrived in the Ukraine, their lifesavings had become worthless paper. Again they had to start a new life from scratch.

The *Doulos* team sent to help them consisted of eighteen or twenty people, including South Koreans, Malaysians, a Filipino, a South African, a Swiss, an East German (Russian-speaking) and several other nationalities. In addition there were five Turks who had sailed with the ship from Istanbul. The idea was to offer the Tartars practical assistance in establishing their homes, helping to build block houses with rough bricks, digging gardens, planting fields, carrying water. Some of the women would run a children's programme to keep the young ones occupied while their parents worked. The team knew they were going to work, but the full force of what they were getting into hit only when they arrived, viewed the primitive living conditions and felt the burning heat of a blazing sun.

Devrim Leonard, a teenage Turk with an American father, stayed with another *Doulos* man at the village mullah's home. He tells about his experience:

> When we came there, I didn't like it at the beginning. I was tired, fed up, bored and I didn't like the home I was staying in, that of the mullah who was like the Muslim

minister or priest. These people hadn't been allowed to go to Muslim schools or mosques to recite the prayers and practise their Muslim beliefs, so they didn't know much about Islam. Even the mullah himself didn't know to pray five times a day. He didn't know the prayers or the proper washing style. They had just founded this village two years ago and so they had no mosque.

On our second day I was working in the mullah's garden when Ester, one of the other Turks on our team, came to see if there was anything she could do to help. The mullah's grandson, who had become fond of her, watched her approach. As she bent down, a little golden cross on a chain around her neck slipped out from under her blouse. The little boy's observant eyes spotted it immediately. When Ester left a moment later, the boy turned to Devrim and asked, 'Are you a Christian?'

'Yes,' Devrim said, 'I'm a Christian.'

'Mummy!' yelled the child, 'Come quickly! These people are Christians!'

They took us into the house and started asking us questions. 'How come you're Christians? Why aren't you Muslims? You're Turkish, right? You should be Muslims. You're very bad people.'

A friend was visiting one of the grandsons and, of course, the grandson didn't waste any time telling him that we were Christians.

'Are you *kafirs?*' he asked, turning around and staring at us. (*Kafir* means infidel or pagan, one of the worst names you can call a person.)

I was annoyed and a bit sad. Then the mullah's wife told us we couldn't stay there any longer. We would have to leave the next day.

The team met every morning at 8:30 to talk about the day and pray and have devotions. So I told them about the situation. We then prayed for the mullah and his family.

After devotions we went back to the mullah's house and were surprised to see that there was an immediate answer to our prayer. The mullah and his family treated us like we were good friends they hadn't seen in a long time, whereas just a few hours before they had told us that they didn't want us there. They were so friendly, I could hardly believe it.

After that when we were working in the garden, they'd come and say, 'Oh, don't work so much! Don't work so much! Sit down and rest a couple of hours.'

We'd sit down and rest for two minutes, then get up and work. Fifteen minutes later they would say again, 'Oh, come inside. Come inside. That's enough work. Rest for the remainder of the day.'

We would have felt guilty doing that while they were working, so we'd be working every day from about 9:30 in the morning till 8:00 at night. We had a good relationship with the family. The mullah's wife would call us 'my sons' and she was really kind to us, as was the mullah himself. Twice I stayed up all night playing chess with the mullah. It was nice to be able to beat somebody!

The grandmother offered to give me her granddaughter in marriage. She was joking, of course. The girl was only seven years old. It became a big joke for us, as team members would tease me, saying, 'Oh, you can get married now! Lucky you!'

Since there were so many people on the team, we did a little International Night for the village, practising every evening for a week. We did a drama and some worship dances. I played the guitar and a couple of others played the fiddle and the trumpet. We did an interview with the ones in their national costumes which they had brought with them. Someone shared a message which was translated into Russian.

When I got home, the mullah's daughter began talking with me. She was a very intelligent lady who had been an engineer with a big company but now she couldn't even find work in a factory because there weren't any jobs. She asked me about Jesus.

'You people worship Jesus Christ and we worship Allah,' she observed. 'That's the main difference between us.'

'Now, wait a minute,' I said. 'Let a Christian tell you what Christians believe instead of listening to other people.'

I had promised myself back in Istanbul that I would find out the difference between Christianity and Islam. I pointed out some of the similarities. We all believe in one God and the Bible teaches us to be perfect in a sense. The Koran also teaches people to do good things. Then I told the family a little about the other *Doulos* man staying with them. They were surprised to hear how much a person can change just by reading the Bible. I told them a few of the Bible's teachings and they were very interested. They kept saying, 'Oh, the Bible's such a good book.'

Then they started asking about Christians and the things, particularly the bad things, that Christians did. I said, 'You don't just say "I'm a Christian" and you become one. You have to show it.'

The mullah was sitting next to me. The whole family had come and were listening. I pointed to the mullah's cap

412

and said, 'If I put that on my head and walk around saying, "I'm a Muslim", would I be a real Muslim? I wouldn't. The same is true of someone who wears a cross and says "I'm a Christian". It doesn't necessarily mean he's a Christian. He has to live the way Christ says to live.'

That interested them and they started saying more good things about the Bible.

'Would you people like to have a Bible?' I asked.

I was able to give them a Russian Bible and show them a few good places to read. The daughter stopped speaking with me and started reading the Bible.

It was interesting. This mullah didn't own a Koran. Nobody in the village owned a Koran. The mullah didn't even know the Islamic prayers but now he has a Bible. I believe the Lord put me in that house for a special reason.

When we left the village the family was sad and kept saying, 'Come again. Come again and speak with us. You can stay here with us.'

'I hope I can come back again,' I said.

The work we did had not been easy. We worked really hard, doing heavy stuff. When I returned to the ship every muscle was aching. But I was happy.

Doulos, *God's ship, was still in business, staffed with* douloi *utterly committed to serving Jesus Christ as Lord and Master and, in doing so, becoming servants of the people to whom they would proclaim Christ. Doulos staffed with* douloi *willing to offer their lives in mundane but demanding behind-the-scenes labour; staffed with* douloi *willing to follow directives even when those were unappealing; staffed with* douloi *trying to be faithful in service to the Master they loved.*

Doulos, *God's ship, was still in business. And so was her Master. Treating his* douloi *as friends. Sharing in their joys. Putting a comforting arm around them when they were in pain. Coming to their aid when they floundered. Accepting them as they were while seeing in them what they could become. Involving them in the things that lay close to his heart.*

*That has been the story of* Doulos.

413

# Facts and figures

In 1992 *The Guiness Book of Records* listed *Doulos* as the world's oldest active ocean-going ship. Built in 1914 in the USA, she served for many years as a cargo vessel before being converted into a passenger ship. Here are some of her vital statistics:

| | |
|---|---|
| Gross tonnage | 6804 |
| Maximum draught | 5.5m |
| Length | 130.35m |
| Beam | 16.54m |
| Port of registration | Valletta, Malta |
| Call sign | 9HKF |

Between 1978 and 1996 *Doulos* sailed under a number of captains, some of whom served for one or two voyages only. Eight, however, served for at least six months:

| | |
|---|---|
| Ronald Wright | (UK) |
| Dallas Parker | (USA) |
| George Booth | (South Africa) |
| Carl Issacson | (USA) |
| Richard Prendergast | (UK) |
| Pertti Merisalo | (Finland) |
| Michael O'Reilly | (Australia) |
| Graeme Bird | (New Zealand). |

Seven chief engineers served for a period of at least six months:

| | |
|---|---|
| Rex Worth | (UK) |
| Mike Poynor | (USA) |
| Sigge Johansson | (Sweden) |
| Yan Yin Tong | (Singapore) |
| Johannes Thomsen | (Denmark) |
| Tim Wilson | (UK) |
| Bryce Pearce | (Australia) |

Serving as ship's directors have been

| | |
|---|---|
| George Miley | (USA) |
| Dale Rhoton | (USA) |
| Frank Dietz | (USA) |
| Allan Adams | (Australia) |
| Mike Strachura | (USA) |
| Bernd Gülker | (Germany) |
| Mike Hey | (Australia) |

Miscellaneous statistics for the period 1978–1996:

| | |
|---|---|
| Total number of visitors: | 13,205,877 |
| Educational books sold: | 4,557,635 |
| Christian books sold: | 2,940,213 |
| Bibles and New testaments sold: | 771,361 |
| Attendance at programmes on board: | 2,267,046 |
| Nautical miles travelled: | 212,694 |
| Countries visited: | 83 |
| Ports visited: | 231 |
| Total port visits, including return visits: | 352 |

Ports with highest number of visitors:

| | |
|---|---:|
| Taichung, Taiwan (September 1988) | 201,710 |
| Kingston, Jamaica (December 1981) | 167,289 |
| Veracruz, Mexico (February 1982) | 160,246 |
| Tuticorin, India (January 1988) | 159,850 |
| Callao, Peru (September 1980) | 148,864 |

Ports with highest attendance at on-board programmes:

| | |
|---|---:|
| Rosario, Argentina (April 1981) | 30,000 |
| Cape Town, South Africa (October 1986) | 29,700 |
| Mar del Plata, Argentina (January 1981) | 27,800 |
| Belem, Brazil (September 1981) | 27,000 |
| Callao, Peru (September 1980) | 25,000 |

Ports with highest number of educational books sold:

| | |
|---|---:|
| Tema, Ghana (August 1986) | 108,000 |
| Buenos Aires, Argentina (March 1981) | 101,630 |
| Port Louis, Mauritius (November 1995) | 89,346 |
| Dubai, United Arab Emirates (March 1994) | 80,958 |
| Abidjan, Ivory Coast (July 1986) | 74,128 |

Ports with highest number of Bibles sold:

| | |
|---|---:|
| Singapore (July 1987) | 22,596 |
| Port Kelang, Malaysia (June 1987) | 11,881 |
| Port Kelang, Malaysia (March 1996) | 11,498 |
| Manila, Philippines (October 1988) | 11,357 |
| Cagayan de Oro, Philippines (July 1991) | 11,274 |

*International Address:*

> OM Ships,
> Postfach 1565
> D-74819 Mosbach
> Germany

*British Address:*

> Operation Mobilisation
> The Quinta
> Weston Rhyn
> Oswestry
> Shropshire SY10 7LT

# The George Verwer Collection

George Verwer has inspired and encouraged thousands in their Christian discipleship. Now three of his best-loved book, *The Revolution of Love*, *No Turning Back*, and *Hunger For Reality* are brought together in this three-in-one collection. The trilogy points us to love as the central theme of Christian life, calls us to effective service and revolutionizes our lives so that they are consistent and productive.

"*Immensely readable and full of the practical aspects of spiritual principles.*" Evangelism Today

"*A wealth of good material.*" Martin Goldsmith, Church of England Newspaper.

Over 100,000 copies sold.

**George Verwer is the founder and International Director of Operation Mobilisation. He has an international preaching ministry based in Britain.**

1-85078-296-2

solway